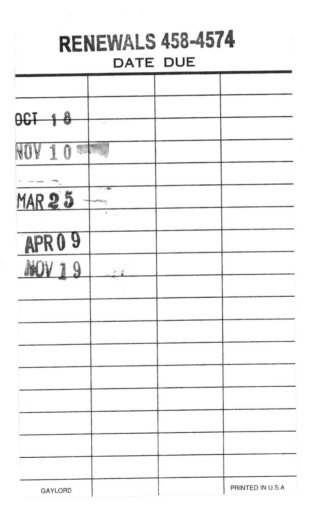

RECOVERED MEMORIES
OF TRAUMA

RECOVERED MEMORIES OF TRAUMA: TRANSFERRING THE PRESENT TO THE PAST

C. BROOKS BRENNEIS, PH.D.

INTERNATIONAL UNIVERSITIES PRESS, INC.
Madison   Connecticut

Library of Congress-Cataloging-in-Publication Data

Brenneis, C. Brooks.
   Recovered memories of trauma : transferring the present to the
past / C. Brooks Brenneis.
      p.   cm.
   Includes bibliographical references and indexes.
   ISBN 0-8236-5788-4
   1. False memory syndrome.   2. Recovered memory.   I. Title.
RC455.2.F35B74   1996
616.89—dc21   96-39645
                                                                    CIP

Manufactured in the United States of America

*To my Mother and Father, and
to Ginger, Michael, David, Sara, and Leah Nell*

CONTENTS

Acknowledgments	ix
Preface	xi

1. The Shadow of Unremembered Past Trauma   1
2. Trauma, Dreams, and Symptoms   17
3. Belief and Suggestion in the Recovery of Memories of Childhood Sexual Abuse   41
4. Memory Systems and the Psychoanalytic Retrieval of Memories of Trauma   61
5. A Special Traumatic Memory   79
6. Memories of Abuse or Reactions to Technique?   101
7. Multiple Personality, Invasive Therapy, and Recovered Memory   125
8. Suggestion and Influence in the Therapeutic Process   149
9. Conclusions: Reweighing the Evidence   165

References	175
Name Index	193
Subject Index	199

ACKNOWLEDGMENTS

It is a pleasure to acknowledge those who have helped me with this book. Although my name appears on the title page, many people have made contributions of substance and support along the way. None of them, however, should be held responsible for whatever mistakes and misinterpretations it contains, nor should any of them be assumed to hold opinions identical to those expressed here.

This book evolved piece by piece. Some of the pieces were informal discussions; some were shared experience, ideas, and reference material; some were encouragements; and some were critical commentaries. Bill Swift, Larry Shriberg, Michelle Jacques, Richard Levine, Marion Becker, Jim Gerndt, and John Kihlstrom all played much appreciated parts. The ready encouragement of Margaret Emery, Editor-in Chief at International Universities Press, to pursue a contrary point of view on a controversial subject was more than welcome.

Several people deserve special mention. As the book unfolded, my close associates Mark Trewartha and Joe Kepecs read and reread nearly every word and offered not only support but invaluable comments from the vantage point of superb clinicians. The book itself might not have been written had it not been for the repeated urgings of my very good friend Bob Nicholas who, from the start, saw a book in my ideas. Dee Jones, whose time was made available by Ned Kalin, chairman of the University of Wisconsin-Madison department of psychiatry, was a partner every step of the way. Her tireless and skillful efforts made a beautifully prepared manuscript out of my patchwork quilt of writings and rewritings. The book would not have existed at all were it not for Grace's steadfast reluctance to find memories where none were to be found and her courage in allowing this therapeutic material to be shared. The patience, encouragement, and interest provided by my family, Ginger, Michael, David, Sara, and Leah Nell, were beyond measure and reasonable expectation. For years, under the trying conditions of my preoccupation with this project, they were willing listeners, careful readers, and sources of information and insightful comments. I am profoundly grateful to them.

A final person needs to be acknowledged. One does not always know at the outset who will have exerted the greatest influence over one's career and professional identity. Jean Schimek, my friend and colleague for many years at Yale, has been that person for me. His standards of exceptional scholarship, critical thought, clinical wisdom, and personal integrity have been a model for me. I hope this book embodies, in good measure, his lofty standards.

Parts of Chapter 2 and Chapter 5 were first published in slightly different form in *Psychoanalytic Psychology* (1994), 11:429–447; Chapter 3 was first published, with minor changes, in the *Journal of the American Psychoanalytic Association* (1994), 42:1027–1053; a portion of Chapter 7 was first published in *Psychoanalytic Psychology* (1996), 13:367–387; and portions of Chapter 4 were first published in the *Journal of the American Psychoanalytic Association* (1996), 44:1165–1187.

PREFACE

Sexual abuse, and childhood sexual abuse in particular, is a sensitive topic. Often shrouded in secrecy, shame, and terror, in many instances there is no other direct evidence of its occurrence aside from the memory of its victim. Memory itself, however, is complex: no longer regarded as a static entity, memory for past events is continually recast and reformed depending on the conditions and circumstances of its recall; no longer regarded as a unified entity, memory may be explicit and subject to voluntary recall, or implicit and only visible in pattern recognition, intrusive imagery, and learned action patterns.

Because questions about memory for sexual abuse may be open to misinterpretation, I must, at the outset, indicate precisely what type of memory is and is not under examination here. Explicit autobiographical memory which has been more or less continuously available prior to any therapeutic encounter warrants validity without reservation and is expressly excluded from this discussion. Because they represent quite different circumstances, purported memories recalled by children under clearly coercive and leading questioning have also been omitted from consideration.

The focus here will be exclusively on memory for abuse and trauma which is identified by certain indirect clinical signs and recovered from total conscious, volitional inaccessibility by adults in psychotherapy. Many sources assure us this is not an uncommon clinical circumstance. When referring to clinical reports, I have endeavored to confine my observations, as much as can be determined, to those which fulfill these conditions; although, because this distinction is not easy to assess even in reports which strive for clarity, I may, at times, inadvertently be in error.

With the exception of the clinicians discussed in the chapter on multiple personality, most of the therapists whose work is examined have identified themselves as psychoanalytically oriented. This is worth noting not because they are representative of analytic practitioners (for they are not), but rather to indicate that recovered memories of trauma do not occur only with poorly trained, undisciplined therapists.

Regardless of my care to restrict these comments to memory wholly recovered in therapy, some readers may be concerned about the wider implications they may generate. Questions about the validity of such memories, unfortunately, can be read as discounting the existence of child sexual abuse, as discrediting adult women and men as witnesses to their experience, and as impeaching the integrity of psychotherapy and those who provide it. Because such questions can be misconstrued, however, is not a sufficient reason to shy away from asking them, and asking them would seem to be part of our obligation as clinicians and scientists. Very often the dispute about recovered memories is framed as occurring between clinically naive researchers and research naive clinicians. These characterizations have some truth to them. I hope the reader finds this text well informed about both clinical and research matters and that the author fits neither of the above categories.

This book parallels the course of my thinking about the issue of recovered memories of trauma, and, at the cost of some simplified discussions early on, I have gambled that this will make an engaging format for the reader. I would locate my starting point very differently now than I would have at the outset. At the beginning, I took for granted that I was a reasonably informed and well-trained analytic therapist. Consequently, whatever I assimilated from the clinical literature and from the less substantiated but equally influential clinical lore was granted a degree of credibility which I had little reason either to be aware of or to question.

Memory of trauma could be repressed, as it was then described, and could be identified through certain clinical signs. Careful reading of these signs allowed the knowing therapist to bring forth previously hidden memories, often of early sexual abuse. The growing research on sexual abuse indicated that it was far more prevalent than we had ever thought and buttressed these implicit conclusions.

Doubts formed incrementally, while efforts to satisfy these doubts led in directions I did not anticipate and gave me an entirely different perspective on where I was when I began. Several circumstances spurred me on, and describing them may be a good way to introduce the reader to the work that follows. In the early 1990s, Mark Trewartha, a clinical colleague, and I spent several evenings trying to sort out questions and problems associated with past sexual abuse. Both of us were seeing patients we thought might have been sexually abused but who did not have memories of those suspected events. What kind of material prompted us to consider unremembered sexual abuse, and why was it convincing? I decided to review my notes and collate evidence from one patient, Grace, for whom this question seemed most compelling. I was surprised and impressed at how well this material lined up with the writings about abuse with which I was then familiar. Still, Grace did not remember being abused and this left me wondering what kind of evidence might be regarded as conclusive, even if circumstantial. Certainly other clinicians must be wrestling with this dilemma, but the literature seemed more to offer assurances than to pose questions.

My response was to write up Grace's case, with as much "raw" clinical data as possible, and raise the question: Given this information, had she or hadn't she been abused? Admittedly, the premise of the paper was flawed—there was, after all, no definitive answer—but I was startled by what I took to be one reviewer's dismissive attitude toward. my questions and mistrust of my material because I was sharply critical of an article the reviewer found convincing.

At that point, I shelved "Grace" and decided to pursue a more focused question: Did some dreams contain literal memory of trauma? Many of Grace's dreams portrayed sexual exploitation. Did this mean, as several articles indicated, that unremembered experiences were being transparently replayed in dream content? I picked a simple strategy—locate published accounts of dreams paired with trauma and compare one with the other. Later my inquiry broadened to include research efforts to influence dream content with high-intensity presleep stimulation. This quiet pursuit, leafing through dusty journals in the stacks, received a fortuitous boost.

In the fall of 1993, Elizabeth Loftus presented a paper (1993d) at a conference in Madison, Wisconsin, and I took the opportunity to meet with her. I expressed some of my doubts that dream content directly reflected memory and referred to an influential paper by van der Kolk, Britz, Burr, Sherry, and Hartmann (1984) comparing dreams of combat veterans with those of nightmare sufferers. This paper served as a cornerstone in Alpert's construction of unremembered incestuous abuse from dream content (1994), a prepublication draft of which I had carefully studied. Loftus encouraged me to contact van der Kolk and request access to the dreams and memories collected for that study. Van der Kolk directed me to Ernest Hartmann who had been responsible for that portion of the research. I was unprepared for Hartmann's response that neither dreams nor memories had been collected, and that the conclusion—of exact correspondence between dream content and combat experiences—was based solely on the dreamers' subjective assessments. While I had no doubt this reflected a reasonable conclusion, I was now quite determined to check concrete data—actual dream texts with trauma texts. It was with less surprise that I discovered how often an exact correspondence between dream content and trauma was asserted and how seldom I could find any direct evidence to support this conclusion. If dreams were being used to recover unremembered events, then it would be important to know that dreams really did mirror events in some exact fashion.

In the process of struggling to understand the inferences drawn about unremembered events in clinical publications, I had to learn some very basic information about memory. Along the way, I received much encouragement and many papers from Loftus, Steve Lindsay, John Kihlstrom, Peter Ornstein, and Steve Ceci. If I have failed to grasp the intricacies of memory, it has not been for want of very able assistance. Reading this literature reminded me of the value of carefully stated and tested hypotheses. Arguments about theory—and there are many associated with memory—were fought with data derived from exacting experimental designs. The clinical literature, with its preference for theory over data (Spence, 1994), began to invite more caution.

This caution led me to read reference lists with considerable care, and gain. In this book, I have tried to be precise enough in my references to allow the reader to review carefully both my sources and my interpretations of them. To this end, I have confined myself, with very few exceptions, to publically available, professional sources. Although many of my arguments would be easier to support using the vast lay literature on recovered memory, because that literature is so uncritical, those arguments would also be easier to dismiss or discredit.

Of course, the main reason to review references is to learn more, and in several instances I found more than I could ever have hoped for. Initially I had little interest in multiple personality disorder (MPD), and was led to it only via the concept of dissociation. For a variety of reasons, dissociation had come to replace repression as the mechanism used to account for the absence of memory in sexual trauma victims, and dissociation was most prominently displayed by MPD patients. My reading took me to an article by Fahy (1988) which contained a reference to a work by Wilson and Barber (1983), a work so obscure I have not found it cited in any other clinical papers aside from my own. It turned out, however, that fantasy proneness, the topic of the paper, was well known to a select group of experimentalists interested in the broad area surrounding hypnosis. Wilson and Barber present a cluster of individuals whose lives center around vivid, private fantasy. The experiential phenomenology of these individuals matched, to an extraordinary degree, the phenomenology of MPD patients, including imagining themselves to be other people and enjoying richly sensory fantasy. These fantasy prone individuals showed an astounding capacity for retrieving vivid, detailed memories for early life events like first birthdays and for events unattended to at the time of occurrence. Except in a one sentence footnote toward the end of the paper, Wilson and Barber take all of these memory feats at face value, but clearly here was a group of people exquisitely prepared to validate clinical assumptions about lost and reclaimed memories. It was less apparent, however, how this process might unfold.

The "missing link" was supplied in a paper by Belli and Loftus (1994). They used "source monitoring" theory to explain how the mind discriminates between memories of past thought and fantasy, and memories of past actions and events. Typically, memory for actions is densely encoded along sensory dimensions while memory for thought and fantasy is more likely to be encoded along cognitive lines. Consequently people with very rich sensory fantasy may be prone, as Wilson and Barber found, to entangle memory of events with memory of fantasy. An alternative reading of recovered memory, not as memory at all, began to take shape.

While discussing these ideas with Don Lynam, a graduate student in psychology at the University of Wisconsin-Madison, he called my attention to Orne's seminal paper on demand characteristics (1962). Orne captured the process of influence and suggestion quite differently from what I had imagined it to be. Where I anticipated deliberate indoctrination foisted upon a more or less passively receptive subject, Orne saw shades of influence, covertly expressed, and running back and forth between, in his examples, experimenters and subjects. This turned out to be the barest beginning of the literature on covert influence. Compelling, painstakingly accumulated evidence now makes it indisputable that powerful ideas may be triggered and inculcated without either participant's conscious awareness. In fact, the absence of conscious awareness may potentiate the effects of influence. As patient or therapist we are quite capable of intuiting, without conscious awareness, the unconscious beliefs of others, even ideas which, when raised to consciousness, are disavowed.

My thinking took me a long and unexpected way away from where I began. It would be a serious mistake, however, to read the following as a tract against the malevolent influence of analytic therapy. Therapy rests upon a foundation of influence from which is built its benefits as well as its liabilities. An adequate, if demanding, safeguard exists to place checks on rank influence. We need to accept that unwarranted influence can never be ruled out and that it can only be tracked down by an informed, skeptical

mind. This book illustrates the difficulty of maintaining that safeguard and the possible outcome when we do not.

In presenting evidence which challenges the validity of therapeutically recovered memories of trauma, it is now nearly a requirement that one acknowledge the existence of real childhood
sexual and physical abuse. To construe anything written here as
a disavowal of the existence of the abuse of children would grossly
distort the arguments I have made. Some children and, I would
contend, some adult psychotherapy patients have been exploited
and damaged by their respective caretakers. For the therapist's
part, it is unthinkable that this is anything but unwitting and
unknowing. Still, one in no way cancels or discounts the other.
We have a moral and a professional obligation to address both
real and metaphoric abuse. If this book lessens, to any degree,
the likelihood of our zealous therapeutic quest for past events
which might not have occurred, it will have well served its
purpose.

1 THE SHADOW OF UNREMEMBERED PAST TRAUMA

Shortly after her divorce, Grace wrote out a dream about:

Lying in bed, barely asleep. L (her ex-husband) crawls into bed
on the other side and pulls me toward him. Neither of us speak.
He forces one of his legs between mine, trying to separate them.
I resist, in silence. He reaches down with his hand to spread my
legs. Suddenly I am aware that it is not me now that is in bed with
L, but that it is myself at a very young age. I see it perfectly. It is
L as he was several years ago; and I am the same exact child who
comes up just above your (CBB) waist, who wears a pale blue dress
with puffed sleeves and a sash in the back, who wraps her arms
around you and clings to you, burying her face in your side.

Later Grace dreamt about "a bear in the house—forest bear,
black, brown. My brother Y had it in his bedroom the previous
night but was not attacked. The bear disappears during the day,
but is in the house. I am afraid to come to my bedroom this
night—but prefer this fear to searching out the bear during the
day." When she woke from the dream, Grace had an immediate

1

desire to "run to you (CBB) and bury my face in your chest," the sense of which was "I can't face it."

After three years of intensive therapeutic work, the implication of these dreams seemed nearly incontrovertible: Grace was reexperiencing unremembered past sexual trauma. So many clinical indications pointed this way, and seemed so baffling and inexplicable when viewed any other way, that it was difficult to bear in mind that Grace had no direct memories of any such experiences and that the absence of such memories was consequential. A tide was moving toward certainty, at least to some reasonable degree, while doubts seemed rooted in sand.

GRACE

In the mid-1980s I received a telephone call from "Grace."[1] Clearly concerned about herself, but expecting that her contact with me would be quite brief, Grace accepted my invitation to come and talk with me more specifically about her situation. But matters worsened, and weekly meetings were replaced by sessions two and three times a week. Inexplicably, in rather short order, this very capable and independent woman found her life and well-being tied to her therapeutic relationship with me. It was difficult to know at times whether she hated or was grateful for her attachment to me. Her life-threatening turmoil was wildly inconsistent with her personal resourcefulness, and left us puzzled as to how to account for this discrepancy. Perhaps some very specific issue had created this massive but localized psychic fault line.

Grace, a woman in her mid-forties, had been married for about twenty-five years when I first saw her. Her husband, L, was a successful attorney and they had two children, a 17-year-old daughter and a 13-year-old son. Her parents were both alive: mother was a housewife and father an insurance salesman. Grace

---

[1] "Grace" has expressly consented to the publication of clinical material from her psychotherapy with me. Although some demographic information has been changed to disguise her identity, none of the clinical material has been altered.

was the middle child; her older brother was an accountant and her younger sister was a housewife with a family.

Grace describes herself as a dutiful and obedient child. Her family was close emotionally and quite traditional in its assignment of parental roles. The only notable early experience was a three-week hospitalization for pneumonia at 6. Grace was an active, outdoorsy child with many close friends. As she grew older, spiritual life was as important to her as closeness to nature.

Grace is in almost all respects a remarkably sensible woman and parent. While she is emotionally in tune with her children and their adolescent struggles, she has a no-nonsense, down-to-earth approach which is both firm and caring. She has remained close with a number of friends from adolescence. A dancer as a youth, she continues to maintain her excellent physical conditioning. After her children reached school age, Grace worked part-time as a legal secretary. For the last ten years, she describes a broad-ranging awareness of her inner life and has no difficulty reporting dreams and fantasies in exquisite detail. Literary and scriptural references and allusions seem to come naturally to her, and without affectation. Strikingly, she cannot tolerate any degree of conflict with her hard-driving, opinionated, and critical husband. She defers without reflection, and in retrospect feels considerable guilt about her inability to stand up to her husband, especially when he is harshly critical of the children. About one year prior to contacting me, she had surgery for cancer. This had been a time of deep spiritual crisis for her. No recurrences of the cancer appeared in the ensuing years.

Grace's presenting concern was that the substance had gone out of her marriage and she was thinking of divorce. This level of concern was rather quickly replaced by a deeper phrasing: for a number of years she had had conversations with herself, the substance of which was that there was no integrity to her life with her husband and she was living an emotional and spiritual lie. Perhaps it was time to invite an outside listener to these conversations. Within the first months, however, whatever casual or deliberate tone was attached to these questions was lost to a rising sense of panic. She revealed that the conversations with herself included the thought of suicide, then the possibility of suicide, and finally the inevitability of suicide. Life had lost its meaning;

something at the center of her had failed to hold and she was hanging onto a thread.

This downward spiral, which took her by surprise and was unprecedented in her life, continued over the next several years. She was unable to continue work, and hung on the edge of panic, disintegration, and suicide. She relied on her contact with me to maintain some degree of control over her dread and despair while she tried to hold onto her daily routines. She made gutsy efforts to stay involved with friends, keep up with her physical conditioning, and to continue to be a real parent. After divorcing her husband, there was an acceleration of terrifyingly explicit exploitative sexual dreams. About four years into the treatment, she began to emerge from this dislocated state, shaken and unsteady, but increasingly on her feet. She was able to stand up to her now ex-husband and increasingly protect the children from his harshness. Although aware that something still felt dislocated at her center, she was able to reconnect emotionally, found a much more rewarding relationship with a man, and returned to work. Recently, she wrote to tell me that she continued to do well, was remarried, and had moved to be nearer her daughter.

In the therapy, we were faced with the question of how to account for the rapid and steep drop in her level of functioning and the development of desperately suicidal feelings in a woman who seemed in most other respects creative, resilient, and emotionally accessible. The possibility of unremembered early sexual trauma seemed at first only a remote consideration, and then an increasingly likely one until the appearance of literal and symbolic dreams of sexual exploitation made it a nearly inescapable conclusion. As with a vexing puzzle, if only one arrangement of the pieces seems to fit (Freud, 1896b), it must represent the solution. In fact the clinical data are so massively and comprehensively in accord with the possibility of unremembered trauma that some readers will no doubt regard any uncertainty about the solution as signaling a lack of courage to see what is plainly there to be seen. Indeed, this is what makes "Grace" such a compelling example.

EVIDENCE OF TRAUMA

At the most fundamental level, trauma, of whatever nature, appears to shape and channel behavior in distinctive ways (Terr, 1979, 1988, 1991; van der Kolk, 1987). Thought of as the psychic trademarks of trauma, these patterns may include highly stereotyped imagery, repetitive behavioral sequences, and dissociation, a specific defensive adaptation to overwhelming stimulation. While one might not necessarily infer trauma directly from the presence of such features, their appearance certainly alerts the clinician to the possibility of past trauma.

Grace's experience was shot through with these trademarks of trauma. The monotonous consistency of the imagery in her prolific, detailed dreams was remarkable: three-quarters of over three hundred dreams centered around some form of water. While some of the water imagery was placid, most of it was destructive or foreboding: icy slopes, dark depths, cascading torrents, and rising floods threaten her again and again in her dreams. Explicit suicidal fantasies also centered on water; Grace imagined cutting her wrists in a tub, leaning over a dock on a pond, and leaning into a rapidly moving stream. A peculiar, repetitive behavioral sequence was also in evidence. Frequently during the beginning years of treatment, Grace would report awakening in the night doubled up with fear. She would cower, fall to the floor, and there, prone, flatten her body tightly against the floor. Throughout, she describes crying out in desperation, "No, no, please God, not now." Asked to elaborate, all Grace could say is that she had no idea what triggered her panic, and that her pleas were directed against the possibility of going crazy out of fear.

Dissociative experiences were everywhere. Grace reported "disconnecting," that is, having the sensation of seeing her body but not knowing where she was. Once she found herself lost in a field in the dark, and was afraid to go home because, she wrote, "home felt hollow, as if no one lives there."[2] Numb and paralyzed

---

[2]As the therapy advanced, Grace found it helpful to write down her more terrifying experiences, including dreams. Often she would bring these accounts to our sessions, but just as often would dispose of them by dropping them off between sessions in my waiting room.

trancelike states were frequent, often in conjunction with self-destructive impulses. Immediately after being aware of a wild rage, Grace wrote, "gradually the wild inside went away. I became empty. Nothing mattered. I felt myself sinking, down deep to a part of me that is dark and quiet and empty. Empty, empty, empty. When a thought formed at all, it was about my option, my emergency option [suicide]." On another occasion, Grace wrote, "I got stuck Tuesday afternoon." Her living room felt all white and her experiences like a kaleidoscope: "There were voices, not my voice, saying 'Do it, you know you want to! Do it! You know where they are [pills]! You know you want to die.' " Finally, she said inwardly, "Yes, I want to die. Yes I do." "Being stuck helped, because I couldn't move. I sat there with my hands parting, spread in front of me."

Moreover, although not necessarily associated with trauma, Grace provided numerous dreams of extraordinarily graphic violence, often self-directed. She dreamt, for example, of "a view of the back of my head, with a clear round bullet hole and my hair matted with blood." In another dream, she saw the "expressionless, detached" heads of two women, with bloody bits and pieces of their heads sprayed behind them. Further, in a third dream, Grace wrote that she had given birth but, "there is something dreadfully wrong. The inner thighs of the baby are ruptured. There is blood all over, especially on the infant's inner thighs." As in these instances, many of Grace's dreams were so filled with imagery of rupture and penetration that it was difficult to think of them only as manifestations of internalized rage.

All of these experiences, bewildering as they were, were doubly so because Grace had no context for making sense of them. Where were they coming from? What did they mean? Some form of trauma became a possibility in part because there seemed no other plausible explanation for them. Could, for instance, the blood on the infant's ruptured thighs be a clue to something more specific?

Grace's relationship to her husband reflected a profound lack of agency and autonomy. Not unlike Kluft's (1990) depiction of the "sitting duck" syndrome, Grace had cast herself under her husband's spell, where she felt, in nearly all respects, his responsive and deferring captive: his will was her will. According to

Kluft's notion, someone so readily victimized may well have patterned that behavior after an earlier victimization.

The degree of Grace's subservience was both extreme and in sharp contrast to her usual presence of mind. Anytime Grace was aware of her husband's pain, unhappiness, or annoyance, she automatically reoriented her awareness to his needs, opinions, and desires. The degree to which Grace lost not only her feelings but her critical abilities was evident in her delighted and warm response to a card in which her husband declared her his first and only love. Only much later did she realize that she was neither his first nor currently his only love. For a long time, every encounter with him came as if on a clean emotional slate. Trouble could be regarded only after the fact. After many years of therapeutic work, Grace described the magnitude of his influence in these terms: "When things have been very bad for me, and I feel more whole with you, that will last until I'm about a half-mile away. When I've seen him, the effect can last for days."

Like a frightened animal caught in a powerful beam, Grace was paralyzed in his presence. "The moment I saw him I was afraid. He was aloof, powerful, critical, threatening. Probably he was hurt and angry and that's how it came out. When he is that way, I get paralyzed. My mind freezes. I can't say anything unless it is to agree with him. 'Sure, fine.' 'Yes, that's a good idea.' 'Whenever is best for you.' 'I think you're right.' "

In addition, there was a highly eroticized, dangerous quality to being under his spell. Identifying the snake in this dream as her husband, Grace wrote:

A magnificent snake appears from behind a boulder. It is full of light and has a tiny diamond pattern of bright green, sapphire blue, and white that sparkles like diamonds. It is stunning. It makes its way to me and slides its head back and forth along my hand, the hand holding the knife. I am frozen. I try not to act afraid, but I am terrified. It then begins to coil itself around my arm and slide slowly up my arm. I cannot scream. I cannot breathe.

Grace indeed appeared to be a "sitting duck" in her relationship to her husband. She had little ability to define or locate her own perspective in his dazzling presence. Realizing, after the fact, that fear had once again paralyzed her mind and she had once again allowed herself to be taken advantage of, she was aghast and full of primitive rage toward herself. We had to ask: What could occasion such intense rage? What was this dynamic with her husband replaying? Where before had she been exploited, mesmerized and pliant, invaded and fearful?

Although difficult to interpret, there was something of a parallel in her relationship to God. From her early adolescence, Grace recalled several experiences of being drawn up into God and held. Aware of intense longing, she subsequently decided that these experiences defined how she knew she was alive. When, later in adolescence, they ceased to occur, Grace felt bereft.

In the last few years, her tie to God had ruptured. Prayer, once a source of great strength and solace, had become impossible because Grace could no longer tolerate being alone with God. Her feelings ran amuck: so full of hate toward God was she, Grace could not be quiet enough to pray. Grace's claim against God was that he had abandoned her, and she would, with reluctance, describe internalized shouting matches, laced with obscenities on her side, between her outraged God and her equally outraged self. We had to wonder, what transformed this embracing relationship into one in which any degree of intimacy, once so prized and precious, was terrifying and intolerable. Could some symbolism apply to being drawn up to God? Could a loving, protective "father" have betrayed her trust and given good cause for both outrage and fear of closeness?

These issues were repeated in magnified form in the transference. A central image in the transference was that of a lifeguard. In an early dream, Grace encountered a swimming pool at which was posted a sign: "No Lifeguard on Duty—Swim At Your Own Risk." Thereafter references to me as the lifeguard were frequent. For example, after an anxious phone call to me, Grace said she felt like she was "inside the lifeguard's ropes." My encouragements to use the "safety line" of the therapeutic relationship gradually to face her unknown terrors were designed to provide support while stretching her tolerance for anxiety.

There was, however, another side to her experience. The lifeguard protected her from physical danger and disintegrating anxiety, but also became the source of great turmoil. On one hand, Grace recurrently pictured herself as a child burying her head on my chest or kneeling with her arms wrapped desperately around my legs, pleading with me "not to let [her] go!" On the other hand, security could destroy her. A story she heard on the radio summed up her plight. A fire in a horse barn stirred up so much commotion that the horses tethered in the pasture broke their restraints and rushed into the burning barn to their death. They were so frightened, they went to the only security they knew, even if it meant their death. Similarly, Grace was repeatedly thrown between desperate attachment and the dread of being overwhelmed.

Although Grace reassured us that the therapy had given her an alternative to the burning barn, it was clear that at times, the therapy *was* the burning barn. Within that context, I was seen as both igniting the flames and oblivious to their consuming potential. Time and again, I was told, not only to hold on, but to stop posing questions, to stop looking beneath the surface of things, to stop stirring things up. On one occasion, having written out a disturbingly explicit sexual dream, she added to her account: "I hate it. I hate it that you will say that it is my dream, that I am the author of it. I hate to think that I am actually telling you this and I hate that I am so messed up that I think that I should tell you this. This isn't working. I just want to wish this whole thing away. It seems to be getting bigger and worse instead of better." Such frequently voiced feelings represented Grace's outraged sense that my participation sometimes amounted to unjustified overstimulation and the biased pursuit of sexual content. Nonetheless, as indicated above, Grace had to acknowledge that, as we began to piece together and attach content to her fears, her dreams became more explicitly sexual and that she produced the very graphic sexual scenes she so despised.

The bystander who, faced with commotion and cataclysm, failed to see or ignored what he saw was another recurrent transference image. "How could you let this happen?" was a charge frequently leveled at me. As was often the case, the depth of Grace's despair at not being seen to be in trouble was most vividly presented in a dream. Her dream of the baby with ruptured and bloody thighs continued. She wrote:

I am desperate, possessed. I am screaming and crying for help. "Help! Help! Someone please help!" I am going crazy because no one comes, even though I can hear people moving about in the hall outside my door. I crawl out of bed, around a corner in my room to a big glass window that looks out onto a nurse's station. There are many nurses in there. I am weak, but I pound on the glass and shout to get their attention. They are busy about their work and don't notice me. I am frantic. Finally, a woman looks up. I catch her eye. She smiles and appears friendly. She looks familiar. I catch her eye. I gesture to her that I need help. She smiles and nods and turns back to her work, putting something in a drawer. I am on fire with anger and frustration.

The dream offered a transparent view of someone who is supposed to be there to provide care and assistance but who is pointedly not paying attention. Grace's agitation reflected not only her need for help, but also her sense of being ignored. The lifeguard was looking elsewhere while someone was drowning and screaming for help.

These persistent transference patterns left me with more specific questions, but now with more specific answers waiting in the wings. Can transference patterns like this be taken as literal reenactments? Did her explicit image of being held, as a frightened child, by me as an adult have any literal antecedent? Could it represent a situation which might have been exploited? Is it significant that the images of me as invasive and overstimulating, as promoting sexual content, were generally manifested in male figures? Similarly, what does it mean that the figures to whom Grace's distress was invisible were often, as in the dream, women?

These more sharply focused questions helped arrange the clinical data into what appeared to be more coherent pieces. Meaning could be glimpsed where before only uncertainty was seen. For example, at one juncture, I wondered if Grace would appreciate seeking a consultation for herself about our work. Without hesitation, she told me that she couldn't ask for one because she had "to be faithful to this! I have to say I trust you, I trust this!" When I commented that this seemed to be more a matter of will than belief, Grace agreed emphatically. I then wondered what might have happened between her and someone else that might have made her feel she had to trust them even though something else might make her question it. Her immediate response was, "I can't think about this anymore. I need to get quiet." Viewed from the perspective of the answers forming in my mind, Grace's distress at my question looked like confirmation of the possibility that her trust had been betrayed in some situation in which betrayal could not be revealed or acknowledged. Similarly, I began to wonder whether her panicked nighttime cries of "No, no, God not now" referred to real past events with real people. Maybe it wasn't God who took her into Him.

The appearance of explicit dreams of sexual exploitation seemed to provide the best conceivable evidence for the possibility of unremembered past sexual trauma. In a three- or four-month period after her divorce, Grace presented a series of dreams which portrayed explicit, coerced sexual contact with an older man. In one of these dreams, she recognized the face of the man forcing his tongue deep inside her mouth. "Not now Uncle Joe, but Uncle Joe like forty years ago," adding that although not a child in the dream, Grace too was much younger than her current age. With manifest sincerity, Grace thought it inconceivable that this dream might represent or reflect an actual experience with her uncle.

Other dreams were more explicit and precise. In the dream which began this chapter, Grace was having her legs pried apart by her husband, but as a terrified young girl. Grace wrote up this dream and disposed of it by leaving it in my waiting room. The text continued: "Then it is as if I had caught myself in the act of dreaming this dream. I am horrified and terrified and confused at seeing L with this child. It's chaos, and then the me that is now, as I am now yells 'Stop, stop!' This is one of those dreams—I don't want any more of those dreams, no more, no more." Talking about it later, Grace wondered if, like an angry director crashing onto a set yelling "Cut! Cut!," she were trying to rescue that little girl from harm, or from additional harm. It was hard to avoid the impression that Grace's intense revulsion carried with it a certain implication of reality: she seemed to react as if the dream reflected actual events. Telling me such dreams, moreover, was invariably accompanied by an explicit pressure not to tell. Repeatedly Grace would let me know that something inside her was warning her, and insisting, "Don't tell him."

The image of herself as the "exact same child" was recurrent and specific; she was always attired in the same blue dress with puffed sleeves, and identified the image as herself, in reality, at 7 or 8 years old. "This exact same child" appeared in several dreams as well as in Grace's frequent desires to clasp onto me. Invariably, this child was frightened to the point of desperation, and invariably, mute. Even when Grace appeared as an adult in these dreams of coerced sexual contact, she screamed only on the inside while giving the outward appearance of silently going along. If protest was registered, it was, as in the above dream, an adult Grace looking on in horror at the mute terror of her child self.

Like missing puzzle pieces, other material reinforced a notion of child rape and of delayed emotional reactions. In one poignant dream, Grace recounted hearing her son respond to her call in an odd tone of voice. Going to his room, she found him "crying, frightened, enraged, despondent, and confused." Her son told her, "I've been raped" and when Grace awakened, she realized she was experiencing her son's feelings and that the dream was about her. Soberly and hesitantly, Grace added that she now remembered something, that this was how she felt the last few years with her husband.

Discounted or inaccessible feelings emerged. Long separated from her husband, during a visit he startled her with a sudden embrace. A few days later, while taking a shower, Grace found herself washing her mouth over and over again. She then realized how violated she had felt, and how repulsed she had been by their sexual contact during the last few years of their marriage. She hated herself for permitting it, and was dismayed that, "I didn't know how I felt about it until a few days ago." If it was possible to block recent feelings so completely, was it unthinkable that earlier, similar feelings could also be totally inaccessible?

And were wholly inaccessible feelings and memories unthinkable given Grace's ferocious determination to keep such a possibility out of mind? On several occasions, I was told, when the evidence seemed most indicative, that "I don't want to know about it if I was sexually mistreated. I just want to let it alone." Again, a dream captured the tone, not only of Grace's narrow-eyed resistance, but perhaps, of her abuser's demand for secrecy.

Grace was out hiking and saw a bearded man with a girl who was too big for a back-pack, but nonetheless was being carried in one. The girl was tightly wrapped in a blanket, which covered her mouth so that she could not talk. With an ominous tone, the man said to Grace, "Don't even think about asking about her."

Eventually Grace offered the "bear in the house" dream about a concealed attacker lurking invisibly during the day, but poised to invade her bedroom at night. Her dread was preferable to searching out the bear during the day. Given the preceding cumulative evidence of past trauma, I commented on the possibility that the dream might be about someone from her household entering Grace's bedroom, with Grace feeling great dread but unable to face her attacker directly. Grace responded that she had no such memory, and in addition, felt frightened at the implication that there was a deeper layer of meaning beyond the feelings about her husband whom she identified as the bear in the dream. Further, she remarked that she could follow my interpretation if it were applied to a third person but not if it was applied to herself. Grace ended with what amounted to a plea: "It's not my dad—I just want you to know that. You don't know him. It's not him."

Interpretations, like the above, unfolded bit by bit. Cautious wonderings about the possibility of some unknown early trauma were followed by more specific hypotheses as the material began to seem more consistent with and suggestive of sexual trauma. As these tentative interpretations took on more clarity, Grace's material seemed to open up, as if, having glimpsed the truth, the truth could more clearly reveal itself. In general such interpretations worked at the outer edge of her tolerance. Like a rapidly spinning but unbalanced wheel, Grace feared she might simply shake apart if she took these possibilities seriously.

REVIEWING THE EVIDENCE

Over time, I formed a very specific idea of what Grace's unremembered past trauma might have been. On a number of occasions, and for a period of time when she was about 8 years old, Grace was kissed and forcibly fondled on the genitals, perhaps with efforts at intercourse, by an older man at night in her bedroom or in the bathroom. Her attacker might have been someone who otherwise ought to be trusted; someone else who might have protected her was oblivious to her plight.

A reconstruction along these general lines makes sense of much of the clinical data. The contemporary nighttime panics could be seen as reenactments of her childhood terror—her efforts to plead for mercy, and, by lying prone, to protect herself from invasion. Later dissociative episodes recapitulated her earlier attempts to disconnect from her terror. Her subservience to her husband could easily be seen as repeating the almost mesmerized passivity and compliance of a young girl too frightened to protect herself and too frightened to let herself remember how she felt or even what happened. The repeated internal message "not to tell" may reflect some earlier threat of silence and secrecy. The repetitive dreams of foreboding water suggest that water may have played some part in her trauma, hence the possibility that some of the abuse occurred in the bathroom. Finally, her agitation at the mere thought of past trauma might be seen both as confirming the notion that she had something powerful and disruptive hidden from herself and as revealing the depths of her earlier distress. At this juncture, one simple fact stands against this reading of the evidence: Grace did not recall or recover any memories of these hypothesized childhood events.

This simple fact prompts one to ask, just how good is this evidence? In the late 1980s and early 1990s, one could align it with a growing literature on trauma and childhood sexual abuse. My awareness of this literature was casual rather than systematic, but seemed sufficient to note the broad outlines of an emerging set of conclusions. Childhood sexual trauma was real and occurred much more often than was generally accepted by the psychoanalytic community (Wolf and Alpert, 1991; Simon, 1992). Such trauma led to significant psychological problems and produced characteristic signs of traumatization (Terr, 1988, 1991), including repetitive playback dreams, behavioral reenactments, and the "sitting duck syndrome" described by Kluft (1990). Impressively massive, repeated trauma could be unavailable to consciousness (Terr, 1991); that is, people could be genuinely unaware of having been victims of early sexual abuse. It had even been demonstrated that some people could not only come to recall previously unremembered trauma, but also find documentary evidence to substantiate those recovered memories (Herman and Schatzov, 1987). Finally, some dreams apparently could be regarded as relatively transparent windows through which unremembered trauma could be seen (Alpert, 1994).

Collectively, these findings substantiated my clinical inferences. Yet, despite the support derived from this literature, in my mind the case refused to be decided. More accurately, the case closed and reopened several times over. Although suggestive, the evidence remained circumstantial and not entirely conclusive. Perhaps Grace did not recover memories because there were none to recall. Perhaps her reluctance to consider the possibility of past abuse was to be taken at face value and reflected honest disagreement rather than defense. Did her voice of protest count, and if not, why not? Was the evidence, however circumstantial, good enough? Questions initially focused in two areas: Given my reliance on the capacity of dreams to capture and reflect memory, how well researched was the literal relationship which was said to exist between past memory, trauma, and certain dreams? And, if patients could not directly reveal their traumatic past, how accurately could these patients with concealed trauma be identified by certain signs and symptoms thought to be characteristic responses to trauma?

In trying to answer these questions, I learned many things I did not know, and worse, many things I thought I knew, but did not. I also discovered that, in these respects, I was not alone. And only later, with more careful examination, did I find significant flaws in the research I had used to direct my thinking.

2   TRAUMA, DREAMS, AND SYMPTOMS

DREAMS AND TRAUMA

Dreams have long enjoyed a privileged position in psychoanalytic theory and clinical process. In recent times the "royal road" provided by dreams leads not only toward the dynamic unconscious, but also toward memories of actual traumatic events. Over and over, clinical experience appears to teach us that the past, especially a disruptive past, may be viewed, often quite literally, through a window in certain dreams. Strikingly realistic, repetitive, and anxiety provoking (Huizenga, 1990), these dreams are held, both clinically and conceptually, to the side, away from ordinary dreams. We call them "traumatic dreams." Broad-reaching anecdotal clinical evidence has given this class of dreams a kind of conceptual independence which tempts us to think at times that we have found a transparent dream window through which the past may be seen clearly.

Some of the impetus for this shift from psychic to material reality no doubt is driven by our increased recognition of the existence of actual traumatic experience in the early lives of many of our patients. While some patients can declare this knowledge

17

from the outset, it is at least as common for them to present
without conscious memory of any past traumatic experience
(Wolf and Alpert, 1991). For these patients, the analytic process
often results in the gradual reconstruction or recovery of quite
specific memory regarding early trauma. While the evidence
which accrues to point the analytic inquiry in the direction of
trauma is broad and complex—including distinctive defenses and
behavioral and transference reenactments—very often a central
role in the discovery process is accorded to dreams.

The history of this use of dreams begins with Freud (1918)
and Nunberg (1932), returns in the fifties and sixties (Greenacre,
1953a,b; Rosen, 1955; Niederland, 1965; Sachs, 1967; Stewart,
1969), and then mushrooms in the last decade (Schuker, 1979;
Jucovy, 1986; Dowling, 1987; Greenberg and van der Kolk, 1987;
Williams, 1987; Marcus, 1989; Myers, 1989; Bernstein, 1989, 1990;
Raphling, 1990; Kramer, 1990; Lisman-Pieczanski, 1990; Sherkow,
1990a,b; Eyre, 1991; Alpert, 1994). In each of these reports,
dreams are used as a central or primary source of evidence in
the analytic reconstruction of repressed childhood trauma. What
follows is a critical examination of the relationship between
dream content and trauma, and the conceptualizations upon
which the notion of a "traumatic dream" is based.

The concept of a "traumatic dream" asserts a connection
between a real (known or unknown) event and the manifest content of a dream. The connection is in the nature of a *homomorphism*, that is, a similarity in outward appearance between the
dream and the "event." This "event" not only leaves tracks, but
tracks which follow a pattern homologous to the event. In conceptually setting aside such a group of dreams, we have presumed
some very specific and potentially unique operations of the dream
process. The general and ordinary process of dream formation
involves subjecting internally and externally generated images to
a series of transformations which are integrated and assembled
to form the manifest dream. This set of transformations includes
Freud's (1900) displacement, symbolization, condensation, and
secondary elaboration. In a traumatic dream, images associated
with a potent real "event" may be unaffected by this broader set
of transformations or, more precisely in line with our definition,

may be affected only by a restricted set of limited, literal transformations which preserve the original, or a clearly homologous form, of the material stimuli.

THE ISOMORPHIC TRAUMATIC DREAM

In principle, there exists a special case in which the trauma and the dream are isomorphic, or absolutely identical. This special case is a unique psychic phenomenon and deserves a close look. The above depiction of the dream process as the interpolation of a set of transformations between some form of initial images or experiences and the dream product, grossly simplifies matters. There is seldom such a thing—in any isolated or objective form—as an "initial image." Beyond this, one must also include the level of arousal or stress which exists in an individual throughout the period of dream production. The period of dream production, rather than a REM interval, is referred to because the processes which are integral to the final production of a dream must include wide-ranging perceptions and memory storage which long predate the actual interval of dreaming. Recall of such stored material, as well as the final fashioning of the dream, and the verbal communication of the dream to a second party, are also subprocesses in the formation of what is called, finally, a dream.

We have enumerated perception, memory, recall, fashioning, and communication as phases in the production of a dream. Each of these junctures, or complex subphases, is open to the interpolation of transformations. The concept of an isomorphic traumatic dream asserts that such "complexly motivated psychic products" (Renik, 1981, p. 177) may be generated which *completely* bypass transformative processes to yield an absolutely faithful reproduction of the traumatic event. These transformative processes must be bypassed at *every* phase or juncture—perception, memory storage and retrieval, fashioning, and communication—of dream production. In addition this must be accomplished under conditions of extreme stress or arousal, circumstances that we believe increase rather than diminish the impact of such personal transformations. In short the existence of

an isomorphic dream requires cameralike objectivity at every processing phase from an individual in a state of extreme distress
and peril.

Whatever weight is carried by these considerations could be
undone by the presentation of a counterexample. Can we find
an isomorphic pairing of trauma and manifest dream? A careful
review of the literature leads to a surprising conclusion: Statements of equivalence are made but actual texts are almost never
presented. Bonaparte (1947), Renik (1981), van der Kolk et al.
(1984), and Terr (1979, 1990) make explicit reference to dreams
which are "exact replicas" (van der Kolk et al., 1984, p. 188) of
a trauma, or "accurately [repeat them] in faithful detail" (Renik,
1981, p. 175). The *only* quoted texts are to be found in Terr's
(1979) study of children abducted and buried at Chowchilla. One
(of two cited) "exact repeat playback . . . dreams" (p. 587) reads
in its entirety: "I dream when the man gets on—when we get on
the vans" (p. 589). Impressively, van der Kolk et al. based their
"exact replica" conclusion on the dreamers' statements of equivalence without collecting *any* dreams (Hartmann, personal communication, 1993).

In addition, there is no research evidence that discrete images or experiences may be literally transposed into manifest
dream content. As reported by Freud (1900), Maury applied a
variety of stimuli (tickling with a feather, smelling cologne, being
pinched lightly, etc.) to a sleeping subject. While each of the
stimuli seems to have had a discernible impact on the ensuing
dream, the form of that impact was never identical to the stimulus. Fisher's study (Fisher and Paul, 1959) found that subliminally
presented images only marginally affected dream content. No
literal inclusion of the images occurred.

A much more powerful experimental test is offered by Witkin
and Lewis (1965). Their elaborate and scrupulously constructed
experiment permits us to explore carefully the question of
whether highly charged presleep stimuli find expression in subsequent dreams, and, more informally, whether the presleep stimuli
can be derived from the dreams. Subjects were shown movies with
explicit and charged bodily and sexual implications, and then
reported dreams from later REM awakenings.

Let us approach the latter question first by providing some of the dream imagery without indicating its likely source: (1) a troop carrier plane with people, parachutists jumping out of it; (2) a hot closet; and (3) white gloves on a girl's arms (pp. 829–830). These images were culled by the authors from many dream reports as among the most vivid and clear-cut representations of aspects of a presleep film. It is *not* obvious, unless one knows the film, that all refer to a vivid birth scene. The authors suggest that the troop carrier is derived from the pregnant woman, the closet from the vagina, and the white gloves from the obstetrician's bloody gloves.

There is no doubt that film images find expression in the dreams, but impressively there are *no* literal transpositions of any of the presleep films into the manifest dreams. Witkin and Lewis conclude that: "the identification of an element in a dream as related to a pre-sleep stimulus relies on the intuitive interpretation of a symbolic or metaphoric dream translation" (p. 829). The body is replaced by "congruently structured and functioning mechanical objects" (p. 835). These transformations are highly personal, and often focus on peripheral details, or central details which omit significant portions of the films' latent meanings. We are left with the conclusion that not only can we not divine the film from the dream alone, but also that, having seen the film, we could not predict the dream images. They are apparent only when one knows the film.

In an even more dramatic study, DeKoninck and Koulack (1975) presented subjects with a film about industrial accidents in which a worker is impaled by a board and dies. Even this level of intense stimulation did not result in a single exact reproduction of a film element in any dream from any subject.

Nonetheless, some clinical evidence indicates that under specific conditions occasional pieces of literal dream incorporation of traumatic experience do occur (Bonaparte, 1947; Rappaport, 1968; Wilmer, 1982, 1986; Lisman-Pieczanski, 1990; Chasseguet-Smirgel, 1992; A. Siegel, 1992).

The lion hunter's dreams are a classical example (Bonaparte, 1947). W, a professional ranger and hunter, is on horseback when lion A approaches him from the front and attacks. W manages to evade this lion, only to be snatched by a second lion, B. B grabs him by his shoulder and drags him off to the base of a tree. W unsheathes his knife and strikes three times at B, wounding it, and causing it to retreat. W climbs the tree and, to avoid falling, straps himself to the tree. Lion A returns and prowls around the tree. W's party hears his cries and finds him. Three days later, after much travail, W is attended by a physician and miraculously recovers.

One of the dreams reported by W, as best as can be determined by Bonaparte, the most proximal to the trauma, is as follows:

> I am out hunting lions, find a troop of them and fire at and hit one and it at once charges me. I fire again but the shot does not go off. I run to a tree close by, climb up it, and get out of reach of the lion whereupon a very big bull buffalo appears and starts butting the tree with his head. The tree sways to and fro and I fall. Then I waken to find it is only a dream for which I am terribly thankful [p. 5].

This dream retains the core of the trauma—W is confronted by a lion and escapes to a tree from which he fears being dislodged—but is nonetheless remarkably altered. The knife becomes a gun, and the initial close encounter a remote one. Lion A reappears as a bull buffalo who butts rather than prowls around the tree. Finally, in the trauma B attacks W and then W attacks B; while in the dream, this action sequence is reversed.

For a second example, a woman who lost her home in the 1991 Oakland, California firestorm dreamt that she was, "suddenly watching a woman burn alive in a building. I was watching her. There was nothing I or anyone else could do. She was terrified as she clutched the front of the charred building—flames all around her . . . " (A. Siegel, 1992, p. 5). The fire and its destructive implications for this helpless woman are literally portrayed. However, even here a substitution has been made: It is not her house which burns in the dream but another building and another woman. Significantly, as a child this woman's family home had been destroyed by fire.

In a similar fashion, Rappaport (1968) dreams about his concentration camp experience; and combat soldiers dream about combat (Wilmer, 1982, 1986). In all of the above, the dreamer was cognitively prepared for the trauma (because it was in the line of duty, had happened before, or was repeated), traumatized as an adult, and had access to memory of the trauma. As may be gauged by the lion hunter's dreams, without knowledge of the trauma, no observer could identify which dream elements were relatively untransformed.

In sum, there is no empirical evidence, and only limited clinical evidence to support any isomorphic transposition of traumatic experience into dream content, except under the very restricted conditions noted above. Even then dream transformations are so encompassing that it is impossible, without knowing the trauma, to identify which dream components are isomorphic.

Freud's conclusion about Maury's experiments is equally applicable to the clinical and research evidence we have reviewed: "we may have a suspicion that the sensory stimulus which impinges on the sleeper plays only a modest part in generating his dream and that other factors determine the choice of the mnemic images which are aroused in him" (1900, p. 29). Material reality is always transformed, and only when the mind is specifically prepared is it even partially transformed in a literal sense.

THE HOMOMORPHIC TRAUMATIC DREAM

When we examine dream texts which can be paired with trauma texts, it becomes apparent that the relationship between them is homomorphic not isomorphic (see also Grinker and Spiegel [1945] and Kanzer [1949] for dream responses to war trauma; Levitan [1965], to shocking news; Horowitz [1986, pp. 217–226], to witnessing a suicide; Terr [1985], to a friend's rape and murder; Terr [1990], to being injured in an accident). A range of examples will make this clear.

Rappaport (1968) reports the following dream from a middle-aged Polish concentration camp survivor: "She and hundreds of other women were pulled high up in an open elevator and then all blood and fat was sucked out of the women and pumped through pipes into a big kettle" (p. 726). The dream leaves no doubt that the dreamer sees herself as an indistinguishable unit in the Nazi's bestial, inhuman rendering of fat.

An Israeli colonel, who as a child during World War II wandered through central Europe on his own, dreams recurrently that: "I am on a conveyor belt moving relentlessly toward a metal compactor. Nothing I can do will stop that conveyor belt and I will be carried to my end, crushed to death" (Felman and Laub, 1992, p. 79). There is no mistaking this man's view of his helplessness in the face of the Nazis' relentless, crushing power.

Also a concentration camp survivor, Rappaport, after discussing many of his own dreams, makes this observation: "I never dream about specific traumatic experiences in the camp such as . . . [recounts specific memory]" (p. 729).

These are instances of massive and repeated trauma. It is impossible to track the precise transformations which lead to the metaphoric renditions presented in the dream. Circumscribed traumatic events permit this. Accompanied by his wife and others, Loewenstein's (1949) patient suffered a violent canoe accident in which he was separated from the others and swept away by a torrential current. Clinging desperately to his canoe for miles, he barely managed to hang on while pulled underwater through powerful rapids. He emerged "helpless and exhausted" near the rest of his party and was carried to shore.

Loewenstein writes that "the night after the accident" the patient had the following dream:

> He is shut in the highest room of a tower. An elderly woman is trying to prevent him from escaping. He succeeds in diving through the floors, ceilings, and walls of the different rooms of the tower, one after the other. He arrives below in a yard, shut off by a large porte-cochere. He hesitates to ring for the concierge and dives through the door, turning outside to the right with a feeling of enormous relief [pp. 449–450].

The patient's dream *on the night of the accident* has so fully transformed the trauma that it is highly unlikely it can be deciphered from the dream, and yet so aptly conveys the trauma that once it is described, the homomorphism between trauma and dream is immediately obvious. The traumatic event has been simultaneously rendered and transformed beyond recognition into an almost mythic and fanciful escape.

A significant number of the dreams Terr (1979) reports from the Chowchilla children abducted and buried for hours in a dimly lit truck trailer have this same quality: an expressively apt metaphor which simultaneously personalizes and conceals the details of the original traumatic experience. Examples include: (1) "I had a dream in a castle. I was a princess with a big giant catching me, grabbing me. He grabbed me by the shirt and ripped it off." (2) "Someone will get me and take me away in the ocean. You'd go down and down with the fish. The shark would eat me" (pp. 589–590).

A final example is provided by the dream of an evacuee of the 1991 Oakland firestorm (A. Siegel, 1992). A man whose home was unexpectedly saved from destruction by an air-dropped fire retardant, dreamed: "In my house watching the flood waters rise. Soon I look out the window and the ocean waters are coming right up to the edge of the house . . . water starts leaking in. . . . Then as I watch out the window, the flood recedes like in the movie the Ten Commandments" (p. 6).

In *all* of these examples, no element from the preceding trauma is literally transposed into the manifest content. Heinous Nazi crimes become large-scale fat rendering; their relentless power an unstoppable conveyor belt moving toward a metal compactor. Being held in an engulfing river is depicted as being held captive by an elderly woman in a tower. A big giant replaces kidnappers, while the buried truck trailer is replaced by being down in the ocean with the fish. Biblically receding waters represent miraculously delivered fire retardant. At the same time each element is transformed, the experience of the trauma is reassembled in such a way as to provide a highly personalized recapitulation of the experience.

This review of the transformations interposed between trauma and dream emphasizes the unpredictability of the relationship between trauma and dream content. Literal recreation in the dream of some traumatic circumstances does occur but only under very restricted conditions. Much more prevalent, however, are transformations which scramble the specifics. The dreamer's position in the event is not necessarily an invariant. The dreamer may be omitted and his role even reversed (the soldier killer becomes the potential victim [Kanzer, 1949].

Even though we can enumerate and describe the types of transformations interposed between specific experience and certain manifest dreams, we cannot determine the rules by which these transformations are applied. In other words, while substitutions and reversals, for example, are regularly employed, we cannot predict what specific content may be subject to transformation by substitution or by reversal. We cannot even say what content is most likely to be subjected to a particular type of transformation. Similarly, it is impossible at present to infer from any given dream content what type of transformation has been applied during the process of dreaming.

Another complexity may be noted. The dreamer's *relationship* to the event which generates a homomorphic dream spans a wide and varied range. Within the sample of dreams reviewed here, the dreamer may be the agent of the event (wartime killing, Kanzer [1949]); the object or victim of the event (accident, Loewenstein [1949]); witness (suicide, Horowitz [1986]); relative of a victim (sister of Chowchilla victim, Terr [1990, p. 230]); indirect witness (friend who heard what happened to victim, Terr [1985, p. 520]); and spared potential object (Oakland firestorm, A. Siegel [1992]). Being the object of the event is *not* the only position which results in a homomorphic dream.

IDENTIFYING A DREAM BASED ON TRAUMA

Before a clinician can begin the task of reconstructing material reality from dreams (i.e., using them as a form of memory), he or she must be able to identify which dreams contain references, be they literal or metaphoric, to a past traumatic reality. The patient cannot do this directly because we have restricted ourselves to patients with, as is often reported to be the case, no direct recall of trauma.

Which dreams are based on trauma? Numerous psychoanalytic solutions have been proposed to this problem. Among the many properties of dreams thought to point toward a link with trauma, those most frequently noted are stereotyped repetition and intense distress in conjunction with some element of realism

(Freud, 1937; Greenacre, 1956; Stewart, 1969; Renik, 1981; van der Kolk et al., 1984; Pulver, 1987; Myers, 1989; Huizenga, 1990; Alpert, 1994). Huizenga (1990) reports on a patient with direct memories of incest as a child who has dreams with exactly these qualities.

It is relatively easy to demonstrate that however accurately traumatic dreams are captured by these criteria, they are not the only dreams which can be so described. Indeed, quite a number of "typical" dreams also fulfill these criteria: the nearly ubiquitous dreams of examinations ill prepared for, of appearing naked in public, and of being chased. One would be hard pressed to assert that all of these dreams are based on trauma.

Similar conclusions may be drawn from Hartmann's (1984) investigation of subjects suffering from long-standing, frequent, disruptive nightmares. Hartmann identified fifty subjects who reported suffering from, on average, four sleep disrupting nightmares per week. Almost all of these people described this as a long-standing pattern which extended back to childhood. The nightmares themselves were harrowing, repetitive, and "real": Typically the dreamer was being "not only chased, but attacked, or hurt . . . in many cases the dreamer was actually caught, beaten, stabbed, shot, or mutilated" (p. 60). Hartmann notes the context of the threat as including war, riot, catastrophe, or torture. In other words, the content of these dreams, and the subjects' pattern of dreaming, resembles that of traumatized subjects: The dreams repetitively portray the dreamer as a helplessly terrified victim or object of mayhem and so distressed as to disrupt sleep.

In fact, Hartmann was so struck by the phenomenological parallels between these dreamers and trauma victims that he made an extremely careful investigation of these subjects' backgrounds for evidence of serious trauma such as sexual or physical attack, and witnessing death or catastrophe. Finding no historical support, he concluded that serious trauma did not play a part in the highly charged dream experience of these subjects.

Several reports (Bernstein, 1990; Huizenga, 1990) make note of strikingly explicit sexual dreams in cases where there is evidence (preexisting memory and possible external confirmation) of early sexual trauma. There are also a number of articles (Stewart, 1969; Williams, 1987; Alpert, 1994) where these kinds of dreams are reported, but where the confirmatory evidence consists of reconstructions and recovered memories. While it may be that such dreams are reliable indicators of repressed early sexual trauma, this contention cannot be supported by these reports in which dreams generate reconstructions which are then used to validate the dreams as trauma based.

The case may be made that *no* formal or content properties intrinsic to the manifest dream itself have been identified which justify classifying a dream as being of traumatic origin. The import of this conclusion is *not* that traumatic dreams do not exist (indeed they are quite common), but only that there are *no defining characteristics which pertain only to or to all dreams of traumatic origin.*

An argument continues to be made, however, that an adequate foundation of evidence exists to validate extracting inaccessible memory from dreams (Alpert, 1995). Nevertheless, there are too many complexities and uncertainties both in the relationship of dream content to memory, and in the identification of dreams derived from traumatic experience, to warrant any degree of confidence in doing so (Brenneis, 1994b, 1995). Repetitive, anxiety provoking dreams do not point exclusively toward trauma. Even though dreams may homomorphically recapitulate traumatic experience, in the absence of firm knowledge of the material reality upon which the dream is based, this congruence may be extremely obscure. No one can adequately justify why one type of transforming link should apply to a certain dream element and why a different type of link should apply to another dream element. There is no firm ground for asserting that some types of dream elements are most likely to be taken as literal while others are understood as metaphor and still others as reversals. Although all of these types of transformations occur, we have no basis, as yet, for predicting what type of transformation will be applied to a given experience, and consequently no basis for inferring that a given piece of manifest dream content has been subjected to a particular type of transformation. Any presumption of literal pairing between dream and traumatic reality finds little substantiation in the clinical and empirical literature. The inference of trauma and traumatic content from dreams is fraught with often unrecognized uncertainty and follows no clear-cut or well-substantiated path.

FROM DREAMS TO SYMPTOMS OF PTSD

If we broaden the circle of presumed indices of trauma beyond dreams, other types of problems arise. The diagnostic category of posttraumatic stress disorder (PTSD) exemplifies these inconsistencies. Like the concussion of a violent explosion, the impact of trauma ripples forward in time and inward to the deepest layers of personal experience. Focus on public, collectively experienced trauma such as military combat (Sonnenberg, Blank, and Talbott, 1985), on privately experienced trauma such as incest (Herman, 1981; Gelinas, 1983), and on natural and manmade disasters (Horowitz, 1986; Terr, 1990, 1991), has sensitized professional awareness to issues of trauma. We are now attuned to the emotional significance of these experiences and to their long-term and often debilitating shaping of psychic functioning (Gelinas, 1983; Horowitz, 1986; van der Kolk, 1987). A growing literature reevaluates earlier clinical material (Masson [1984], Freud; van der Kolk and van der Hart, [1989, 1991], Janet), and calls for placing trauma in a central and comprehensive psychopathogenic role (Chu, 1991). As we have become more sensitized to the consequences of trauma, the highly specific cluster of symptoms and behaviors—often designated as posttraumatic stress disorder (PTSD)—which characterize the psychological impact of trauma, is seen with increasing frequency.

With this expanded interest in the effects of trauma has come the revelation that some especially pernicious forms of traumatic experience may not be directly accessible to consciousness. In particular, memories of childhood sexual abuse may fester for decades and only be recalled or remembered in the process of psychotherapy. The current literature (M. Williams, 1987; Dewald, 1989; Olio, 1989; Bernstein, 1990; Kramer, 1990; Alpert, 1994; Brenner, 1994; Person and Klar, 1994) offers many such accounts, and one finds numerous assertions that these circumstances are commonplace (van der Kolk and van der Hart, 1989; Wolf and Alpert, 1991; Kuppersmith, 1992).

The clinician who suspects a history of trauma in a patient who genuinely does not remember it confronts a difficult problem: Can trauma be recognized by its after-effects, in the absence of direct recall? The psychological markers of trauma, aside from direct memory, may be thought of as falling into two categories. The first reflects what might be called, for the moment, indirect memory; that is, psychic experience which captures some literal aspect of the unremembered trauma but which may not be recognized by the individual as an expression of memory. Certain dreams, flashbacks, and repetitive behavioral sequences (van der Kolk et al., 1984; Terr, 1988, 1991; Rynearson and McCreery, 1993) are considered to be exemplars of indirect memory. The second category may be thought of as systemic reverberations of the traumatic experience. Without necessarily being tied to specific content, trauma sufferers, for example, may startle more easily or have more readily disrupted sleep patterns, reflecting a generalized heightening of central nervous system (CNS) functioning (Ross, Norton, and Wozney, 1989). In a different vein, trauma victims may also involuntarily alter their state of consciousness to form a psychic barrier against overwhelming stimulation and affect, and consequently, give evidence of dissociation. The appearance of dissociation, regarded by some to be generated only by trauma, is considered to betray the existence of unrecalled trauma (van der Kolk, 1987; Spiegel, Hunt, and Dondershine, 1988; Braun, 1990; Davies and Frawley, 1991a).

Do these indices provide solid ground for the clinician to identify the unsuspecting victim of past trauma? It might be thought that a straw man proposition lies behind these questions; namely, that any clinician would be convinced of the existence of an unknown past trauma by this type of essentially circumstantial evidence. This proposition construes the inexact art of clinical inference and interpretation as if it were an exact science. Nevertheless, the footprints of precisely this kind of thinking are visible whenever a clinician accepts an offering in the form of a previously inaccessible memory of trauma as an expected or unremarkable outcome from a patient with a symptom cluster similar to the above. Specific clinical instances of this thinking appear with some regularity in the literature (Schuker, 1979; M. Williams, 1987; Olio, 1989; Kramer, 1990; Alpert, 1994; Brenner, 1994; Person and Klar, 1994). A more general and broader version appears in conclusive statements like Chu's (1991):

The re-experiencing or reliving of previously dissociated experiences must be recognized, whether in its full-blown form of flashbacks or in many kinds of partial forms. It is only with the recognition of the presence of old trauma and the acknowledgment of the importance of trauma in producing emotional disturbance and psychiatric illness, that these patients can be effectively treated [p. 331].

The imperative voice ("must") and the exclusive qualifier ("only") presume a certainty about the relationship between symptoms and trauma which may turn out to be less than absolute.

It is essential to note that the level of evidence required by the clinician to identify the victim of unrecalled trauma is of "necessity," not just "sufficiency." By linking documented and remembered trauma (such as combat experience) with their consequences, most studies demonstrate that trauma is sufficient to produce certain psychological effects. In order to deduce the occurrence of unremembered trauma, however, the evidence must demonstrate that these effects can only be generated by trauma. In other words, trauma is necessary to their appearance and no other conditions or circumstances produce these same effects. For example, if terrifying, realistic, and repetitive dreams can be seen in nontraumatized chronic nightmare sufferers, such dreams cannot be taken as evidence of unremembered trauma. Clearly, this is a much more stringent requirement and places a premium on a search for other conditions which mimic or replicate typical responses to trauma. Those who make this search do not return empty-handed.

FLASHBACKS AND BEHAVIORAL REENACTMENTS

The intrusive reexperience of traumatic events, in dreams, flashbacks, or actions, is a primary diagnostic marker for PTSD (DSM-III-R, APA, 1987; DSM-IV, APA, 1994). Implicit in this criterion are the notions that such dreams, flashbacks, and action sequences represent memory of the experience and occur only to the immediate victims or objects of trauma. As was demonstrated with dreams, both of these assumptions can be shown to be much too exclusively framed. Flashbacks and repetitive action patterns need not reflect any significant memory component, nor do they occur only to the direct victims of trauma.

Rynearson and McCreery (1993) studied the responses of eighteen subjects to the homicide of a family member. Vivid, intense images reenacting the murder appeared as repetitive intrusive waking images to all but one of the subjects (and also as repetitive nightmares for most). Nonetheless, the images which replayed the murder were only apparently authentic, for just one of the subjects had actually witnessed the homicide. Rynearson and McCreery conclude that "abundant and elaborate fantasized projections embellished the visual imagery" (p. 259). Without doubt, these family members were deeply affected by the death, but these vivid ideational products (flashbacks) do not guarantee the direct and immediate involvement of the subject as a witness, or do they reflect direct memory of the homicide. Similar conclusions may be drawn from a study of children's reactions to a sniper attack at school (Pynoos and Nader, 1989). Some children who were not at school during the attack report vivid flashback memories of events they had only heard about.

Frankel's (1994) historical review casts additional doubt on the necessary association between flashbacks and trauma, and further erodes the notion of the flashback as a "historically accurate revisualization or memory" (p. 321). Identifying the psychiatric origin of the term in the 1960s in the reexperiencing of imagery connected with hallucinatory drug use, Frankel follows its evolution into the literature on Vietnam combat veterans and finally into the literature on early childhood trauma. In the process, the term metamorphosed from a description of the return of altered states of awareness and amorphous imagery with little claim of accurate memory, into one with an implicit and nearly absolute claim of both memory and accuracy. Frankel, however, cites one study (Rainey, Aleem, Ortiz, Yeragani, Pohl, and Berchou, 1987) in which patients produced flashbacks of impossible events, and another (Maloney, 1988) in which the female partners of Vietnam veterans absorbed imagery from them and experienced it as their own. Based on his comprehensive survey, Frankel concludes (1994) that "dependence on the concept of a flash-back to validate such recall [of childhood trauma] is entirely unsupported by any evidence in the literature" (p. 332).

We can draw a parallel here to the data reviewed on homomorphic traumatic dreams. Bystanders, relatives, and possible but absent victims may present flashbacks and dreams of events which have occurred to others. Expanding the criteria for PTSD, as is done in DSM-IV, to include exactly such individuals (i.e., witnesses, relatives, and close associates), further muddies the water. Modifying criteria in this way means that more people may be retrospectively identified as having suffered trauma, but with less certainty that they were directly and immediately the victim. This may be of little consequence in many regards, but introduces a large element of uncertainty when working backwards or deducing the existence of unremembered traumatic events from these types of symptoms.

Traumatic experiences also generate repetitive and stereotyped action sequences (Blank, 1985; Terr, 1988, 1991; Dewald, 1989; Kramer, 1990) in which critical elements of that experience are reproduced, oftentimes without individuals' awareness that trauma is being reenacted. Blank offers several examples of Vietnam veterans who unconsciously duplicate overwhelming combat experiences; and Terr cites instances of children's activities which replay traumatic events. But stereotyped actions, often quite complex and accompanied by great anxiety, are also routinely performed in compulsive rituals. Typically, although individuals behaving in this way may not know why certain actions must be carried out, the actions themselves reflect coherent symbolic meanings. Consequently these action sequences may be indistinguishable from those of trauma victims.

Postural and behavioral sequences like these have appeared in other, telling contexts, and been mistakenly taken as the repetition of traumatic experiences. In the late 1800s Charcot's meticulous observations of hysterical patients at the Salpêtrière found recurrent patterns in their postures and behaviors. Of particular interest is the third phase, that of passionate attitudes, which include postures of crucifixion, ecstasy, and eroticism. In this phase of grand or full-blown hysteria, the patient "experienced various false sensory or mental images . . . ," and would "babble and shout, repeat phrases and gestures . . . " (Drinka, 1984, p. 83) from which Charcot would detect experiences from the patient's past. Rather than reflecting indigenous aspects of hysteria, or revealing the patient's past experiences, however, these well-organized behavioral patterns turned out to have to do with something of a historical accident. Because their buildings were condemned, about 1870 a group of epileptics and hysterics were transferred and housed together under Charcot's care at the Salpétrière (Drinka, 1984). The hysterics' apparently characteristic posturings and behaviors had nothing to do with past experiences but evolved through a complex shaping process which included action models provided by the epileptics, Charcot's passionate interest, and the fame won by these patients throughout the European medical community. Similarly, Janet (reported by van der Kolk and van der Hart, 1989) found the stories and histories of past trauma represented in the automatic and repetitive behaviors of his hysterical patients. Janet's case of Irene, used by van der Kolk as an exemplar of enacted memory of trauma, reveals the flaws in tying unremembered trauma to behavior, and will be carefully explored in chapter 5. In any event, serious doubt must be cast on any association drawn between repetitive behaviors and past trauma in these patients who seem to have a special capacity for psychic and behavioral plasticity.

SYSTEMIC RESPONSES

The possibility emerges that the manifestation of PTSD-like symptoms may have as much to do with personality as with literal trauma, especially when one focuses on the presumed more systemic responses to trauma. Heightened CNS functioning, for example, is clearly visible in the disrupted sleep and repetitive, horrific nightmares suffered by Hartmann's subjects (1984), although Hartmann found no evidence of trauma in their histories. Intensified CNS functioning unassociated with trauma is also indirectly reflected in the research reported by Southwick, Krystal, Morgan, Johnson, Nagy, Nicolaou, Heninger, and Charney (1993).

Using the administration of yohimbine, Southwick attempted to identify the biochemical pathways which activate the behavioral and experiential features of PTSD, including panic attacks and flashbacks. Parenthetically, it is worth noting that this research presumes flashbacks to be factual and veridical. Aside from verifying combat experience from military records, no effort was made by Southwick et al. to collect combat memories from the veterans and to compare those memories with the evoked flashbacks. Careful review of their data (along with previous research with panic disorder patients [Charney, Heninger, and Breier, 1984; Charney, Woods, Goodman, and Heninger, 1987]) lead them to conclude that PTSD patients and panic disorder patients respond in a highly similar fashion to yohimbine and therefore may share a "common neurological abnormality" (p. 272). This raises the possibility that an "altered sensitivity of the noradrenergic system" (p. 272) may underlie both PTSD, and PTSD-like symptoms which appear in a specific group of nontraumatized subjects. These subjects might include both chronic nightmare sufferers and panic disorder patients. The threshold for the experience of uncontrolled stress may be very low in these subjects.

DISSOCIATION

The relationship between dissociation and trauma is similarly confounded by personality variables. Many writers regard the appearance of dissociation to be directly linked to trauma. Some recent research points to dissociation as a defensive response to severe, recurrent trauma (Carlson and Rosser-Hogan, 1991; Bremner, Southwick, Brett, Fontana, Rosenheck, and Charney, 1992), especially experienced early in life (Kluft, 1987; Braun, 1990; Chu and Dill, 1990; Davies and Frawley, 1991a, 1994; Spiegel and Cardena, 1991). In the extreme, the argument is made that dissociation only appears in response to trauma. Van der Kolk and Kadish (1987) argue that, "except when related to brain injury, dissociation always seems to be a response to traumatic life events" (p. 185). More pointedly, in their summary of research of trauma, Davies and Frawley (1991a) declare, "our belief is that dissociation, more than any other clinical phenomenon, is intrinsic to the intrapsychic structure and organization of this patient group [survivors of childhood sexual abuse] and, to a large extent, is pathognomic of it" (p. 7). A more tempered view is offered by Chu and Dill who regard the link between dissociative experience and childhood trauma as "strongly suggest[ive]" (1990, p. 891).

This linear link between trauma and dissociation may be questioned along two lines: Trauma is not uniformly associated with dissociation, and dissociation need not be uniformly tied to trauma. A comprehensive review by Tillman, Nash, and Lerner (1994) reveals several weaknesses in the evidence for a tight link between trauma and dissociation. In particular, they cite the problem of confounding the effects of trauma with other more nonspecific factors, such as level of psychopathology (Nash, Hulsey, Sexton, Harralson, and Lambert, 1993) and pathogenic early environment (Nash et al., 1993). In addition, they discuss the possibility that dissociation may compromise the accuracy of reports of early trauma. Beyond these methodological reservations some empirical work directly contradicts the tie between trauma and dissociation. For example, in Holocaust survivors, where traumatic experiences are severe and well documented, dissociation does not appear as a major posttraumatic feature (Krystal, 1991). Tillman et al. (1994) conclude that although "intuitively attractive, empirical research has not produced a clear demonstration" (p. 407) of the link between trauma and dissociation.

It is also possible that an alternative pathway, unconnected with trauma, exists for the development and expression of dissociative phenomena. Several studies indicate that somewhat less than 5 percent of the population may be characterized as "fantasy prone" and mimic the cognitive dexterities seen in dissociative experiences (Wilson and Barber, 1983; Lynn and Rhue, 1988; Rhue and Lynn, 1988). Most of these individuals are highly hypnotizable and readily amenable to altered states of consciousness. Capable of extraordinary psychic absorption and segregation of consciousness, these individuals describe an immediate, detailed, multisensory fantasy life "as real as real" (Wilson and Barber, 1983, p. 352). Such dissociative phenomena are a routine aspect of the mental life of fantasy prone people. Most of these subjects do not report histories of early abuse or trauma, and given their tendency "to confuse their memories of their fantasies with their memories of actual events" (p. 353), the validity of abuse histories which are reported may be open to question (Lynn and Rhue, 1988). On balance, the hypothesis may be offered that a class of dissociative experiences exists which may be accounted for by fantasy proneness without traumatic implications.

PERSONALITY VARIABLES

There is a fair amount of evidence to indicate that what is reflected in PTSD-like symptoms has as much or more to do with psychological aspects of personality than with objective or clearly defined trauma. Just as some individuals resist the appearance of PTSD symptoms (Lee, Vaillant, Torrey, and Elder, 1995), others seem to be especially sensitive to even ordinary stressors. A cluster of personality and cognitive attributes seems to be associated with a lowered threshold for experiencing trauma and manifesting PTSD-like symptoms.

Boulanger (1985) studied 275 Vietnam veterans six to sixteen years after their return to the United States. While 36 percent of the veterans exposed to heavy combat could be diagnosed with PTSD, a remarkable 17 percent of the noncombat and non-war-zone veterans also suffered from chronic symptoms of PTSD. Boulanger observed that, within her sample, "men of unusually unstable families tended to show traumatic stress reactions not simply to combat but also to the stressors of everyday life" (1985, p. 27). Weighing all of his data (including interviews, sleep studies, and projective and objective psychological tests), Hartmann (1984) felt that the picture of apparent traumatization of chronic nightmare sufferers was best accounted for by the notion of thin or permeable psychological boundaries. Sensitive and empathically attuned to others, they "let things through" (p. 104) to such a degree "that normal fears and angers 'get through' more and become more vivid and frightening for them than for most of us" (p. 105). In his review, Frankel (1994) voices a similar possibility, noting the presence of imaginative proficiency, absorption, and suggestibility in individuals most likely to report flashbacks.

These factors may tie into hypnotic susceptibility. For instance, Spiegel et al. (1988) found that Vietnam veterans diagnosed with PTSD tended to be more susceptible to hypnosis than
veterans without PTSD. Although Spiegel et al. speculate that
trauma, via dissociation, may create a greater responsiveness to
hypnosis, in the context of the above studies, a more persuasive
argument can be made for the reverse; that is, that a certain type
of psychological porousness, thin-skinnedness, and imaginative
absorption lowers the threshold for experiences of trauma. The
dissociative proclivities manifested by fantasy prone individuals
fits snugly within this roughly sketched profile.

The core of PTSD and its symptoms may then have more to
do with "who" than "what." In the absence of direct memory of
something traumatic, PTSD-like symptoms may be taken to reflect
hidden trauma when in fact they more accurately indicate someone whose threshold for the experience of trauma is compara-
tively low, in part because of their relative openness to experience
and their capacity to absorb what surrounds them. This constellation of attributes lies at the heart of an alternative view of recovered memory of trauma which will progressively emerge in
subsequent chapters.

SUMMARY

This discussion of PTSD, although extended, has been far from
comprehensive because PTSD itself has not been the principal
issue. The main points have been that vagaries exist in the memory trail left even by known trauma; an uncertain relationship
obtains between trauma, symptoms, and memory; and certain psychological and cognitive attributes critically influence what is experienced as trauma and as memory. There is no doubt, on the
one hand, that indirect memory, like repetitive dreams and
flashbacks, and systemic reverberations, like heightened CNS
functioning and dissociation, may be produced by trauma. On
the other hand, however, although trauma may be a sufficient
condition for the appearance of such symptoms, it is not a necessary condition. All of these symptoms may also be produced without immediate exposure to significant trauma. In short, trauma,

in the absence of direct memory, cannot be validly inferred from PTSD-like symptoms: False positives exist. Moreover, again in the absence of direct memory, intrusive, repetitive, nonvolitional ideation has no indisputable claim as memory. The content may, as Frankel puts it (1994, p. 331), be "true, false, or confabulated," without a certain or plausible procedure for untangling one from the other, and further without knowing if any objective or factual truth resides within that content.

The material presented in this chapter argues that some individuals may present the presumed clinical signs of trauma without having been exposed to literal trauma. Taken to be victims of hidden trauma, memories of trauma recovered from such individuals must necessarily be historically false. Consequently, two explanatory models are required to account for the recovery of previously inaccessible memory of trauma; one if the memories are valid and true, another if they are invalid and false. The next chapter explores two divergent explanations for this phenomenon and introduces more precise concepts for discussing memory.

3 BELIEF AND SUGGESTION IN THE RECOVERY OF MEMORIES OF CHILDHOOD SEXUAL ABUSE

The recovery of inaccessible memories of childhood abuse, particularly of a sexual nature, has become a frequent aspect of current analytic clinical reports. Questions about the validity of these recovered memories are difficult to address, not only because of the complexity of the data and the processes involved in recovery, but also because such questions are easily taken beyond a scientific and into a political realm: to question may be to discount. Nonetheless, to shy away from the issue of validity may lead to a subtler form of discounting: to place a finding beyond examination erodes its strength. We are in the difficult position of considering that some, but not all, recovered memories may be valid. No blanket generalization is adequate or sufficient.

Some patients, never having forgotten, recall further memories in analysis. Some patients, never having known as adults, recall details of entirely forgotten abuse. The most comprehensive investigations of the recovered memory phenomenon (Loftus, 1993a; Wakefield and Underwager, 1992) place a crucial dividing line between these two instances. No one seriously doubts the basic authenticity of the recollections of the former group who

41

have retained some memory of abuse. Such a distinction, however, is frequently not made either in clinical or research work.

This chapter will explore the problem of how recovered memory and analytic process are related in the specific but considerable subgroup of patients who have completely repressed memories of abuse prior to treatment. The underlying question will be: How do we account for the derepression, recovery, or appearance of heretofore unavailable memory? Two paradigms will be critically examined: first, that the analyst's belief in the existence and ultimate accessibility of repressed memories of early trauma creates a potential for the suggestion of memories; and second, that precisely the same beliefs are a necessary condition for their emergence. Implicitly, the first model tends toward the conclusion that such recovered memories are likely to be invalid or at least heavily influenced by the analyst. Implicitly, the second model tends toward the conclusion that such memories are likely to be valid.

The contrasting nature of the paradigms may be illustrated in the following clinical excerpt (Bernstein, 1990, pp. 81–82). After relating a dream about a boat which gets bigger and bigger, a woman associates to a boat cleat with a line around it. The patient recalls how she panicked when her boyfriend held her around the neck: "Never do that!" she told him. Following an association to her father's hands on a line, teaching her how to tie lines, the analyst asks, "Is that all he taught you to do with your hands?" The patient replies, "Oh my God! . . . my hands around his penis. . . . That's why the boat gets bigger and bigger!"

What has transpired here? Has the analyst, by asking an open-ended question, allowed the patient to recover an inaccessible memory? The clinical data, beyond what is presented here, support the idea that the analyst's direct, well-timed, in tune, and encouraging question has freed the patient to remember what might have been unrememberable in isolation. Or has the analyst posed an apparently open but highly suggestive and leading question? One might also conclude that the patient has been pointed in the direction of the analyst's unspoken but easily completed thoughts and filled in those thoughts rather than recalled an inaccessible memory.

A careful survey of recent clinical literature (Wolf and Alpert, 1991) concludes that many patients enter treatment unaware of memories of childhood sexual abuse. Some sources (Kuppersmith, 1992) estimate that as many as 50 percent of patients fall into this category. The recovery of memories of abuse in these patients is often reported but seldom explicitly described (Schuker, 1979; Dewald, 1989; Kramer, 1990; Bernstein, 1990; Alpert, 1994). Schuker's report, for example (1979), is typical:

> Shortly after I stated that I believed it was indeed possible that she had been sexually assaulted (citing her nightmares, phobia of men, and aggressive perception of sex as evidence), she then remembered an actual episode with many corroborating details.
> At age 4–1/2 she had been molested by a stranger in a field near her house. . . . Within a short time in treatment after recovering this memory and discussing it (accompanied by a brief increase in violent dreams, sleep disturbance, phobic feelings) there was a striking improvement in her level of functioning and relating to others [pp. 569–570].

In the following discussion, a suggestion paradigm and a belief paradigm will be used to account for the therapeutic recovery of previously inaccessible memory of childhood sexual trauma.

SUGGESTION

The topic of suggestion is a sensitive one in psychoanalysis and in the clinical psychoanalytic process, having been historically a favored position from which to challenge or disqualify many now well-established analytic observations. Nonetheless, even within psychoanalysis, the possibility that the analytic process is influenced by suggestion recurs, inasmuch as it is frequently argued against, especially in relation to analytic reconstructions (Freud, 1937; Blum, 1983).

Suggestion operates in the analytic process along a continuum, at one end quite direct and overt, at the other, more subtle and covert. The analyst suggests quite directly, for example, that free association is a useful psychological process, and by his or her open interest that dreams are revealing and relevant (Greenson, 1967). At the same time, although seldom stated directly, the analyst's active involvement implicitly suggests and imperceptibly seeds a variety of beliefs—such as in the existence of new perspectives and meanings, and hope. For the most part these suggestive influences are highly beneficial and unobjectionable. It is with beliefs in the existence and retrievability of fully repressed memories of childhood traumatic events that the role of suggestion becomes more problematic.

Basic assumptions about the nature of memory are critical to this discussion. Historically, psychoanalytic theory has presumed that long-term personal memory, however distorted or transformed in conscious recall, exists as a relatively objective permanent record in the brain. This view of memory is implicit in Freud's thinking, whether expressed as a notion of objective perception (see Schimek, 1975a) or his archaeological analogy for memory (Freud, 1937): "All of the essentials are preserved; even things that seem completely forgotten are present somehow and somewhere, and have merely been buried and made inaccessible to the subject" (p. 260). Currently, the idea that ultimately valid repressed memories from childhood may be recovered presupposes a similar view that some form of indelible, relatively stable, and decipherable memory traces of repressed childhood experience remain in the brain. Penfield's work (1969) on brain stimulation generated apparently hard scientific evidence for such a permanent record conception of memory. From this point of view, suggestive influences would then have to overcome or compete against solid, if inaccessible memory traces.

In recent years, new evidence (summarized by Loftus and Loftus, 1980; Loftus, 1993a; Kihlstrom, 1994a,b) has raised significant questions about what might be characterized as this relatively static view of memory. Memory is now regarded as a dynamic and highly plastic process, never independent of present time and never independent of present context. From this vantage point, it is no longer so convincing to counter reservations about the validity of recovered childhood memories, and the role of suggestion in their recovery, by recourse to the idea of an indelible, stable (if repressed) memory record.

The present context of memory most relevant to psychoanalysis is the analytic dyad. The roles of both analyst and patient are integral to the argument that memory, specifically derepressed memory of childhood trauma, is vulnerable to influence and suggestion. In its subtlest form, suggestion may resemble a seamlessly wrought dance in which each partner both leads and follows, and in which both take apparent spontaneity for authenticity rather than possible artifact. Neither participant need be aware that suggestion is occurring. This is a critical point, for although on occasion the process of suggestion of early abuse is deliberate (M. Williams, 1987; Alpert, 1994), the arguments which support a suggestion paradigm do not require that the process be at all conscious. Suggestion does not require deliberate or witting action from either participant, and in fact operates most powerfully when all participants are unaware of its influence (Ofshe, 1992).

It is somewhat inaccurate then to assign altogether disjunctive roles to clinician and patient for a process which may be more reflexive and symmetric than reactive and asymmetric. Nonetheless, let us begin with the role of the analyst as one who contributes the germ of an idea about repressed events, and the role of the patient as one who elaborates that idea.

Much of what is now understood about the plasticity of memory and its susceptibility to influence and suggestion comes from a well-grounded body of experimental research on eyewitness questioning and reports. Loftus (1979; Loftus, Donders, and Hoffman, 1989; Loftus and Hoffman, 1989; Loftus, 1993a) carefully documents the vulnerability of memory to the conditions under which it is elicited and to falsification by misleading embedded information. Details embedded in questions about perception later return as part of the memory of those perceptions. For example, after viewing a film of a traffic sequence, a question about the kind of car seen beside a stop sign often elicits the recollection of a stop sign where none was present in the film. While such findings are never uniform or found in all subjects, this research indicates the easy access of planted information to memory. Once internalized as an experienced perception, such details tend to be highly durable, and even subject to further elaboration.

In the powerfully charged emotional crucible of the therapeutic relationship, the potential always exists for influencing perceptions and memory by pointed questions, tentative hypotheses,

or implicit biases such as in the retrievability of repressed childhood experiences. In this light, we cannot easily separate out the
influence of suggestive processes whenever reconstructions are
made about the existence of repressed childhood traumatic experiences.

Kramer's presentation (1990) affords a glimpse of these dynamics:

> I reconstructed that she was telling me of being touched, being
> carried against her will, and being made to touch (or to rub)
> something (a penis). . . . The patient then remembered that when
> her mother was angry because her husband had abused her, she
> would make him sleep with one of the children. . . .
>   She began to remember hitherto repressed memories: of be-
> ing carried to the "other bed," of being told to touch something,
> of not knowing whether he was the nice daddy or the fearsome
> one [p. 161].

While Kramer's reconstruction may have led to valid memories,
those memories cannot be completely divorced from their context; that is, a suggestion that present associations have a prior
reality base. Under the influence of the analyst–patient relationship, a buried assumption by the analyst may resurface as a memory in the patient. This form of association, *presented or taken as
memory*, exerts an enormously reinforcing effect on the behavior
of the analyst who will now feel confirmed and thus more likely
to offer comments with this bias. The patient cannot fail to notice
the affirmed response of the analyst and be similarly reinforced.
A powerful mutually reinforcing loop, based more on process
than substance, may be created.

It is not necessarily or primarily content which is suggested,
for most often the reconstructed content is clearly embedded in
the patient's previous associations. Rather, as in the above, what
is suggested is the belief, however tentatively voiced, that a particular material reality underlies these associations. Most broadly
stated, the analyst's implicit belief must be that memory of real
childhood events may be wholly lost to consciousness, can be
recovered, and are evidenced by a given set of associations.

These beliefs surface directly in an atypical use or handling
of dream content (e.g., Schuker, 1979; M. Williams, 1987; Alpert,

1994). For a small subset of analysts, manifest dream content is interpreted literally and taken to reflect accurate memory of otherwise repressed childhood events. The analyst's belief, implicitly conveyed in interpreting dream material as equivalent to relatively undisguised repressed childhood memories, establishes a specific suggestion (this particular material embodies a real event). However, the analyst's belief also establishes a more general axiom that highly derivative analytic associations (here manifest dream content) can directly reflect repressed memories of long past events. This perspective on analytic material may be given with potent directness, as is evident in Williams' comment that "on many occasions, I explained [to the patient] that these dreams had preserved experiences and impressions of an indelible nature" (p. 152), where it is clear Williams believes these experiences are not merely subjective impressions. Additional force must have been lent to this perspective by her conclusion that, "the analytic process only moved forward when the patient could grasp and work with the trauma of molestation" (p. 157). Given the strength of Williams' convictions, one can sense how powerfully Williams would be influenced by any form of agreement from the patient, and, reciprocally, the patient by Williams' overt or covert response.

This example makes it possible to point to another facet of the dynamic of suggestion: an anxious patient seeks comfort and direction from and affiliation with a perceived expert. Suggestion operates in areas of doubt and uncertainty. Williams' comments are authoritative; they convey conviction on the part of someone trained and experienced in these issues. The force of her convictions creates for the patient what amounts to a stacked deck: solace and direction require affiliation, and affiliation in turn requires some measure of agreement or acceptance of the beliefs of the analyst.

In some degree, these are essential and inescapable features of the analytic dyad: the analyst is always implicitly the authority, for the patient has sought out him or her on that basis; the patient is always in pain and looking for something from the analyst; and finally, the process always depends upon some measure of willingness to be open to the ideas of and a relationship with the analyst. In addition, the analyst, no matter what the circumstance, cannot avoid filling in aspects of what is communicated from his or her own subjectivity (Blum, 1983).

Nonetheless, in special circumstances the role and impact of these vectors may be potentiated toward more invasive suggestion. These unusual but special circumstances occur when a diffusely and powerfully anxious patient, who derives particular comfort in aligning with a supportive authority with unambiguous views, finds an analyst with a corresponding witting or unwitting presentation. The suggestive outcome of such a pairing may take many forms, but one outcome could be the joint confirmation of the analyst's beliefs. This represents a stable solution to an unstable situation. Both participants gain what they are implicitly seeking: the analyst, confirmation of his or her beliefs, and the patient, cognitive clarity and affiliation with an accepting authority.

This line of thought argues that the alleged derepression of memories of childhood trauma actually reflects a concordance between analyst and patient based more on suggestion than historical truth. The argument would be immeasurably strengthened if it could be shown that similar configurations can generate fabricated behaviors or demonstrably false memories of allegedly repressed past events. Experimental research, and historical and contemporary events provide this evidence.

Loftus (1993a) describes a procedure for "experimentally implant[ing] memories for non-existent events that, if they had occurred, would have been traumatic" (1993a, p. 532). A trusted family member recounts to a younger family member a false and frightening story about the younger person being lost in a mall at age 5. In one instance, within two weeks the subject recounts a greatly elaborated version of the story as if based on personal memory. When told later that two stories had been told to him about his younger years, one true, one false, this subject selected the true memory as the implanted false one. In her broader studies (Loftus and Pickrell, 1995), approximately 25 percent of subjects fully or partially remembered false experiences of crying while lost in a shopping mall. Hyman, Husband, and Billings (1995) attempted to create false memories for a variety of childhood experiences such as the loss of a pet, going to the hospital, and tipping over a punch bowl at a wedding. About one-quarter of their subjects recalled these false events, and 50 percent of these subjects provided elaborate detail for their false memories.

One may discount the "lost-in-the-shopping-mall" variety of example as relatively trivial, especially compared with memories of sexual abuse in childhood. Recent events (summarized by Loftus [1993a]; and thoroughly detailed by Wright [1993a,b]), however, provide a chilling real life demonstration that elaborate memories of abuse may be created. Paul Ingram, the chief civil deputy of the sheriff's department in Olympia, Washington, was accused by his adult daughters of sexually abusing them as children. Although he initially denied all such allegations, after intensive questioning by detectives, and sessions with his minister and collaborating psychologist, Ingram eventually recounted his participation in extensive sexual abuse of his children and in far-reaching satanic cult rituals, including murder.

Richard Ofshe (1992), a social psychologist, examined Ingram after many of these recitations had been presented. Ofshe told Ingram that a son and daughter had alleged that, as children, he had forced them to have sex in front of him. This idea was fabricated by Ofshe and no such incident had been alleged or offered by Ingram or his accusers. Within days, Ingram presented detailed memories of these made-up allegations. Loftus notes that this case is relevant because similar techniques are employed in many cases of the recovery of repressed memories; for example, imagining of events (focusing on dream content would be an analytic equivalent) and using authority figures to validate the authenticity of events. Reviewing much clinical and experimental data, Loftus argues that a mechanism does exist "by which false memories can be created by a small suggestion from a trusted family member, by hearing someone lie, by suggestion from a psychologist . . . " (1993a, p. 533).

A piece of analogous historical data from psychiatry briefly described in chapter 2 bolsters this conclusion. In the lecture halls of Salpétrière, Charcot was able to demonstrate a rich array of exotic postural concomitants to hysteria. These postures were felt to be integral aspects of hysteria. But, as Drinka (1984) carefully documents in his historical review, what appeared to be independent phenomena were really constructions woven from an active if unwitting interplay between the expectations of doctors, frightened young women, and models available from longer standing hospitalized hysterical and epileptic patients. The more the young women's postures conformed to the doctors' expectation, the more attention the young women would draw. The more often the doctors saw these increasingly shaped behaviors, the more convinced they were about the validity of their observations. Shaped by a mutually reinforcing and continuous loop of influence, patients produced distinctive postures taken at face value by all. Doctors expected to see them, patients were rewarded for producing them, and audiences were unfailingly impressed by their repetition. One may substitute repressed memories of abuse now for postures then; the process is identical.

If processes such as these describe the mechanisms by which false memories are constructed, some gain must accrue to each participant for the outcome to take a stable and solid form. After all, it is noted that even if such memories might be false, patients do not immediately embrace them but rather attempt to resist and discount them (Davies and Frawley, 1991b). Where is the gain in this? An answer has already been hinted at: even if some distress results, clarity is preferred to confusion and obscurity, affiliation is preferred to isolation, and an external locus of causation may be preferable to an internal one. These are not uncommon choices in individual and group psychological processes, and could apply, in different measure and manner, to both analyst and patient.

The eventual relief and shared sense of good work described in clinical reports following the recall of a previously repressed early trauma may be read as support for these considerations. For example, before recovering the memory of being molested at $4^1/_2$, Schuker (1979) reports of her patient that "she developed the fixed idea that her disappointment in her father as a rescuer might have stemmed from his having sexually assaulted her. She tried hypnosis to 'help remember' and obsessed about this for years" (p. 569). A state of confusion and doubt reaches closure with the recovery of a memory. Since the absence of memory can never be conclusive, recovery of memory affords the only clear-cut resolution of doubt.

Nor are therapists immune from the draw of clarity and closure. Terr (1990) expresses this appeal forthrightly: following a lead offered by her respected teacher, Selma Fraiberg, Terr "loved the idea of guessing what had happened to someone entirely from a repeated dream. It intrigued me. It was like an easy solution to a complex mind teaser" (p. 209). The mind appears to prefer closure, especially if it strengthens the bond to an important other.

The explanatory paradigm of reciprocal suggestion between analyst and patient has several weak points. The experimental data described above, while persuasive in its own realm, only roughly generalize to the analytic situation. Although this does not rule out its occurrence, the necessary authoritative posture of the analyst reads more like a maladaptive countertransference than an accurate depiction of sound analytic perspective. Nonetheless, as we will examine in chapter 6, the stance advocated by Davies and Frawley (1991a), and employed by Williams (1987), bears a striking resemblance to this posture. Even so, patients are characterized as if they were not possessed of a mind of their own, and as if their critical abilities were not nurtured or encouraged. The suggestion paradigm presumes a significant degree of naiveté in both patient and analyst. In addition, the experimental research reflects contrived and/or deceptive conditions while the real life example of Paul Ingram incorporates an extraordinary element of threat and coercion. Neither of these qualities is fairly ascribed to the analytic situation.

Arguments in favor of the suggestion paradigm also carry a degree of skepticism about the recovery of memories of early trauma which is difficult to get around. Since the factors which facilitate suggestion include inherent qualities in the analytic situation as well as any measure of direct or indirect belief on the analyst's part, every derepressed memory of trauma taken seriously by the analyst may be suspect. Little room is left for the recovery of historically valid trauma. Since we must leave open the possibility that some valid memories have been recovered, this may be a too inclusive hypothesis.

BELIEF

To consider the role of belief in the recovery of early traumatic memory requires that the view of memory taken above be reassessed. Many clinicians would not recognize or find agreement with the view of memory inherent in the suggestion paradigm. Where this paradigm focuses narrowly on memory's literal error-proneness, the belief paradigm takes a broader view. Plasticity and distortion are not regarded narrowly as errors, but broadly as in the service of higher order representational processes. Dreams, for example, seldom if ever reflect objective reality, and consequently may be thought of as full of error if taken as memory statements of real events. On the other hand, as we saw in chapter 2, dreams may be thought of as personalized or metaphoric commentaries on real events. Understood correctly, or interpreted correctly, some measure of the underlying events may be taken. Errors are regarded as superficial to a metaphoric memory which carries the potential to reveal deeply what is disguised on the surface.

Memory may be taken more broadly in another sense. Memory need not be restricted to ideational contents produced consciously or deliberately as memory. To put this more concretely, memory is not confined to formulaic statements which begin as "I remember . . . " or "I have a memory of. . . . " Memory is embedded not only in ideational productions but also in many varieties of behavior. Repetitive sensorimotor patterns are based on memory as much as are direct verbal expressions. In other words, there exists an extensive class of expressive behavioral patterns which may be thought of as memory counterparts.

The distinction drawn here corresponds roughly to two classes of memory described in the cognitive psychology literature (Squire, 1986). "Declarative memory" consists of the explicit facts, episodes, and routines of life which are accessible to direct verbal recall. Those who demonstrate the plasticity (error-proneness) of memory seem to be studying declarative memory. "Procedural knowledge," however, is "implicit and it is accessible only through performance, that is, by engaging in the skills or operations in which the knowledge is embedded" (Squire, 1986, p.

1614). The sensorimotor forms of memory described above may exist as a subset of procedural knowledge. The restricted conditions under which procedural memory is accessible are an essential aspect of this variety of memory.

Examples of sensorimotor memory may be found in both the psychoanalytic and psychiatric literature. Although given a variety of labels, such as "somatic memory" (Kramer, 1990) or "motor enactments" (Dewald, 1989), singularly odd repetitive behavior patterns or sensory experiences have been linked to early (and sometimes repressed) trauma. Kramer (1990) concludes that, "in certain patients who have suffered childhood sexual abuse, the memory as such is not available or is only partially available. However 'somatic memories' of the trauma persist and carry with them some of the actual sensation, fear, anxiety, anger, revulsion, and pleasure that accompanied the childhood seduction . . . " (pp. 163–164). For example, R frequently described a chemical smell in the office which made her anxious. Over time that smell was associated with alcohol and also semen. Later in treatment, R recalled being sexually abused by her drunken father.

Similar findings are reported by Dewald (1989). At times his patient would roll her head back and forth in a vigorous fashion, rub her face with her hands more and more rapidly, or pull on the finger of one hand with a comparably jerky motion. These movements were regarded "as serving an unknown communication function for issues, memories, or experiences that could not yet be put into words" (p. 1004). Eventually the analysis translated these "motor enactments . . . as avoidance of oral penetration during fellatio, wiping ejaculate from her face and seeking to decontaminate herself" (p. 1005) after overt sexual encounters with her father when she was a child. In the process explicit memories were recalled.

An even more astounding finding is reported by Pulver (1987). He gives details of a young woman's dream and intense sensorimotor experiences in an immediately subsequent hypnopompic state. These sensorimotor experiences match quite literally traumatic medical procedures (recounted in physician records which Pulver does not mention seeing himself) performed on her on several occasions between 6 and 14 months of age. Rosen (1955) and Bernstein (1990) offer similar examples of childhood trauma pieced together from dreams, sensations, and smells.

Based on her extensive research on trauma victims, Terr (1991) concludes that "behavioral reenactments" are among the most common responses to childhood trauma, and occasionally are even found with children exposed to trauma before the age of 12 months. These "behaviors and physical responses repeat something of the original set of thoughts or emergency responses" (p. 13), often in the form of repetitive or stereotyped play. In addition, tactile, positional, or olfactory memories may also follow from trauma.

A specific and striking example of exact behavioral repetition is well known in the analytic literature. Because of an esophageal atresia which required the prompt establishment of esophageal and gastric fistula, Monica (Engel and Reichsman, 1956; Panel, 1979) was fed through her gastric fistula for the first 22 months of life. The most striking finding of the 25-year follow-up study of Monica was that she bottle-fed her babies in the exact position in which she was fistula fed, that is, with the baby flat on her lap. This style was unique in the family and rationalized (her arm got too tired to cradle the baby) without reference to her early experience of being fed.

In summary, these reports offer justification for regarding memory as a highly complex, multisensory faculty in which present behavior may reproduce aspects of repressed childhood traumatic experience. In some instances, current repetitive motor or somatic patterns (procedural memory) appear to be exact, or nearly exact copies of forgotten experiences. In one instance, external verification of the prior traumatic experience is unassailable (Engel and Reichsman, 1956).

Such reconstructions require an elaborate and painstaking synthesis of verbal, behavioral, and somatic data. They also require a belief on the order of a willingness to consider that material reality may well be reflected in and accurately reconstructed from these rather unusual types of psychic experience. This presumption is described as a "belief," as opposed to a scientific conclusion, for two reasons. First, to be regarded as a conclusion such a presumption would require some measure of external validation, but the clinicians who work within a belief paradigm do not report seeking or considering questions of validation (Sachs, 1967; Schuker, 1979; M. Williams, 1987; Dewald, 1989; Kramer, 1990; Davies and Frawley, 1991a; Alpert, 1994). In addition, although there is much support for the idea that trauma can give rise to the types of procedural memories described above, the relationship is not a reflexive one. As we saw in chapter 2, there is solid documentary evidence that such "procedural memories" may be found in some patients who have not suffered trauma. In other words, prior inaccessible trauma cannot be presumed from the appearance of experiences like the apparent somatic memories referred to by Kramer (1990).

Second and more significantly, for many of these clinicians, a willingness to believe that repressed memories lie behind a set of the patient's current associations is seen as an essential ingredient in appropriate technique (Davies and Frawley, 1991a; Alpert, 1994). The belief paradigm argues that this communication creates what amounts to a necessary holding environment in which the unrememberable may be remembered. In this respect, the necessity for precisely these conditions might be thought of as required for the state-dependent retrieval of a special subset of procedural knowledge.

Procedural knowledge (and consequently sensorimotor forms of memory) may be quite context dependent (Squire, 1986). Some forms of learning which occur in a highly specific context (e.g., a certain pharmacological state) influence memory in such a way that its retrieval is "state-dependent" (Eich, 1980). The encoding specificity principle (Tulving and Thomson, 1973) declares that the greater the similarity between the learning and retrieval state, the greater the likelihood of access to stored information or memory. Recall of certain types of memory may only be possible under certain parallel conditions. In this broader context, the belief paradigm rests on an implicit notion that only a specific type of therapeutic alliance creates an atmosphere in which current stressful affective states may emerge which parallel earlier stressful affective states. Unless those precise affective states reemerge, freed by an atmosphere of accepting belief, learning (memory) which has occurred in earlier versions of comparable states will remain inaccessible.

The form in which this belief is conveyed varies from outright assertion (M. Williams, 1987; Alpert, 1994) to general presumption (Dewald, 1989) to direct and explicit reconstruction of specific objective events (Sachs, 1967; Schuker, 1979; Bernstein, 1990; Kramer, 1990). This expression of willingness to believe fits into a larger constellation of the availability and introjection of a caring, supportive maternal figure who is not bound to silence by denial. This may well be related to what Davies and Frawley (1991a, p. 15) characterize as the necessity to "[allow] ourselves to enter, rather than interpret, the [patient's] dissociative experience. . . ," for only when we occupy a "shared field" can we begin to comprehend their internal processes. Regarding dissociation as intrinsic to the psychological makeup of the adult survivor of childhood sexual trauma, and in large measure pathognomonic of it, they argue that the experiential intricacies of dissociative phenomena are a " 'royal road' to otherwise unavailable, split-off experience and *memory*" (p. 15; emphasis added). The stuff of dissociation is regularly comprised of precisely the types of somatic, sensory, and motor experience previously characterized as memory equivalents.

Davies' and Frawley's formulations posit the existence of a fully developed, primitively organized, but dissociated child-self which seeks "acknowledgment, validation, and compensation" (p. 16). They regard it as imperative that the therapist of such a patient realize they are treating two people: "an adult who struggles . . . ultimately to forget and a child who, as treatment progresses, strives to remember and to find a voice with which to scream out. . . . " The child-self, they argue, can only be heard, and ultimately validated by an exquisite, experience-near attunement to the nuances of the patient's dissociated feelings and perceptions. This is possible only from a therapist who is prepared to see the potential for repressed memory in such phenomena, and validate memories as they are authenticated by the unfolding analytic process. Davies and Frawley convey that to do otherwise is to discredit or dismiss emerging memories and the feelings associated with them. This deals the patient two critical blows: "It represents a secondary betrayal of the child whose original abuse was ignored, denied, and unattended to by the significant adults in his life" (p. 33), as well as representing a damaging assault to an already enfeebled sector of reality testing (also, Alpert, 1994). Davies and Frawley declare in no uncertain terms that the treatment stance must convey a solid belief that "we can speak of these things now . . . I will be right here with you as you recall these events" (1991b, p. 896).

This emotionally nearby position, along with its direct expression of belief, provides a required bridge for a gap in psychic structure. Bernstein (1990) states unequivocally that "the introjection of a caring, maternal figure is essential to the recovery of memories of the incest trauma" (p. 88). Gabbard (1991), in his commentary of Davies and Frawley, points out that the "uninvolved mother" as an internalized object is often implicated in the object world of the female childhood sexual abuse victim. This lends a special importance to the therapist who, in contrast to such an internal object, can see and will believe what has been ignored, and does not remain silent or emotionally removed.

Fundamentally, what may be involved is that only in this way can a specific form of therapeutic alliance be created which allows for the reemergence of current affective equivalents of early affective (traumatic) states, and only then can state-dependent learning be retrieved. Very similar arguments have been made to account for childhood amnesia (Wetzler and Sweeney, 1986) and postanalytic amnesia (Trewartha, 1990).

The analytic processes by which these memories are recalled involve the assignment of meaning to primitively organized and primitively communicated experience. Ambiguous and contradictory images abound and shift decisively over time. Stable meanings and memories derived by necessarily inexact inferences from this flux may be at worst fabrications and at best approximations with a wide range for error. In this context, the question of validation assumes paramount importance.

Validation may be sought from existing documentation, such as court or hospital records, from interviews with witnesses, and even from admissions by perpetrators. Although admittedly a difficult prospect, the gravity of the alleged actions would seem to justify attempts to seek out independent corroboration. In a review of the literature on the reconstruction of childhood trauma in multiple personality, Frankel (1993) concludes that external verification of these trauma is seldom sought and seldom noted. Later reports refer to earlier reports as if the question of validity had already been settled. The skepticism warranted by Frankel's observations would seem to be substantially countered by the research of Herman and Schatzow (1987). This oft-cited study found that, of a group of fifty-three incest survivors, 74 percent (39 of 53) were able to validate their memories by finding corroborating evidence from the perpetrator, other family members (including similarly affected siblings), or physical evidence such as diaries. These findings weigh heavily in the direction of validity where memories are recovered.

In the specific area under review here, recovery of memories where none were conscious prior to treatment, the power of this study may be diluted by several factors. Fourteen (of the 53) subjects were apparently fully amnesic of childhood abuse prior to joining the treatment groups in the study but recovered memories during the treatment. It is impossible to tell from the statistics presented how many of these women were able to verify their memories with external evidence. The bulk of the verification could have come from the other (39) women who are described as never having forgotten their incestuous experience or as having some recall prior to the study. In addition, the members of the fully amnesic subgroup are depicted as obsessed with doubts about the reality of their suspected early incestuous experience. Some had tried hypnosis and sodium amytal interviews to resolve these doubts. Herman and Schatzow also note that "in response to the intense stimulation of hearing other group members' stories, these patients reported recovery of additional memories" (p. 7). These are precisely the conditions which favor the suggestion paradigm: isolation and doubt coupled with the offer of support and affiliation, and the ready availability of positively regarded models. Moreover, although L. Williams' (1994) research demonstrates that, upon inquiry, documented childhood sexual abuse failed to be reported by a significant number of her subjects, the definitive presentation of the recovery of a previously inaccessible memory of authenticated childhood sexual abuse has yet to appear in a scientific publication.

Further reservations may be registered from the vantage point of process. Just as the suggestion paradigm seems to offer no avenue for belief, the belief paradigm seems to offer no avenue for doubt. Doubt is regarded as a failure to support a patient who has already been injured by disbelief. Doubt represents a replication of one aspect of the trauma, the withdrawal of support from someone who could bear witness.

COMMENTS

Although the weight of evidence to this point seems decidedly to favor the suggestion hypothesis, these paradigms may form a vexingly confounded complementary series. Clinically, the analyst confronts a serious dilemma. Leaning in the direction of doubt, from the belief paradigm, threatens betrayal; leaning in the direction of belief, from the suggestion paradigm, promotes fabrication. On the other hand, if one does not believe, no memory can be tolerated; and if one does believe, whatever memory appears is suspect.

There is no obvious way to differentiate these paradigms on the basis of predictions, for they predict the same outcome, assigned inverse valence: belief (suggestion) leads to memory (false). If we return to Bernstein's example cited above, we are no closer to any definitive answer about how to read the clinical process. How one reads that piece of analytic process is determined overwhelmingly by which paradigm one favors rather than by some discernible aspect of the data. Vivid, affectively charged, and apparently genuine presentations of repressed memory do not guarantee authenticity. Similarly, even directly expressed belief and blatantly suggestive questioning do not conclusively invalidate authenticity. We cannot, as yet, discriminate false from genuine recovered memory either on the basis of process or presentation. Considering, or not considering the possibility of an early traumatic experience carries great implications for real people in the real world. At some points, we as therapists may find ourselves forced to choose between bearing false witness or failing to bear true witness, without knowing with any certainty which we are doing. Neither of these alternatives is without potent clinical consequences, both within therapy and beyond it. With this much at stake, these hypotheses deserve to be examined with greater care and at closer range.

Ultimately, the belief hypothesis stands on the integrity and durability of a certain type of memory. Ultimately, the suggestion hypothesis stands on the comprehensive power of covert influence. A more searching evaluation of these explanations requires that they be examined through the lens of what is known about different types of memory, and about the power of suggestion. Is it possible for splinters of memory not only to survive undeformed, but to permit an accurate reconstruction of the whole from which they fractured? Can a splinter of memory for an objective event be distinguished from a splinter of thought? Can suggestion create not just memory, but abhorrent memory? If so, where would the content come from? Let us turn first to the belief hypothesis and the integrity of memory.

4 MEMORY SYSTEMS AND THE PSYCHOANALYTIC RETRIEVAL OF MEMORIES OF TRAUMA

Reconstruction of earlier events, circumstances, and experiences has always been an integral facet of psychoanalytic practice. Over time, the nature of what has been reconstructed has shifted from suspected early sexual trauma (Freud, 1896b) to more atmospheric affective and ego states (Wetzler, 1985) and, most recently, back to suspected sexual trauma. Subtle trends are also visible within these shifts. For example, reconstructions relating to sexual events now appear to lean toward direct, invasive, and aggressive contact, as opposed to an earlier inclination toward experiences of passive viewing, such as with the primal scene (Freud, 1918). While these trends are by no means absolute, the nature of what is being reported has clearly altered in the direction of explicit sexual and coercive acts in which the patient has been a participant.

Another shift is also visible and critical: reconstructions now are more likely to be described as retrievals. Instead of calling what emerges a construction, something put together which may or may not have a literal material validity, it is conveyed in terms which suggest the retrieval of more or less objectively factual memory. A degree of credibility is assigned to these current retrievals comparable to the credibility Freud initially accorded to (and then withdrew from) his earliest clinical findings.

There is, however, some justification for this confidence. In contrast to the collateral scientific resources available to Freud, present-day analytic therapists have access to a growing body of theory and research on the impact of trauma. Based on the experiences of military veterans, predominantly from the Vietnam war, and soon extended to the experiences of rape and physical assault victims, the concept of posttraumatic stress reactions integrates and provides a framework for understanding responses to traumatic events. Special encoding and retrieval mechanisms are thought to exist for experiences wrought under enormously high arousal. Extreme arousal itself may also have the tell-tale effect of altering one's state of consciousness to such a degree that it is "dissociated" from normal consciousness.

As described in a host of recent articles (M. Williams, 1987; Dewald, 1989; Bernstein, 1990; Kramer, 1990; Alpert, 1994; Brenner, 1994; Davies and Frawley, 1994; Person and Klar, 1994), analysts have made use of these ideas to guide technically and explain theoretically the processes by which previously inaccessible memories of trauma are retrieved. In so doing, the findings of trauma research are extrapolated beyond their base of evidence, from subjects known by external documentation or by accessible memory to have been traumatized, to subjects thought to have been traumatized but for whom there is no direct memory of trauma. This critical distinction is often not clearly made in clinical reports although the citations above all appear to describe the retrieval of memory for traumatic experiences for which the patient had no preexisting conscious memory.

On the one hand, then, contemporary analytic retrievals of trauma tend to involve horrific acts of sexual violation and betrayal of the patient based on indirect evidence. On the other hand, these retrievals employ the findings of trauma research beyond their original target population. In their own right, both counts warrant a serious appraisal of these recent clinical trends. This chapter examines the assumptions embedded in the retrieval of previously inaccessible memory of trauma from the vantage point of current cognitive theory and research on memory.

MEMORY SYSTEMS AND TRAUMATIC MEMORY

Segments of the "memory pie" have received a variety of labels. With some consistency, however, contemporary cognitive science has identified two interlocking but often independent forms of memory: implicit (sometimes called early, indirect, or procedural) and explicit (sometimes called later, direct, or declarative) memory (Tulving, 1972; Squire, 1986; Kihlstrom, 1987; Roediger, 1990; Tulving and Schacter, 1990; Schacter, 1992). Although the "declarative/procedural" labels (Squire, 1986) were used in the previous chapter, in line with what appears to be the predominant nomenclature, hereafter I will use the labels "explicit/implicit" to refer to essentially the same distinctions in types of memory. A lively and unfinished debate continues between those who think that the differences between these two forms of memory are best explained by positing the existence of separate brain systems (Squire, 1986; Schacter, 1992) and those who argue they are best explained by differential processing within a single system (Roediger, 1990).

Explicit memory is directly accessible to consciousness and can be volitionally evoked and declared. Available for deliberate access, explicit memory includes general knowledge based on experience and verbally or iconically coded accounts of specific personal experience. Autobiographical memory may serve as a shorthand designation for the latter sector, that of volitionally available personal memory. This segment of memory is familiar not only because it appears in consciousness but also because it contains and conveys a continuous sense of selfhood.

By contrast, implicit memory is accessible only in context and by active demonstration. It is embedded in some basic (and advanced) cognitive and behavioral skills, and inseparable from automatized actions based on these skills. Tulving and Schacter (1990) write that the products of implicit memory "do not provide a basis for awareness of previous experience" (p. 305). Knowledge of the circumstances of learning, or even the very act of learning, need not be represented in awareness, and consequently awareness of previous experience derived from implicit memory may be unreliable. Pattern recognition for previously encountered sensory forms may occur automatically without reaching consciousness. At a more complex level, language development draws upon implicit memory or knowledge of deep grammatical structure. Such memory is only demonstrable by language performance. Implicit memory is a fundamental aspect of the "cognitive unconscious" (Kihlstrom, 1987), the vast, dynamic, working mind which never reaches consciousness.

Some dimensions of both implicit and explicit memory exist in a state of being primed and require a specific trigger to be activated. While explicit memory operates through consciousness, implicit memory does not. In a rough shorthand, explicit memory usually refers to "knowing that" (information) and implicit memory, to "knowing how" (to do or recognize) (Cohen and Squire, 1980).

The concept of a special traumatic memory (van der Kolk, 1987; van der Kolk and van der Hart, 1989, 1991; Davies and Frawley, 1994; D. Siegel, 1995) occupies an area of implicit memory. The necessity to defend against extraordinary levels of arousal generates an altered (dissociated) state of consciousness which imposes specific restraints on the encoding of experience. As the use of linguistic channels is dampened, the use of sensorimotor channels is augmented. This eclipsing of linguistic forms of encoding severely limits the accessibility to consciousness of traumatic experience, and consequently restricts the degree to which the trauma can be consciously assimilated and organized. The role of explicit memory falls as the role of implicit memory rises.

The result is a set of primitively encoded "unsymbolized" (Davies and Frawley, 1994, p. 28) or "inflexible and invariable" (van der Kolk and van der Hart, 1991, p. 431) stimulus primes outside of consciousness and beyond volitional control which may be automatically activated given an appropriate trigger. The encoding specificity principle (Tulving and Thomson, 1973) helps identify potential triggers: because greater similarity between the learning and the retrieval state increases the likelihood of access to or reactivation of stored memory, these implicit traumatic memories are most likely to be cued by conditions which closely resemble the original affective and physiological traumatic experience. Similar *state* and *sensory* stimuli both may operate as instigating cues. Thus, van ker Kolk and van der Hart (1989) conclude that traumatic "memories are reactivated when a person is exposed to a situation, or is in a somatic state, reminiscent of the one present when the original memory was stored" (p. 153), and that this "occurs automatically" (1991, p. 431) in such circumstances.

Serious challenges to the sufficient or even necessary relationship between trauma and dissociation were raised in chapter 2, and will be further elaborated in chapter 7. Nevertheless, dissociation, as a state and as a process, is thought to play a pivotal role in traumatic memory in large measure because it opens the door for the concept of state-dependent learning and retrieval. Current theories of traumatic memory (Kluft, 1987; van der Kolk and van der Hart, 1989, 1991; Braun, 1990) suggest that experience which, under less overwhelming stress, might be accessible to volitional recall by the dominant state of consciousness is dissociated and now dependent upon the evocation of the same state of consciousness for its retrieval. Thus, some traumatic memories appear only in altered states of consciousness such as in repetitive dreams, flashbacks, and stereotyped behavioral sequences. Despite much evidence to the contrary, dissociative states thus are regarded as providing at once a marker for the presence of hidden trauma, a defensive response to unbearable stimulation, and a vehicle for the expression of implicit memory.

A special condition arises when explicit autobiographical memory of trauma fails to be encoded and the only traces are in implicit memory (D. Siegel, 1995). In the last several years, many cases (see below) have appeared in the analytic literature which exactly fit this condition. Because these traumatic experiences have not been integrated into ordinary consciousness and linguistic modes, they tend to be reexperienced as raw, disengaged, sensory–affective experiences with the same intrusive impact as the original trauma (Davies and Frawley, 1994). Implicit traumatic memory produces or activates in sensation and bodily enactments what has not been processed and cannot be recalled by explicit memory. In addition, an exact parallel between implicit and explicit memory is proposed by both van der Kolk and van der Hart (1991) and Davies and Frawley (1994). Davies and Frawley specifically alert the analyst to this likelihood: "adult patients' stereotypic behaviors, dreams, seemingly inexplicable fears, or recurrent intrusive thoughts often accurately convey details of previous trauma" (p. 97).

Numerous examples of the application of these ideas may be found in the recent clinical literature. It is important to note that, as best as can be determined, all of the explicit memories of abuse retrieved by the patients cited below were inaccessible prior to analysis. Kramer (1990), using the notion of "somatic memories" of early trauma, reports on a patient who frequently described a chemical smell in the office which made her nervous. In the course of the analysis, that smell was associated with alcohol and with semen. Eventually the patient retrieved memories from an unspecified age of having to rub her drunken father's penis. A similar report by Dewald (1989) employs the concept of "motor enactments." His patient repeated several stereotyped movements of her face, hands, and fingers which were interpreted as literal enactments of participation in and reaction to being forced as a child to perform fellatio to ejaculation on her father. Memories, from younger than 7 years of age, consistent with these interpretations, were retrieved.

Both Williams (1987) and Alpert (1994) cite cases in which repetitive, anxiety provoking dreams provided the basis for retrieving memories of early abuse. Between 2 and 3 years of age, Williams' patient was repeatedly stimulated anally by a trusted male servant. Alpert's patient recovered memories of masturbating, mutually masturbating, and performing fellatio on her father from ages 3 to 7. The manifest content of the patient's dreams was regarded as a direct reflection of the nature of trauma unavailable to explicit memory. The notion that repetitive dreams portray rather undisguised depictions of inaccessible trauma is frequently reported as a well-established clinical fact (see also Person and Klar, 1994; Brenner, 1994; Davies and Frawley, 1994).

Making use of repetitive dreams of "endless assault and penetration of her by vicious men" (1994, p. 1060), "strong visual images . . . [recalled] frame by frame, as if in a film" (p. 1063), and extreme nausea associated with the beginning of analytic sessions, Person and Klar enabled A to retrieve explicit memories of being forced, apparently after returning from a date, to perform fellatio on her father. Summarizing four cases Brenner (1994) writes: "all four patients experienced recurrent dreams and/or hypnogogic hallucinations which helped bring their trauma into awareness. The manifest content of this imagery resembled the trauma itself . . . " (p. 835). In one case, the trauma apparently involved repeated instances, during elementary school, of mutual sexualized touching with an uncle who reached orgasm. In two others, the nature of the trauma is described as "severe preoedipal sexual trauma, which continued into late adolescence" (p. 837). The role of altered or dissociated states of consciousness and their contents is highlighted in the clinical thinking of both Person and Klar, and Brenner.

To summarize, in implementing the concept of traumatic memory with patients without explicit memory of trauma, two crucial assumptions are made: (1) state-dependent memory provides an adequate theoretical explanation both for the absence of explicit memory of trauma and for its ultimate recovery; (2) a more or less exact fit exists between available implicit memory (e.g., behavioral and somatic enactments, repetitive dreams, and flashbacks) and unavailable explicit memory of trauma. The following discussion will critically evaluate both of these assumptions.

STATE-DEPENDENT LEARNING AND TRAUMATIC MEMORY

As noted in chapter 3, a state-dependent learning and retrieval model is generally used to link implicit memory of trauma to its corresponding autobiographical memory. Two decisive problems undermine the use of this model in this context: first, almost all state-dependent research refers to explicit, as opposed to implicit memory, and second, the research itself provides only equivocal, lukewarm demonstrations of the phenomenon.

In state-dependent experiments (Eich, 1980; Eich and Metcalfe, 1989; Bower, 1987; Bower and Mayer, 1989; Southwick et al., 1993), subjects learn or experience specific material in state A and the results of recall in states A and B are compared. Typically, performance on remembering simple word lists is studied over brief retention spans, the longest, 35 days (Squire, 1986). Subjects' states have been primarily altered by alcohol or marijuana;

their moods, by listening to Mozart or Barber. This paradigm tests the cued retrieval of autobiographical memory; that is, memory for explicitly recognized prior learning. Subjects are fully aware of the context and general content of what they have learned. The accuracy of retrieval can be matched against known experimental stimuli or life events. No studies are available which attempt to track the learning of implicit memory and its emergence as explicit memory.

Even if we grant the relevance of state-dependent learning to traumatic memory, research on the phenomenon gives no support for the possibility of great accuracy, and therefore little support for the possibility of delineating, in the absence of prior knowledge, accurate from inaccurate recall. Even when state-dependent learning is demonstrable, subjects only retrieve a higher percentage of target items and recall never approaches anything remotely near absolute accuracy. Only relative accuracy is evidenced and those target items accurately recalled cannot be distinguished from those inaccurately recalled without knowledge of the target items.

Reviews of state- and mood-dependent learning and retrieval research yield inconsistent and contradictory results (Bower and Mayer, 1989; Eich and Metcalfe, 1989; Revelle and Loftus, 1990; Eich, 1995), suggesting that the concepts are by no means clearcut or readily demonstrable. Evocations of a mood or state turn out to be exceedingly complex and of questionable equivalence across subjects. When state-dependent effects are produced, they appear only in the absence of "discretely identifiable retrieval cues" (Eich, 1980, p. 157). Any kind of concrete prompt of what is to be remembered overrides these state-dependent effects. Although Bower found limited empirical support for his earlier theory of mood as a retrieval cue for memory, mood dependency effects were visible when the subjects perceived the mood as integral to the learned event or material (Bower, 1987). Far from supporting the absence of emotionally laden explicit memory, these data argue the reverse, namely, that subjects' existing explicit memory for emotionally charged events will be enhanced by the reinstatement of the original "mood."

With the exception of the Southwick study (1993) mentioned in chapter 2, the relationship between implicit and explicit memory has never been studied within the state-dependent mode. No memory tasks even remotely parallel to the recall of complex human experience retained for years have been investigated. Similarly, no states even remotely approximating those experienced during trauma have been studied. If a process like state-dependent retrieval of implicit memory is applicable to the recovery of inaccessible traumatic memories, at present the basic experimental work which might support this idea is weak, inconsistent, and of limited value in grounding the accurate recovery of explicit memory for trauma.

THE FIT BETWEEN IMPLICIT AND EXPLICIT MEMORY

If the state-dependent learning research applies only partially to the problem of traumatic memory, what model might better apply? The clinical circumstances for which some explanatory model is needed are fairly specific. Explicit autobiographical memory is, by definition, absent and unavailable for matching with recall, but isolated (presumed) memory experiences, unrecognized as such, are unconsciously triggered or activated. The model which would appear to best approximate these conditions is the priming of implicit, not explicit memory (Roediger, 1990; Tulving and Schacter, 1990; Schacter, 1992). Implicit memory may be activated by a prime which presents a fragment of the previously encountered stimuli. The circumstances of prior exposure and the content of what has been learned need not be consciously available. In other words, the presence of a previously encountered sensory prime may activate some form of recognition, although not, by definition, an explicit memory; that is, one which can be identified by context and content.

Similarly, the unknowing victims of trauma do not have explicit access to the traumatic event, experience, or context. Yet, it may be argued, via implicit memory, they are primed to recognize the elements of previously encountered sensorimotor experiences. Dissociated traumatic experience is cue-dependent in its retrieval, being prompted "automatically" by conditions or circumstances identical to the original experience. In addition, it is organized along sensory, as opposed to linguistic lines, and therefore stores and responds to specific, concrete sensory forms. In these respects, dissociated (or state-dependent) traumatic memory would seem to be conceptually identical to implicit memory. This conceptual equivalence carries much significance, because it can be argued (Schacter, 1992) that implicit and explicit memory represent related but quite separate brain systems.

As demonstrated in the clinical examples above, dissociated or implicit memory is thought to fit like a hand in the glove of explicit autobiographical memory. This idea is especially critical, for, if the relationship between implicit and autobiographical memory can be regarded as exact and inflexible, the possibility of social influence or shaping can be ruled out in the reconstruction of autobiographical memory. The absence of existing autobiographical memory of trauma, the specific condition under consideration here, further heightens the importance of what can be established about the relationship of implicit and explicit memory.

Some clinical evidence supports the notion of an "exact fit," especially for involuntary behavior or sensory experience. Blank (1985) reports several cases of Vietnam combat veterans who re-enact specific and general aspects of their wartime experience. Although the subject may be unaware of the enactment's relationship to past events, careful interviewing "unmistakably defines" these "sudden, discrete experience[s], leading to action" (p. 297) as repetitions of a wartime event. Terr (1988, 1991) describes children traumatized at an early age for whom behavioral and visual memory offer remarkably accurate depictions of their trauma. "Exact repeat playback dreams" are noted in children (Terr, 1979) and in combat veterans (van der Kolk et al., 1984). In a carefully controlled study (Southwick et al., 1993), flashbacks judged to be realistic reexperiences of wartime trauma were induced by the administration of yohimbine in 40 percent of veterans with a posttraumatic stress disorder diagnosis. A biochemical reactivation prompts state-dependent implicit memory (flashbacks) which appears to mirror explicit memory (actual combat experience).

A measure of caution may be called for in evaluating this evidence. Knowing the trauma in advance (from observers or reported autobiographical memory) may make the parallel between enactments or dreams and aspects of the trauma easier to identify.

In addition, in some instances (van der Kolk et al., 1984; South-wick et al., 1993) the exact correspondence reported is based only on a subject's report without direct comparison with autobio-graphical memories. A more rigorous "exact fit" test would entail blind matching of implicit memory data (e.g., flashbacks) with autobiographical memory collected separately. Could, for example, an uninformed judge identify the traumas depicted by Terr's subjects' stylized play? Could anyone but Blank, with his extensive knowledge of the Vietnam war, have deciphered the alleged pan-tomine of his subjects' combat experiences? Would blind judges correctly pair the flashbacks prompted from Southwick's veterans with their combat memories? Finally, in the absence of precise historical information, would anyone recognize Monica's peculiar feeding behavior with her children as a repetition of her earlier feeding procedure? As none of these tests has been reported, some skepticism about an exact fit must attach to these data.

As we saw, however, in chapter 2 the preponderance of clini-cal evidence supports a subjective or "inexact" fit between invol-untarily accessible implicit memory and voluntarily accessible explicit memory. Several studies (Pynoos and Nader, 1989; Ry-nearson and McCreery, 1993) demonstrate a marked amount of coloring from external sources in flashbacks. In fact, flashbacks are also reported by subjects who are not eye-witness to or direct victims of trauma, such as spouses of combat veterans (Frankel, 1994), relatives of a homicide victim (Rynearson and McCreery, 1993), and schoolchildren absent on the day of a sniper attack (Pynoos and Nader, 1989). A study (Brenneis, 1994b) of pub-lished texts of trauma paired with corresponding dream texts revealed almost no literal similarity in content although the dream content might quite aptly portray the trauma in meta-phoric terms. Hypnotically altered consciousness so confounds memory that "memory" produced under hypnosis is discredited (Orne, Whitehouse, Dinges, and Orne, 1988). Finally, like the highly specific posturings of hysterics at Salpêtrière indicate, what appear to be repetitive behavioral reenactments (van der Kolk and van der Hart, 1991) may also be significantly shaped or even created by social influence or interaction (Drinka, 1984).

Laboratory research on implicit memory in numerous care-fully designed and controlled experiments (Roediger, 1990; Tulv-ing and Schacter, 1990; Schacter, 1992) provides additional evidence for an "inexact fit" between implicit and explicit memory. In these experiments subjects are exposed to specific perceptual items—words or geometric forms—but given no indication that these items are to be recalled. Amnestic subjects who cannot recall even the event of exposure are used in some cases. At test, subjects are shown words with letters missing and geometric shapes with lines missing. Some of the test items have been previously viewed, and some not. Implicit memory reveals that subjects can more successfully complete items seen previously, even though they cannot recall the items explicitly, or, with some subjects, even recall the earlier exposure event. This priming, however, is only relatively more accurate than for unprimed fragments. Further, many experiments reveal what is called a "dissociation" (or contrasting performance) between implicit and explicit memory. In these experiments, some conditions enhance the performance of implicit memory while having the opposite effect on explicit memory. Other conditions produce the reverse effect.

These "dissociations" provide support for the notion that implicit and explicit memory reflect different brain systems. In fact, some memory theorists argue that, because altogether different memory systems are involved, implicit memories can *never* become explicit (Squire [1994], cited in Lindsay and Read [1995]). The contention that differential processing, not different brain systems, accounts for the distinctions between implicit and explicit memory does not permit such a categorical statement. The differential processing model would seem to allow for the possibility that implicit memory might, under some circumstances, be translated into explicit memory. Nevertheless, while there are many questions to be answered about the processes underlying implicit and explicit memory, neither model predicts an "exact fit" between their contents, nor does any currently available research demonstrate anything remotely approaching this "exact fit."

One might argue that laboratory or experimental results seldom transfer freely into the clinical arena. While there is, indeed, merit to this caution, it also involves a certain duplicity. One cannot ask an empirically derived concept like state-dependent or implicit memory to bear the explanatory weight of traumatic memory while simultaneously dismissing or ignoring the research upon which it is based. If the concept is used, the research must come with it. Moreover, in this instance, the argument that research often works within simplified conditions and circumstances makes matters in the clinical realm more not less difficult, and results more not less dubious. Extending concepts beyond their evidentiary base is risky business.

It is not difficult to demonstrate this point. Even if the perceptual priming of implicit memory provides the best model for the cued retrieval of concrete sensory aspects of consciously inaccessible memory of trauma, the reconstructive task facing the analyst is daunting. Clinical circumstances differ significantly from their experimental counterparts. Research scientists know precisely what perceptual forms have been viewed by subjects and therefore can distinguish target and nontarget items. An explicit standard exists of what is being reactivated or primed. In addition, as with state-dependent retrieval, implicit memory functions with relative but not absolute accuracy. Subjects do not correctly complete every word stem previously encountered, nor do they incorrectly complete every word stem not previously encountered. Finally, implicit memory appears to be mostly organized and primed by form recognition, and there is at present only limited support for semantic priming, or priming for recognition of previously encountered meaning. Memories organized by complex meaning may come closer to what clinicians attempt to reconstruct from the implicit aspects of memory of trauma.

Retrieving explicit autobiographical memory from the priming of implicit memory would seem to involve difficulties akin to asking a memory researcher to reconstruct the contents of an implicit memory exposure from subsequent test performance. For example, given only a subject's later performance on completing a series of word fragments, the experimenter would be asked to list correctly those words previously viewed. This analogy actually understates the degree of difficulty. Analysts, in contrast to researchers, have to deal with the ubiquitous ambiguities of clinical material which never appear in readily identifiable standard forms. Even further, given the possibility of dissociative states which mimic the impact of trauma, the clinician might have some measure of uncertainty that an inaccessible traumatic exposure

had occurred to be retrieved. This does not mean that valid retrieval has not or cannot be done, but rather that, given our
present knowledge of memory systems, it is an extraordinarily
difficult enterprise and potentially subject to a high degree of
error.

To complicate matters further, accurate memories of real
events may be impossible to distinguish reliably from fabricated
memories which are believed to be true. Ceci, Huffman, and
Smith (1994) compared 3- to 6-year-old preschoolers' memories
of real events with 'memories' fabricated in response to the experimenters' repeated urgings to remember an offered, made-up
event. Under these conditions, quite a number of children recalled a fictitious experience of having to go to the hospital to
have one's finger removed from a mouse trap. A panel of over
100 professionals in psychology, law enforcement, social work,
and psychiatry were asked to differentiate the memories of real
and fictitious events. Impressively, as many professionals performed worse than chance as performed at or above chance at
this task. It is quite possible, then, that a clinician's effort to construct explicit memory from implicit memory may become entan-
gled in the equally deceptive task of separating false from
authentic explicit memory.

It is important to make clear that the foregoing remarks do
not gainsay the possibility of entirely inaccessible memories of
early trauma, nor their therapeutic retrieval. What they do cast
doubt upon is the adequacy of a state-dependent learning or implicit memory model either to explain their inaccessibility or to
guide their recovery in technical terms.

CLINICAL IMPLICATIONS

The "inexact" fit which most likely exists between implicit and
explicit memory means that, in the clinical situation, even if an
explicit memory could be recovered, some translation would be
required to piece together autobiographical memory from the
primed fragments of implicit (or dissociated) memory. This translation process opens a window not only for error, but also for
social influence.

A massive body of clinical and experimental literature (Loftus, 1993a; Ceci and Bruck, 1993) details the subtle and comprehensive ways in which autobiographical memory may be altered and even created by interaction with others. Reviewing the social construction of autobiographical memory, Kihlstrom (1994b) concludes: "in the world outside the laboratory, remembering becomes an act of communication, of self-presentation, and of social influence at least as much as it is the retrieval of a representation of the past" (p. 6). Quite aside from this evidence, however, the social component of any expression of memory, whether implicit or autobiographical, within a therapeutic context seems inescapable.

How vulnerable is the psychoanalytic situation to the kinds of covert social influence which might shape and suggest memory? On one hand, the therapeutic context, and the psychoanalytic one in particular, is designed to maximize interpersonal influence (Frank, 1973) via the establishment and exploration of an intimate psychological bond. As we have seen in the clinical reports cited earlier, recovered explicit memories were evoked, shared, witnessed, encouraged, discussed, interpreted, and elaborated. Indirectly if not directly, these analysts presented themselves, and were regarded, as professionals who, by their acceptance, authenticated recovered memory and simultaneously confirmed an emotional bond with the patient.

On the other hand, one can argue convincingly that, within the psychoanalytic community, these clinical reports represent the exception rather than the rule. The disciplined reflective mode integral to psychoanalytic therapy lends itself not only to skepticism about definitive causes and manifest appearances but also to the search for variant and layered readings in analytic material. Moreover, typically tuned to the analytic process and relationship, that same scrutiny facilitates the examination of influence of whatever form. Psychoanalytic therapy cannot be immune to the forces of covert shaping and suggestion, but it is not without resistance to them. While this margin of protection should not be overestimated, neither should it be underestimated. The topic of influence and suggestion will be picked up again beginning in chapter 6.

Our fundamental clinical dilemma remains. The procedures by which inaccessible memories of trauma may be reliably retrieved remain obscure and the possibility of false positives remains real. How do we find our way? Increasingly in recent years, interdisciplinary dialogue has enriched psychoanalytic thinking, and in the present instance some assistance may be derived from memory research within cognitive psychology. In a series of broad, integrative articles, Lindsay and Read (1994, 1995) have addressed many of the cognitive questions tied to the retrieval of hidden trauma.

Memory researchers have articulated five criteria by which the validity of retrieved memories may be indirectly estimated: (1) how memories are recovered, with those recovered through extended, multifaceted, socially influenced searches warranting greater skepticism; (2) the quality of the retrieved memory, with more weight given to detailed recollections than to diffuse feelings, dream images, and "body memories"; (3) the plausibility of forgetting alleged events, with less credence given to the retrieval of multiple repetitions of severe abuse extending into late childhood or adolescence; (4) the plausibility of retrieving the memory, with skepticism applied to events reported to have occurred during the period of childhood amnesia, or before 2 or 3 years of age; and (5) the prevalence rate of the alleged abuse, with more weight given to more common types of abuse. Applying these benchmarks to the clinical reports summarized earlier yields a dismaying conclusion: all of these reports warrant skepticism as judged by criteria 1 and 2; several (Alpert, Person and Klar, Brenner) by criterion 3 as well; and most likely two (Williams, Brenner) by criterion 4. In short, none of the purported memories from any of these studies is remotely credible.

There are no comfortable positions to take in this dilemma between the possibility of inaccessible memories of child sexual abuse and, in some instances, the possibility of therapeutically induced invalid memories. As Lindsay and Read note "from any perspective, the stakes are high"(p. 847). Such stakes compel us to deploy the broadest possible array of information toward a solution. That array requires at least three elements.

If reliable pathways for the recovery of traumatic memory are to be distinguished from unreliable ones, the analytic community first needs detailed, explicit clinical material from which to work. The criteria listed above designate the kinds of data which will be of most use. Reports which present detailed information about the procedures used to retrieve memory and the exact nature and content of the memory will be of the greatest value. Second, the need for independent corroboration of recovered memories of trauma cannot be overstated. No criteria have yet been established which indisputably sort true from false recollections (Kihlstrom, 1994b), even in areas less controversial than trauma. Given the difficulty in distinguishing believed but false memories from accurate memories, only documented external confirmation confers indisputable validity; no amount of indirect evidence suffices. External validation also provides an opportunity to identify and examine the type of clinical process which might lead to the recovery of valid memories. Finally, clinical hypotheses must be measured against what is known about memory systems. In the next chapter, this frame of reference will be brought to bear on the pivotal concept of a special memory for trauma and how that concept comes into play in several clinical examples.

memory may further be characterized as "inflexible and invariable," with "no social component," and "occur[ring] automatically in situations which are reminiscent of the original traumatic situation" (1991, p. 431). Implicit memory provides an engraved image (albeit in action and sensation) of a traumatic experience, cued in its reactivation by some element of the original traumatic condition, and, because it has no social component, beyond the influence or shaping of an interpersonal context. Once available, autobiographical memory eliminates the activation of implicit memories. This is the model of traumatic memory which van der Kolk and van der Hart put forward as "psychiatry is beginning to re-discover the reality of trauma in people's lives" (p. 447).

As this model continues to be elaborated, several features stand out, and are of special relevance to clinical procedures. First, the memory markers of trauma are thought to be primarily sensory and somatic. As van der Kolk so pithily expresses it, the body keeps the score. Memory encoded under extreme duress is shaped by the earliest, most rudimentary mental schema, those of the body. Davies and Frawley refer to these memories as "unsymbolized" (1994, pp. 28, 97) and Davies (1996, p. 201) as "subsymbolic." Second, the memories formed by traumatic experience are thought to be fixed and unassimilated. Person and Klar (1994, p. 22) state that traumatic memories do "not undergo the same kinds of revisions as do other 'memories';" and later add, "their vividness, imagery, and unchangeability mark them as veridical" (p. 28). Moreover, the inflexibility of such memories carries the implication that they are transparent, literal copies of the sensorimotor and somatic aspects of the original trauma (van der Kolk and van der Hart, 1989, 1991; Gediman, 1991; Davies and Frawley, 1994; Person and Klar, 1994). Summarizing the work of trauma clinicians and researchers, van der Kolk remarks that traumatic memories "appear to be less subject to distortion than ordinary memories" (1994, p. 258). Finally, this is a threshold model; it asserts that, at certain extreme levels of stress, explicit memory fails while implicit memory continues to operate (van der Kolk and van der Hart, 1991; van der Kolk, 1994; D. Siegel, 1995). Traumatic memory then entails intact implicit but impaired explicit memory. Without this feature, clearly the concept of traumatic memory would have little interest for clinicians who recover hidden traumatic memories.

Each of these tenets is crucial to the process of recovering memories of hidden trauma. The absence of explicit memory itself must be explained; and, in the absence of explicit memory, repetitive, intrusive imagery and sensation are given priority in identifying the existence and nature of hidden trauma. Lastly, without explicit memory to guide the way, because these images and sensations are regarded as undistorted and concrete, the trauma concealed behind them can be transparently read. Without each feature firmly in place, the process of recovering memory becomes at worst a fallacious quest, and at best guesswork with a wide margin for error.

When assembled, these aspects of traumatic memory begin to sound somewhat contradictory and dubious. Specific sensory primings and intrusive imagery are represented both as unsymbolized and as exact. Organized at the most rudimentary level, they are nonetheless thought to be literal depictions transparently obvious to clinicians. While repetitive inflexibility is regarded as the hallmark of trauma-linked psychic experience, is it feasible to assume that this is necessarily or exclusively the case? In addition, by trying to account for trauma in the absence of explicit memory, the theory seems to paint itself into the corner of predicting that trauma is seldom represented in explicit memory. Let us look at each of these issues in turn.

"Many adult survivors of childhood sexual abuse arrive in treatment with only hazy impressions, if any, of their abuse. Their memories are not semantically encoded but reside within their psyche in unsymbolized, unorganized formlessness" (Davies and Frawley, 1994, p. 98). Nonetheless these formless impressions are the types of psychic material which are consistently characterized as more or less transparent copies of aspects of the original traumatic experience. Regarded as "less distorted" than ordinary memories, they provide the skeleton upon which explicit memory is built. Since explicit memory of trauma tends to be accurate (Terr, 1990; Christiansen, 1992), it is presumed that implicit memory must also be reasonably accurate. This assertion is argued by Terr (1991) and van der Kolk (1994; van der Kolk et al., 1984; van der Kolk and van der Hart, 1991), but as discussed in the previous chapter, implicit memory does not fit like a hand in the glove of autobiographical, or explicit memory. In addition, *no* blind tests have ever been reported in which an observer, without previous knowledge, attempts to match a dream, flashback, or stereotyped behavioral pattern with an independently derived explicit memory. Trauma clearly does generate implicit as well as explicit memory, but it goes well beyond the available data to argue that the step between them is either obvious or exact.

While the ingredients of traumatic memory may be encoded in sensorimotor forms, to characterize them as "unsymbolized" causes further problems, especially when the implication of "unsymbolized" is "undistorted." The question must be asked: Unsymbolized in relation to what? The referent is unstated, but seems most likely to refer to more developmentally advanced perceptions and memories which are demonstrably subject to many shaping, revising, and biasing forces. The problem, however, is that just as subjectivity increases with more symbolically rendered perceptions, so does objectivity. The absence of defined symbolizing processes does not, by elimination, leave objectivity. As Schimek points out, "it is the factual, objective impersonal description of reality that is the product of a lengthy construction" (1975b, p. 860). Consequently, while the elements of traumatic memory are, relatively speaking, unsymbolized, the result is not a set of pristinely observed, discrete percepts and corresponding memory primes, but rather relative formlessness. Without an independent standard, such as preexisting explicit memory, there is no way to validate the shape imposed upon that formlessness. "Exact" only means something in relation to something else, and in this instance that something else, explicit memory, is missing. Example 1 discussed below illustrates these problems.

Clinicians who recover memory recognize inflexibly repeated images and sensations not only as the stamp of trauma upon memory, but as pieces literally transcribed from the original traumatic experience. It is fair to ask if this is necessarily and exclusively the case. By this logic, if some piece of experience is repeated without variation, it becomes a relatively simple task to designate the memory component, because all pieces are identical. No records exist, however, of any dreams, images, or sensations which are repeated over and over again with absolute, unvarying consistency. Although, for example, van der Kolk et al.'s subjects (1984) regarded their dreams as exact replicas of combat experiences, this was not verified by comparing dreams with separately reported memories. When such data are available for trauma survivors, it is quite clear that, for dreams at least, the content is not invariant (Rappaport, 1968; Wilmer, 1982, 1986; Lansky, 1992) but rather oscillates around a prototype. Probably this is what is meant by the fixed content of implicit traumatic memory.

Nonetheless, in the absence of explicit memory, the prototype does not clearly or unambiguously announce itself. Which of a cluster of related intrusive images or behavioral sequences should be designated as the exemplar? One strategy employed by clinicians faced with this dilemma is to derive the prototype by extracting, as it were, the greatest common denominator from the cluster. The implicit traumatic memory corresponds to the prototype which emerges from that process. This technique is not as precise as the geometry utilized by the atomic scientists, as the difficulties encountered in example 2 below will demonstrate.

The difficulties do not end here. Even if the fixed, repetitive experience supposedly generated by traumatic memory is redefined to mean radiating from a central prototype, it is easy to establish that such a feature does not distinguish trauma-linked experience. As noted in chapter 2, stereotyped imagery associated with high anxiety is commonplace. Repetitive dreams about examinations, appearing naked in public, and being chased are not in the least unusual. The horrifying dreams of threat, chase, and mutilation endured endlessly by chronic nightmare sufferers (Hartmann, 1984) provide a more graphic, if somewhat less typical example. Lipinski and Pope (1994) describe several cases in which gruesome mental images had been taken to be flashbacks of hidden childhood abuse. Reconceptualized as obsessive images, and with the patient properly medicated, the alleged "flashbacks" remitted. In a similar vein, stereotyped behavioral patterns appear in ritualized compulsive routines. One would be hard pressed to claim, for all of these repetitive psychic images and behaviors, that trauma lay behind them. Trauma does not lead to absolutely fixed experience; and the prototypical experiential patterns associated with it can be matched by the experiences of individuals whom it would be difficult to argue had been traumatized.

The proposition that traumatic memory involves intact implicit and impaired explicit memory also encounters problems, the primary one being that it is contradicted by almost all of the available research on memory for trauma. A comprehensive review of the literature on the relationship of extreme stress and memory (Christiansen, 1992) concludes that, "studies of real-life events suggest that highly emotional or traumatic events are very well retained over time, especially with respect to detailed information directly associated with the traumatic event" (p. 288). Interestingly, if high levels of distress negatively affect explicit memory, it is memory for peripheral details. These findings specifically oppose those predicted by a special memory for trauma; that theory concludes that it is the peripheral, sensory details, not the central event itself, which are powerfully encoded.

The widely publicized study by Williams (1994) reports that some adults who were sexually abused as children fail to recall that abuse when questioned specifically about it. Taking a conservative view, even if subjects are restricted to those who were older than 6 at the time of the hospital documented abuse, had the most credible documentation, and were sexually penetrated, 40 percent (N=4) of these subjects failed to report the indexed abuse. Because some subjects (68%) from the total sample did not report the indexed abuse but did report other childhood sexual abuse, it is possible that some of the selected subjects also recalled other abuse from childhood. Even so, this study provides the most solid evidence currently available that some people do totally forget traumatic events from childhood. Aside from one anecdotal report about an "itchy beard" (p. 1174), no data are included, however, which indicate that implicit memory for the abuse survives intact. The operation of a special traumatic memory cannot be supported from this study.

An analogous special memory mechanism, that of "flashbulb memories," has been the object of study and spirited debate among memory researchers for many years. To my knowledge, this research, although clearly relevant, has not been cited in any of the literature on traumatic memory. "Flashbulb memories" was the felicitous phrase assigned by Brown and Kulik (1977) to vivid recollections of hearing about the Kennedy assassination. It has since been extended to clear and well-retained memories of the circumstances in which news of pivotal, highly charged public events was received. Memories of hearing about or seeing the explosion of the spaceship *Challenger* have been thoroughly studied (Winograd and Neisser, 1992).

Christiansen (1992), reviewing the evidence for a special memory process associated with flashbulb memories, writes that some memory experts argue for the existence of "an inherent special mechanism that is triggered when an event is highly emotionally arousing, surprising, and consequential" (p. 288). In the flashbulb literature, it is referred to as "a neuropsychological 'Now Print!' mechanism . . . which is supposed to preserve a photographic image of the critical event in our brain" (p. 288). This would seem to bear some similarity to the process ascribed to traumatic memory.

Although there is general agreement that flashbulb memories are sharp and well retained, their accuracy has been difficult to establish. Without knowing what actually happened at the moment of disclosure, it is impossible to check later recall with an established standard. Neisser and Harsch (1992) ingeniously capitalized on a moment in recent history to solve this problem. Right after the *Challenger* explosion, they collected reports from freshmen and then, three years later asked those students to recall their memory of hearing about the event. Most were reasonably accurate in their flashbulb recall, but about one-third of those accounts were "dead wrong" (Neisser, 1991, p. 34). No correlation was found between confidence and accuracy of recall, and only an ambiguous correlation between vividness and accuracy. Most puzzling to Neisser was why people have "vivid recollections which are entirely incorrect?" (p. 34) of salient, emotionally charged events.

The phenomenon of flashbulb memories provides only tepid support for a special traumatic memory. The central event, for example, is never lost in flashbulb memories. Even the need for invoking a special mechanism in flashbulb memory is contested (McCloskey, 1992) and unresolved (Christiansen, 1992). While such memories are generally thought to be accurate, when it is possible to test that memory against a standard, an impressive number of vivid, confidently offered reports turn out to be wholly inaccurate. Neither confidence nor vividness assure accuracy. The existence of a special traumatic memory, and a claim for its essential accuracy cannot be substantiated by flashbulb research.

Trauma encodes both implicit and explicit memory, but overall the support for a special class of memory associated with trauma is equivocal, and the support for extending the concept to cover the total absence of explicit memory is dubious at best. Even so, most likely some instances exist in which explicit memory of trauma is forgotten. Consequently, it is not impossible that explicit memory can be recovered from the traces of intact implicit memory. Examples of this achievement are presented in the professional literature, and offer an opportunity to explore how it comes about and to evaluate the results.

EXAMPLE 1: "A PARADIGM FOR TRAUMATIC MEMORY"

Close appraisal of Janet's case of Irene, cited by van der Kolk and van der Hart (1991, pp. 428–431) as "a paradigm for traumatic memory" (p. 428), provides clinical material to explore the problems discussed above. In the months before her mother died of tuberculosis, Irene, a 23-year-old woman, worked conscientiously both to provide for the family and to care for her bed-ridden mother. Sleep deprived for weeks, she was overwhelmed the night her mother died. Unable to comprehend this event, throughout the night Irene tried to revive her mother and force her to speak. She continued to give the body medication and clean its mouth. At some point, her mother's body fell from the bed and her father, who was drunk as usual, did not help Irene return the body to the bed. Irene persisted in talking to her mother's body.

The next day Irene sought out an aunt who took charge and arranged for the funeral, which Irene attended. Within a few weeks, the aunt brought Irene to Salpêtrière with an amazing symptom: although an intelligent woman, Irene had no memory of her mother's death. When asked about this by Janet during admission, Irene stated that she did not believe her mother was dead, for if she were, Irene would have seen her dead in her room and would have attended her funeral. As neither of these events had occurred, Irene did not believe her mother was dead. Furthermore, if mother were dead, Irene would feel abandoned and alone. As she did not feel this, mother was not dead.

While explicit memory (called narrative memory by Janet) for the night of mother's death and her funeral were completely inaccessible, once in the hospital, Irene is described as suffering from a second amazing symptom—stereotyped activities repeated several times a week. Her activities consisted of a rigidly structured pantomime: "an exact and automatic repetition of the acts Irene had performed during that night" (p. 430). After six months of inpatient treatment and hypnotherapy, Irene slowly began to recount verbally her experiences the night of her mother's death. When finally able to provide a full autobiographical account, it took less than a minute, whereas the version provided by implicit memory took several hours.

Because it is presented in detail by a leading theory builder as an exemplar, the case of Irene can be used to highlight problems central to the expanding theory of traumatic memory. A prime problem has to do with the absence of a memory standard. In order for the theory to assert that implicit memory provides an "exact repetition" of prior actions and sensations, there must exist an accepted standard of what those actions and sensations were and against which the implicit memories can be measured. But, by definition, much of this theory is directed at explaining precisely those instances where no autobiographical memory is accessible. Consequently, to validate the concept of exactness, the theory forces one to ask: exact in relation to what? How does one know these were precisely the actions and sensations experienced? Aside from assuming it to be true, the possibilities include an unacceptable tautology and a highly unrealistic circumstance. In the former, reconstructed explicit memory provides the standard, while in the latter, a disinterested observer or record provides the standard. The former hardly constitutes independent evidence, while the latter is seldom available.

In the case of Irene, the standard must have been supplied either by Irene's verbal rendition after six months of treatment and hypnotherapy, or by Irene's habitually drunken father. Both would be of questionable validity. Given the ambiguous meaning of behavior to an observer, the fact that links between behavioral enactments and known trauma have been identified in some instances (Terr, 1979, 1991; Blank, 1985) hardly justifies assuming this to be so in all cases, and especially where the absense of any explicit memory leaves one without any collateral knowledge of what actually happened.

The problem is not resolved by modifying the theory to read "approximate" rather than "exact," for some standard (which may not exist or be available) is still required to make sense of the implicit memory actions. Approximate only makes sense in relation to something already known or located. Most of the clinical evidence which compares implicit to explicit memory of trauma indicates that the relationship is one of approximation, but in a highly selective and idiosyncratically transformed fashion. If implicit memory records actions and sensations for approximate repetition, just which ones are selected and how are they transformed? As a comparison of dreams and the traumas from which they are derived readily demonstrates (Brenneis, 1994a), these transformations may be comprehensible when compared with explicit memory or observers' accounts, but they are in no manner predictable.

As soon as the ideas of selection and transformation are introduced, the necessity for a witness to or interpreter of those selective processes is also introduced. It is here that the question of a "social component" of traumatic memory becomes critical in a number of ways.

Van der Kolk and van der Hart (1991) argue that traumatic memory has no social component and is "not addressed to anybody" (p. 431). Traumatic implicit memory automatically traces out the same engraving regardless of social context. Like the concept of exactness which rules out the necessity for a translation, the notion of no social component rules out the possibility of social or interpersonal influence. Is it possible that some forms of memory—here specifically implicit memory of trauma—reside beyond the reach of social shaping or influence? Can the "engraving" metaphor be taken literally to represent something in the form of cortical structuring (van der Kolk and van der Hart, 1989) which is impervious to alteration?

To return to the exemplar case of Irene, is there no social component to her implicit memory actions? This cannot be the case, for her enactments are not noted before admission to Salpêtrière which, as a prominent teaching hospital, is a very public setting. What does it mean that they appear only in this setting? In addition, for Irene's ritual enactments to be described, they must be observed; and for them to be observed, there must be an observer. Any observer creates a social context, and any social context opens the door for influence.

The reverse is also true and, in this instance, may be even more relevant; what Irene might have observed is significant. Salpêtrière housed other hysterics, many of whom had developed their own rituals and mannerisms which were of great interest to the staff. In addition, hysterical patients were often placed in the same wards as epileptics whose illness was also expressed in behavioral forms (Drinka, 1984). Both observing and being observed create an unavoidable social context of influence.

EXAMPLE 2: DREAMS AND TRAUMATIC MEMORY

Alpert (1994) offers the most comprehensive current effort to detail precisely the kind of clinical material which warrants the reconstruction of inaccessible childhood trauma. It is instructive to review her observations and interpretation of dreams not only because she has provided clear data to review, but also because she states her presumptions about dreams and regards the analysis of dreams as "often the most fruitful" category of data.

Alpert reconstructs the following abuse history:

> The abuse took place in the shower when her mother was not at home, and at night in her bedroom with the door open ... it began when she was three and was terminated by her father when she was seven ... the abuse consist[ed] of masturbation by her father while he lay on the floor next to her bed and watched her, mutual masturbation, and fellatio while she pretended to sleep [p. 222].

While the fact of incest is indirectly supported by the presence of dissociative behavior and behavioral and transference repetitions and enactments, the details of the abuse are primarily generated by the analysis of "recurring and related dreams" and based on a conclusion much too broadly generalized from van der Kolk et al. (1984): "the content of repetitive traumatic nightmares have [sic] been found to be exact replicas of actual traumatic events . . . " (p. 225).

Alpert describes the patient's first dream: "she saw the pink wallpaper from her childhood bedroom and heard footsteps coming to get her . . . she did not want to see the man's face yet. Before she awoke she saw a blurry, fuzzy face and a huge man in underpants" (pp. 225–226). Later variations of this dream "involved her father coming into the room at night and doing something to, and later, with her" (p. 226). Alpert concludes that "from these and other more sexually explicit and involved dreams, the sexual events, and her dissociation during the events were reconstructed" (p. 226).

It is well to remind the reader that the following comments do *not* necessarily suggest that Alpert is in error in concluding that her patient was abused. Alpert presents an array of interlocking circumstantial evidence to support her conclusion. What is in question here is only the process by which dreams are used to reconstruct explicit traumatic memories. One may argue that it is much less clear-cut than Alpert contends.

Alpert's patient, Mary, begins with a dream which very closely matches, and eventually offers dreams which are nearly carbon copies of the ultimately reconstructed trauma. Nowhere in the literature is there to be found a dream which so precisely recapitulates a known trauma. As we have seen, the greatest degree of dream literalness occurs in dreams from traumatized adults who remember their trauma and were prepared for it. Even under these circumstances, no dream is actually reported in the literature which comes close to Mary's for veridicality. Mary experiences her traumatic incest between the ages of 3 and 7. One would have to presume that she was capable of forming an objective memory at that time in order for it to be later reproduced so accurately, but this is unlikely.

Taking some dream elements literally implicitly means sorting literal from figurative elements. In one of Mary's dreams, an unknown man enters her bedroom "whose looks were totally different from my father's" (p. 230). This is not taken literally but regarded as a test of Alpert's belief in the reality of the father's incestuous behavior. In another dream Mary is "horsing around" with a man who throws her up in the air and they laugh. This is regarded as reflecting Mary's pleasurable participation in some of the father's incestuous activity. But if father can be represented clearly as the incestuous agent in the bedroom dreams, why must he be presented in disguise in these dreams? Many dreams, we are told, involve Mary "moving her own hands over her body" and she awakes to find that she has not been touching herself (p. 16). In these dreams, Alpert must take the action (moving hands over her body) as a literal reflection of past experience, but discount, or take figuratively the agent of the action. It is not clear on what basis this differentiation can be made.

In a review of dreams based on trauma (Brenneis, 1994a), it was apparent that it was an impossible task to sort those elements which are to be taken at face value from those which are significantly altered. The only way such dream elements can be isolated is by knowing the trauma. As this example demonstrates, in the absence of this knowledge, one is almost inevitably drawn into making contradictory or ad hoc selections on the basis of a preexisting and preferred hypothesis.

EXAMPLE 3: A DEMONSTRATION OF TRAUMATIC MEMORY

Gaensbauer (1995; Gaensbauer, Chatoor, Drell, Siegel, and Zeanah, 1995) presents four cases (the fifth, Robert, has, unlike the others, no independent documentation of the trauma) of children known to have suffered severe trauma before the age of 15 months. Gaensbauer describes each child, and his or her subsequent responses in detail. Based on his assessment of the data, he concludes that each child retained central aspects of the trauma over time which could be seen in a variety of reenactments and communications. Using Terr's metaphor of images "burned in" to the brain, he felt retention could be demonstrated for visual images, multisensory experiences, and a sense of temporal sequence. Aspects of both implicit and explicit memory appear, and, as words become available to the child, nonverbal representations gained verbal and symbolic forms.

In these four cases, there can be no doubts that the child was traumatized. What is at issue, however, is how closely the children's reactions to the trauma follow the pattern outlined by a special memory for trauma. Gaensbauer's analysis suggests that clear and accurate traces of the trauma can be seen in the children's subsequent symptoms, play, and spontaneous images, not only of fragments of the trauma, but of an overall sense of it as well.

How well do these conclusions hold up with Audrey, the case described in greatest detail (Gaensbauer et al., 1995; Gaensbauer, 1995, pp. 131–136)? At age $12^1/_2$ months, Audrey witnessed the gruesome death of her mother who was killed instantly by a letter bomb sent by her ex-boyfriend. A female friend of the mother's was also injured and died three weeks later. According to the report, Audrey was found, unhurt, close to her mother's body. After seven weeks of foster care, she was placed with one of the mother's relatives and her husband. At age $3^1/_2$, in the context of therapy, Audrey was told that her natural mother had died, and sometime between $4^1/_2$ and 6, also in the course of therapy, she was "officially informed" (1995, p. 135) about how her mother died. Before the initial disclosure, the adoptive mother indicated to Gaensbauer that she had not discussed Audrey's natural mother with her. Audrey was evaluated at age $4^1/_2$, and again at age 6, by Gaensbauer, who appears to have had the adoptive mother's full and candid cooperation.

Aside from generalized posttraumatic reactions (such as separation anxiety and speech problems), Audrey displayed a number of more specific responses attributed to her traumatic loss. She was, for example, fearful of a number of things "reminiscent of the trauma" (p. 132): loud noises (the bomb), Santa Claus (presumably because of the red color), and rocking horses (the vestibular sensations associated with the bomb). She frequently described things as "messy all over," and repeatedly mixed red and brown colors together, calling them "icky." Behavioral sequences appeared to reenact the violent explosion and its effects. Audrey would spin around until dizzy and fall down, or lie on the ground and thrash her legs and arms back and forth.

Something similar to the latter behavior was repeated when, at 4½, Gaensbauer asked her how her mother died. The evaluation session began with Audrey pointing a gun at Gaensbauer, and this initiated a discussion of the effects of shooting, which was interpreted to reflect a preoccupation with the explosion. In play scenes comprised of two women and a baby doll provided by Gaensbauer, Audrey held the baby and violently knocked over the female dolls and some furniture. Watching, her adoptive mother was left in tears. When a police figure was introduced, Audrey moved the figure to the chest of one of the female dolls and then upended the remainder of the furniture. During her evaluation at age 6, Audrey picked up a dart gun and proceeded to shoot all the dolls, including "the moms and babies" (p. 136).

The most startling disclosures seem to suggest the availability of some explicit memory for the event. When asked by her adoptive parents, around age 3½, what she was doing when her mother died, Audrey said she was playing with a red and a yellow ball. Later, balls fitting that description could be seen in a photograph of the apartment where Audrey lived with her mother. Even more astounding was Audrey's revelation, during the therapy experience around age 4½, that as a result of the blast, her mother did not have any hair, hands, arms, or legs. The loss of limbs was new information to the adoptive mother; she called the police and, as she reported to Gaensbauer, the police "confirmed Audrey's description" (p. 135).

This case appears to provide ample demonstration that a traumatic event occurring about age 1 year can be encoded, quite specifically and accurately, by both implicit and explicit memory. At issue is not whether Audrey's various behaviors and communications are derived from her trauma, for most likely some of them are, but rather whether they are as specific and accurate as the observers take them to be. The foremost problem is that of the biased observer who knows what happened to Audrey and tends to see her behavior in terms that fit that knowledge. Audrey's reaction to loud noises seems obvious, but less so are her anxious responses to Santa Claus and rocking horses. Falling down and thrashing her limbs about might be a reenactment of what she saw, but not so unusual in a child that it would allow an uninformed observer to draw any conclusions about the existence and nature of prior trauma. Moreover, if, as we are told, her mother's limbs were blown off by the blast, Audrey's thrashing about with her arms and legs would not literally portray her mother's death throes, but perhaps suggest a generalized sense of cataclysm represented bodily, as might be expected of a year old child. The meaning of the doll play quickly reveals itself to the knowing eye (and heart) of the adoptive mother, but would be unlikely to reveal itself so clearly even to a clinically astute blind observer. An additional problem surfaces in the interpretation of behavior and play. The obvious trauma-driven behavior is taken literally, but those aspects of play (such as pointing the gun at Gaensbauer or shooting all of the dolls) which do not clearly fit, are taken more figuratively or discarded. The fearful reactions to rocking horses and Santa Claus are regarded as symbolic representations whose derivation is not obvious.

It is evident that both literal and symbolic representations of the trauma affect subsequent behaviors and communications, but the only way to know how to interpret an item is to know both that a trauma occurred and what it was. The literal and the figurative can only be distinguished by, and the mystery of her behavior only unfolds to, the knowing observer. In the absence of explicit memory, or knowing that something traumatic happened and what it was, the interpretation of a piece of behavior or imagery as implicit memory of trauma courts folly. In the absence of such information, assigning a specific reality referent to something regarded as implicit memory of trauma courts greater folly.

Audrey's recall, at around $4^1/2$ years old, of the absence of limbs on her mother's dead body is remarkable in more than one way. Because of its significance, one wishes Gaensbauer had viewed the police report himself and verified Audrey's recollection. For the sake of discussion, however, let us assume that her memory reflected a reasonably correct description of her mother's body. This memory, although apparently not available at age 6 when asked about her mother's death during Gaensbauer's second evaluation, apparently represents an accurate explicit memory from age 1 year. Even more remarkable, in another light, is the fact that it had not been anticipated by the adoptive mother and so surprised her that she called the police to verify it. This must mean that the adoptive mother had not been prepared for its emergence by any of Audrey's repetitive play or imagery. No mention was made, and surely would have been had it occurred, of dolls being stripped of limbs during play, or of drawings of armless and legless bodies. If accurate, this explicit memory was retained without influencing any other behavior, spontaneous imagery, or communication.

The gap between explicit and implicit memory presented here is an unbridged gulf so wide that, in the absence of the verifying police report, it threatens to impeach the validity of the explicit memory. This particular purported explicit memory bears no discernible relationship to Audrey's enacted implicit memory and could not be predicted from it. The reverse also holds.

THE "SOURCE OF THE NILE"

There is very little empirical support for a specialized memory system for highly charged, consequential experience which encodes implicit memory while preempting explicit memory. Forgetting explicit memory can be demonstrated (L. Williams, 1994) but without evidence of encoded implicit memory. The durable encoding of traumatic experience in both systems is amply supported. The relationship between what is encoded explicitly and implicitly, however, does not approach congruence, and no study has shown that it is possible for a blind or uninformed observer to recognize the contents of one system from the other, to match consistently the contents of one with the other, or to discriminate trauma derived from non-trauma-derived repetitive imagery or behavior. What appear to be implicit memory forms of trauma may have nontraumatic origins, so that the fact of prior trauma cannot be reliably deduced in the absence of explicit memory, or independent knowledge. Elaborate, sophisticated theory building to explain a phenomenon that does not exist amounts to nothing.

Why then, the persistent belief in a memory system which leaves indelible "unsymbolized" or "exact" traces of bits and pieces of past trauma without capturing the central traumatic event? At the core of this belief lies the notion of a permanent, relatively accurate record of experience in the brain. For a time, the work of Penfield (1969) on cortical stimulation lent some support to this idea, but more recent analyses undermine the possibility of any "permanent record" of experience (Loftus and Loftus, 1980). Within psychoanalytic circles, this notion long pre-dates Penfield, and is a primary assumption in Freud's ideas about memory and unconscious mental representation, wryly character-ized as a theory of "immaculate perception" (Schimek, 1975b): "Freud does not question a theory of cognition which takes for granted, from the start, the capacity for objective, veridical per-ceptions and their automatic storage as undistorted memory con-tents" (p. 173). His familiar simile with "an archaeologist's excavation of some dwelling-place that has been destroyed and buried . . . " (1937, p. 259), indicates that such concepts re-mained as much a part of his later, as his earlier thinking. In many respects the notion of a special traumatic memory inherits Freud's assumption that inaccessible or "buried" past experience can be resurrected from the chards of current psychic experience.

Throughout his life, Freud wrestled with the problem of whether the memories so recovered or reconstructed were real in some objective sense. His arguments are so vigorous and dog-matic that they belie the doubts which he could never quite sub-due (Schimek, 1987). From the beginning, in relation to the "infantile scenes" of his hysterical patients (1896b), to the primal scene reconstructed from the Wolf-man's dream (1918), to his deliberations, near the end of his life, on constructions in analysis (1937), his evidence was never quite definitive enough to settle his doubt. There is here an uncanny historical irony in that some of the same arguments put forth by Freud in 1896 resurface in the debate about memories of sexual abuse nearly 100 years later.

In 1990, the *American Journal of Psychiatry* published a letter (Rich, 1990) which questioned the accuracy of reports about childhood sexual abuse. In his reply, Briere (1990) makes no distinction between always remembered and therapeutically re-covered memories, but justifies the data's validity on the basis of three considerations. Somewhat analogous to Freud's reference to the consistency, between patients, of his findings, Briere cites the consistency of findings among researchers, and then mentions two other reasons for confidence which mirror Freud's argumentation from 1896. Briere writes, "specific aspects of subject's vicitimization correlated with symptoms in ways that made intuitive sense and that had been reported by other authors" (1990, pp. 1389–1390). Freud wrote: "another and stronger proof of this is furnished by the relationship of the infantile scenes to the content of the whole rest of the case history. It is exactly like putting together a child's picture-puzzle: after many attempts, we become absolutely certain in the end which piece belongs in the empty gap; for only that one piece fills out the picture ... " (1896b, p. 205). Freud also wrote, "the behavior of patients while they are reproducing these infantile experiences is in every respect incompatible with the assumption that the scenes are anything else than a reality which is being felt with distress and reproduced with the greatest reluctance" (p. 205). Briere (1990) writes, "the clinical experience of the authors and others suggested that adults' disclosures of sexual abuse are typically accompanied by distress, shame, and fear of stigma, as opposed to obvious enjoyment of secondary gain" (p. 1390).

It is important to note here that although consistency, intuitive fit, and negative affect do not add up to validity and equal corroboration, these considerations make sense and are not in dispute when referring to preexisting explicit memory of abuse. Neither Freud nor Briere make this critical distinction in conjunction with their arguments.

The contention that validity is bestowed by negative affect warrants additional comment. Viewed from this angle, distress, embarrassment, and reluctance declare that the patient is holding back something genuinely shameful or distressing. One need not suggest the outright fabrication of emotion to question this equation of shame and reluctance with the veracity of recovered memory. In so reasoning, Freud, for example, seems uncharacteristically hesitant to consider the influence of unconscious motives and forces. Similarly, Briere seems somewhat naive in pairing secondary gain with "obvious enjoyment." It is not hard to think, for example, that even acutely painful feelings can be outweighed by the value of an emotional affiliation with a strong, supportive figure.

The notion that there is some inherent validity assigned to therapeutic material accompanied by manifest distress implicitly limits unconscious influence to a narrow, shallow realm. As we will see in the succeeding chapters, this realm is much broader, deeper, and more inclusive than many clinicians are willing to imagine. Nonetheless, this view finds its way into the clinical writing of experts on the subject of recovered memories of sexual abuse (Davies and Frawley, 1991b, 1994; Herman and Harvey, 1993). The logic of it leads toward murky water. If distress testifies to truth, truth must be accorded to whatever is presented with reluctance, shame, or distress. As will be seen in chapter 7, to follow such a dubious proposition risks extreme credulity. If not all distress is taken at face value, then the clinician must be in a position to distinguish authentic from inauthentic distress, or to accord truth to the distress which comes in expected, or consistent forms. This too seems a dubious proposition by which to guide one's clinical inferences.

What gain could justify venturing into territory with such unreliable (validation by distress, the ill fit between implicit and explicit memory) and unsubstantiated (permanent record in the brain, special traumatic memory) charts? For Freud, in some measure, the answer is clear: only the bold explorer will discover "the source of the Nile" (cited by Schimek, 1987, p. 962) or "the primal event in external reality which would provide a firm material ground for his etiological formulation" (p. 962). Although Freud's metaphor is a distinctly nineteenth century one, it applies equally to the twentieth century practitioner. Even a cursory review of the literature reveals many analysts who have sought, and found, their source of the Nile: Nunberg, 1932; Greenacre, 1953a,b; Rosen, 1955; Niederland, 1965; Sachs, 1967; Stewart, 1969; Calogeras, 1982; Dowling, 1987. Contemporary citations match this number. Clearly Grace's therapist failed in his quest not for lack of determination, but for lack of "cooperation" by Grace. All of these analysts consider the impact of unconscious, conflictual forces in the patient's subsequent psychological course, but these currents are seen as emanating from an event located in real time and real space.

To find an external reality which, like the source of the Nile, accounts for so much, and which has never been glimpsed before, exerts a tremendous pull on some clinicians. How far the influence of that pull may go remains to be seen. If recovered memories are not true, what are they and where do they come from? The following chapters are devoted to exploring these questions.

6 MEMORIES OF ABUSE OR REACTIONS TO TECHNIQUE?

Given the absence of a necessary link between clinical signs and trauma, the inexact fit between implicit and explicit memory, the socially constructed nature of memory, and the limited support for a special traumatic memory which obscures explicit memory, it now seems inescapable that at least some recovered memories are invalid and evolve from suggestive factors in the therapeutic process. Nonspecific suggestive factors alone, however, do not seem adequate to account for the distinctive forms these memories take and the consistent content they represent. Something further must play a part. After all, were suggestion alone a factor, patients might, more or less, simply produce intact, previously unremembered memories of early sexual abuse.

As we have seen, however, such memories do not appear directly in explicit memory, but rather appear piecemeal, experienced as repetitive, terrifying dreams and flashbacks, and as inexplicable somatic sensitivities and behavioral sequences. Because the defensive process of dissociation, and accompanying dissociated state of consciousness, isolates these experiences away from the dominant state of consciousness, patients often regard such experiences as bewildering and beyond their control. The major themes of recovered trauma center on coercion and loss of control, betrayal of trust by a parental figure, and bodily invasion and penetration. When the exact nature of the trauma can be ascertained from the literature surveyed to this point, the most frequently recovered trauma is of a father compelling his daughter to perform fellatio (Dewald, 1989; Alpert, 1994; Person and Klar, 1994).

This chapter will advance the hypothesis that two factors, one relating to the therapist, the other to the patient, may interact to produce these apparent dramatic enactments of childhood sexual abuse. Although located temporally by the therapist and patient in the past, these enactments may actually refer to the patient's present therapeutic experience.

In explicating this hypothesis, I will refer to the published work of several analytic clinicians and view their work in a manner almost totally at variance from their expressed intent. Their work receives special notice because they have presented enough material to allow independent judgments to be made about it. They are to be lauded for this, for methods practiced out of sight can never be checked or reviewed. All but one (Briere) of these therapists are respected members of the psychoanalytic community. While their work is not representative of psychoanalytic opinion, it has nonetheless appeared in standard psychoanalytic journals. Consequently, the argument presented here cannot easily be discounted with the claim that only undisciplined, poorly trained clinicians fit the mold of the zealous therapist described below.

THE ZEALOUS THERAPIST

Clinicians who recover memories of hidden trauma bring specific beliefs to bear on their therapeutic work. That there exists an "inextricable link between dissociation and child abuse" (Davies and Frawley, 1994, p. 210) means that dissociation heralds trauma, even in the absence of explicit autobiographical memory. Dissociation, then, raises an unfailing flag of alert. Dreams, flashbacks, body states, and motor enactments supply the missing memory because it is assumed that they can be read as "memory equivalents," and that they often reflect hidden traumatic experience with transparent accuracy. Accompanied by the total failure of explicit memory, trauma exactly engraves the somatic, sensorimotor, and affective experiences associated with it. The existence of trauma unrepresented in explicit memory, along with the critical role played by sexual abuse in later psychological difficulties, means that the possibility of hidden sexual abuse cannot be ignored. In the most up-to-date literature, this set of beliefs, presented in the form of established tenets, is enumerated by Person and Klar (1994, pp. 1074–1075), and forms the conceptual skeleton of Davies and Frawley's (1994) treatment approach.

The preceding chapters seriously challenge all of these ideas, aside from the pathogenic role sexual abuse can play in subsequent psychological development. Nevertheless, unleavened by serious consideration of alternative hypotheses, these beliefs not only dictate the importance of certain therapeutic material, but also how it is best interpreted and approached technically. While some beliefs reside in the foreground and others in the background, together they form a coherent, internally consistent system which is forcefully imposed upon the clinical interaction by those who recover memories of trauma.

Having decided, on the basis of the kinds of potentially misleading clinical signs described above, that a patient may be a survivor of hidden abuse, these beliefs impart a decisive focus to the therapist's clinical activity. Once locked in, the therapist works to create a similar focus within the patient. Williams' (1987) account illustrates this point. When her patient expressed surprise that Williams regarded her reconstruction of a childhood anal seduction as "the most crucial experience in his early childhood," she offered a detailed, persuasive rationale for that belief (p. 152). "On many occasions" she also explained that his dreams "had preserved experience and impressions [of the seduction] of an indelible nature" (p. 152). At times "the patient would 'forget' previously gained knowledge about the molestation . . ." and presumably be reminded about its existence and effects, one of which was forgetting, "such as a young child does when told about sexual matters" (p. 154).

Similarly, strong beliefs about hidden trauma have a way of compressing clinical data into conforming shapes. When patients

are asked directly during history taking about distressing childhood sexual experiences, Davies and Frawley (1994) indicate that
most nonabused patients handle these questions matter-of-factly,
both verbally and nonverbally. While this may well be true, the
implication is that if a patient is made uncomfortable by explicit
questions about early sexual experience, the therapist should be
alert to the possibility of undisclosed or unremembered sexual
abuse. Verbal denials accompanied by uneasiness may not qualify
as valid disavowals. While anxiety about sexual matters may stem
from past abusive experience, it is surely not the only or even
primary source of uneasiness to be considered. Briere (1994) describes a woman who repeatedly washed her hands, although "not
in a typical obsessive–compulsive fashion." Asked why, the patient
replied that it was because her hands felt slippery. Although many
explanations exist which do not carry the buried assumption of
sexual abuse, the therapist wondered if the slipperiness represented semen. Initially, the patient rebuffed the idea, but eventually came to smell semen and decided the therapist was correct.
She then recovered memories of being made to masturbate her
father whose ejaculate would cover her hands with semen.

Historical information can also be shaded to conform to expectations. Alpert's (1994) summary of her patient's history lines
up the evidence so that it fits with that expected of an abuse
victim. Memory inconsistencies, for example, are seen as typical
of the severe memory deficits of incest victims, and the family
structure is aligned in a manner that is also typical of incest victims. We have seen this inferential pattern before: if certain features are typical of incest/abuse victims who have always recalled
their abuse, these same features alert the clinician to search for
hidden trauma in those without explicit memory. Consistent with
this, Alpert reports that in the initial phase of the treatment "the
focus was on recovering, reconstructing, and reintegrating traumatic memories with their associated affects" (p. 218). During
this time, "Mary placed full responsibility for insight, change, and
interpretations on me" (p. 230), a responsibility Alpert appears
to have assumed.

Secrecy and shame guard access to knowledge about hidden
abuse. "Secrecy is the cornerstone of sex abuse . . . " (Davies and
Frawley, 1994, p. 36). In her depiction of the prototypical scene

of childhood sexual abuse, Davies (1996, pp. 203–204) emphasizes the role of threats, mistrust of caretakers, and fears about disastrous familial repercussions in enforcing secrecy. This veil of secrecy may restrict the individual's explicit awareness of abuse as well as his or her subsequent willingness to consider it as a possibility in therapy. An additional factor bolsters the tense wall of secrecy which protects access to hidden sexual abuse: shame. "Often told" (Davies, 1996, p. 204) that she wants what she really hates, yearns for what she dreads, and enjoys what is actually "searing pain," the abuse victim may doubt her own mind and have a deeply shameful fear, or conviction, that her desire may have played an active role in the abuse. Under terms of shame and secrecy, the hidden abuse victim can hardly be expected to reveal willingly material suggestive of abuse, nor to respond without resistance to the analyst's concern about the possibility of abuse. Hidden abuse cannot be found by passive or faint-hearted effort, and secrets of such magnitude justify active, probing searches.

For the therapist who uncovers hidden abuse, dissociation not only means trauma (Davies and Frawley, 1994) but also provides the principal avenue along which hidden memory may be pursued. Consistently felt by patients as frightening and unpredictable, dissociative states involve a sense of receiving experience passively and outside of their control. Regarding dissociated or altered state experiences as defensive operations, however, justifies a certain amount of therapeutic pressure to overcome the patient's understandable reluctance to enter into such experiences. The heightened importance assigned to dissociative experiences, and the intense therapeutic interest in them is reflected in Davies and Frawley's (1994) advice that "the therapist must accept, work with, and *even encourage* the dissociative states into which the patient enters during treatment. It is through these states that *the truth unfolds . . .* " (p. 94; emphasis added). The implication here would seem to be clear: dissociation, properly understood, speaks the previously unspoken truth, and truth deserves to be pursued.

Where truth must be known and spoken, doubt, uncertainty, and inconsistencies receive special handling. Williams (1987)

frames her patient's reluctance to accept the reality and importance of molestation as resistance motivated forgetting, to be overcome or to be countered with point by point explanation. Alpert
responds to a dream in which the alleged abuse perpetrator
looked totally different from the identified abuser, the patient's
father, by reassuring her patient that she, Alpert, "still knows she
was a victim of father–daughter incest . . . " (1994, p. 230). The
patient's doubts are read as tests of the therapist's willingness to
believe in abuse, and failing these tests threatens the therapeutic
alliance. As with Williams, expressed doubt challenges the therapist to cement the patient's bond to them by overriding the patient's doubt. In a different vein, Person and Klar (1994) marshal
and decisively present a variety of theoretical explanations to
quell any doubts the reader might have about the recovered abuse
discussed there.

Knowing, and by extension, not knowing, is cast in a distinctive light by Davies and Frawley (1994). They wonder, when
themes of abuse like betrayal or intrusions are evident, who
should speak first. The therapist's choices are given—risk paired
with advantage: "For the therapist to name the unnamable first
may feel abusive to the patient . . . ," but not to do so eventually
"may too closely replicate the patient's experience with an un-
seeing, unhearing, unavailable, nonabusing parent . . . " (p. 91).
Reinforced by powerful rhetoric, telling moral implications ad-
here to the therapist's speaking (knowing) and nonspeaking (not
knowing). An act of courage, naming the unnamable, is juxta-
posed with an act of cowardice, replicating the blind, passive,
nonabusing parent. To know is to stand as witness to abuse, while
not to know is to turn one's back. If the same persuasive powers
are brought to bear on the patient as are brought to bear on the
reader, the pressure to conform must be enormous.

To drive home more conclusively the destructive action of
doubt, Davies and Frawley (1994, pp. 163–165) present a caution-
ary tale. By virtue of excessive countertransference allegiances to
mentors, colleagues, and orthodox analytic theory, a therapist
begins to wonder if "she is making too much of the prevalence
and impact of childhood sexual trauma [and] maybe she even
is being suggestive with her own patients" (p. 164). A patient,
struggling for months to accept the reality of her abuse and now

perhaps finally ready to know her father abused her, once again asks the therapist if she really thinks it happened. When the therapist uncharacteristically hesitates momentarily before affirming her belief, the patient is panicked and turns instantly against her. Only after "some time" (p. 164) is the therapeutic rupture rejoined. The explicit message can be simply stated: doubt, even for a moment, breaks trust and breaches the therapeutic relationship. In a word, doubt destroys.

Affiliation with the analyst heals, but requires agreement. Williams, for example, concluded that the analysis with Mr. B only progressed when he accepted the importance and validity she assigned to the recovered molestation. The prototype of an initial exchange about the possibility of abuse proposed by Davies and Frawley (1994, pp. 92–93) further illustrates this point. The patient, Lisette, is described as having been sexually abused by her father, but it seems clear from the passage that the abuse was recovered rather than remembered and undisclosed.

The therapist begins by stating that "you and I have been dancing around an important *secret* . . . we *both know* there's a secret, we *both know* what the secret is . . . " (p. 92; emphasis added). In response to the patient's noncommittal reply, the therapist lists the accumulated circumstantial evidence, including the patient's hate for her body, that the image of a man beside her bed could mean she is reliving something, her anxiety about sexual relations with her husband, her "spacing out" when talking about her childhood relationship with her father, and finally, the absence of clear memories between ages 7 and 15. When the patient continues her apparent failure to comprehend, the analyst suggests both of them have been thinking the same thoughts and introduces the possibility of childhood sexual abuse. The patient denies this; and the therapist assures her that they need not decide now if it really happened, and goes on to wonder why it cannot be talked about. At this point, the patient responds "you *do* know. You *know* I think it happened . . . " (p. 93), after which the therapist endorses the value of working together with such painful possibilities.

If one regards, as Davies and Frawley do, the enumerated clinical evidence as a valid indication of past hidden abuse, this exchange portrays the delicate, tentative introduction of a valuable therapeutic hypothesis. If, on the other hand, one doubts the implicit validity of these same indicators, this exchange portrays a subtle, but powerful indoctrination. Despite the therapist's cautious efforts to designate the idea as tentative, by postponing any judgment about its reality, the language is one of *knowing*. Secrets do not refer to possible events but to real events. All of the evidence the therapist offers points to the reality of what is secretly known. No conflicting evidence balances the accounting. In addition, as the therapist states, what is secretly known is shared knowledge. Agreement with this compassionate, insightful therapist gains affiliation. As the patient clearly intuits and states in her final comment ("you *do* know"), the agreement sought by the therapist is not tentative at all but rather final and conclusive, as if to say, now that we have acknowledged knowing together, we can work together to face these "awful possibilities" (p. 93).

Although the language at the end is phrased as a "possibility," it registers with the patient as a certainty. The same must be said for the analyst. Her comments demonstrate that she has already decided the matter. All of the enumerated evidence weighs in favor of hidden abuse, none of it is questioned, and nowhere is voiced the possibility that abuse did not occur. The data can be seen no other way, and the patient's ultimate response reflects that certainty. While Davies and Frawley describe their recommended stance as being open to the possibility of abuse, it is not equally open to the unlikelihood of abuse.

In fact, none of the works on recovered memory cited here includes a significant discussion of alternative hypotheses. When mention is made of critical views, they seem tacked on (Davies and Frawley, 1994, p. 209), pejoratively rendered (p. 97), and quickly dismissed. It is not surprising then that, aside from Davies and Frawley's citation of an address by Loftus, no references are listed to any standard sources on memory in any of these publications. Davies' (1996) most recent publication is the exception, although her view of the issues remains fundamentally unchanged. In the absence of awareness of some of these sources, serious consideration by these authors of alternative explanations does not occur spontaneously.

Therapeutic zeal dictates what both the patient *and* the clinician need to believe and need not to doubt. It can also instruct the patient how to behave and what to feel. In an effort to ease a patient's distress after disclosures of traumatic material, Davies and Frawley (1994) "find it *helpful to predict* to the patient that she may experience more frequent memories, flashbacks, intrusive thoughts about the abuse, along with intensified affective reactions of rage and terror" (p. 96; emphasis added). Although this may be a valuable technique for patients further exploring already known abuse, for the patient with spuriously generated memories, this helpful warning provides an explicit list of responses expected of trauma victims. The potential for influence is enhanced by Davies and Frawley's insistence ("it is essential" [p. 99]) that the therapist "normalize" (p. 99) somatic memories and hypnogogic and hypnopompic images. The patient needs to be told that "she is not going crazy but is striving to remember an as-yet unsymbolized memory..." (p. 99). Recommended technique, in this instance, becomes detailed instruction in the proper response for abuse survivors. "Striving to remember" is a brave act, while having any doubts means one must be "going crazy."

Spawned by fixed beliefs, technique ultimately becomes coercive: interpretations become indoctrination, and reassurances become instructions about expected behavior; doubt must be combatted by certainty; a mind open to the possibility of hidden abuse is closed to conflicting, ambiguous, or disconfirming evidence; and affiliation with the therapist requires agreement. In significant measure, a script is foreordained, written by the therapist and offered to the patient in exchange for guidance, collaboration, and support. While this text may be overtly or covertly presented, it can exert a decisive shaping power on the pathway followed by the therapeutic process: the therapist can impose control and direction upon a certain type of patient.

Of particular significance is the fact that this overbearing stance may be invisible to the therapist. As was obvious with Grace's therapist, it is possible to miss entirely the degree to which one is in determined pursuit of a spurious clinical supposition because it lies concealed behind the earnest conviction that one is courageously following difficult clinical material. One cannot look for the effects of influence in the absence of careful awareness of being influential. Influential power and awareness of being influential may turn out to be inversely related.

An important note must be added before turning to the patient's participation in what is clearly a two-way dynamic. Although the above commentary has focused particularly on the work of Davies and Frawley, this work is highly consistent with the other published clinical reports of recovered memory discussed here. In addition, Davies and Frawley are widely recognized experts in the area who frequently present at analytic meetings. Consequently, their work can be taken as both influential and representative of therapists who recover memories of abuse.

THE MALLEABLE PATIENT

If influence and suggestion are aptly depicted as a well-executed dance, the patient must be partner to the therapist. All patients bring to a therapeutic relationship varying amounts of distress, longing for help, and uncertainty about themselves and the nature of their difficulties. Consequently, all patients are motivated, in some measure, to listen to and be attuned to a therapist. Beyond this, however, some patients are more attuned, responsive, and malleable than others. Such qualities are not subordinate to any diagnostic category or dynamic constellation, nor do they carry, in and of themselves, any implication of psychopathology. Redrawing the line between dissociation and fantasy proneness will be helpful here. Although somewhat chameleonlike in its appearance, the clinical expression of dissociation characteristically presents two recurrent features: absorbed states of consciousness partitioned off from the dominant state of consciousness; and highly evocative, vivid, sensory experiences whose immediacy conveys a quality of "realness." These are identical to some of the cognitive attributes associated with fantasy proneness.

As described in chapter 2, some especially responsive people can be characterized as fantasy prone, a designation which clusters together a number of cognitive abilities also reflected in hypnotic susceptibility. Three features distinguish the fantasy prone individual and qualify him or her as potentially a very responsive and malleable partner to the kind of therapist portrayed in the preceding section. First, this person brings to psychotherapy a capacity for focused and segmented attention. Oftentimes these individuals feel like passive witnesses to their fantasies which seem to have a life of their own. Mentally, they can be deeply absorbed here, and there, at the same time. While that deep absorption may or may not be equivalent, as is often suggested, to a self-induced hypnotic trance, it clearly mimics what clinicians call dissociation and expect to see in hidden abuse victims. Second, as the label implies, the fantasy prone person brings into psychotherapy a distinctive gift for imaginative thought. Fantasy is a valued activity, experienced vividly along many sensory modalities, and readily granted a suspension of critical thought: fantasy can be seen, heard, felt, smelled, and touched; in short, it is as real as real. Consequently, psychological ideas may be transformed into or directly influence sensory, somatic, or behavioral experiences. For the therapist who expects dissociative states to be loaded in sensory qualities and diminished in linguistic ones, the fantasies of such individuals offer a near perfect fit. Finally, the exquisite attunement of these people to the direct and indirect expectations of others means that they are likely, on the surface, to affiliate readily and uncritically with a knowing therapist who offers direction and support. In a word, they are highly suggestible. Along each of these dimensions, patients who are in some degree fantasy prone may provide exactly what the committed therapist anticipates from hidden trauma victims. In addition, they bring the capacity to respond in ways which further reinforce, for both patient and therapist, the apparent reality of past abuse.

Are there any indications that patients described in the literature who recover memories of trauma match these patterns? No cases are recorded in Davies and Frawley in sufficient detail to answer this question, but other reports offer information which is at least indicative. For example, Person and Klar (1994, p. 1059) characterize A as a "voracious reader" who dove into novels to escape her father's harangues. Alpert (1994, p. 219) mentions that her patient's, Mary's, hobbies included drawing and writing, and that "frequently Mary would spend six or eight hours within any one day acting out fantasies that recreated the past" (p. 220), with the implication that scenes of abuse were enacted. While this seems excessive and likely to be reactive to trauma, Wilson and Barber's (1983) fantasy prone subjects routinely report approaching this level of intense fantasy activity. Dewald (1989, pp. 1001–1002) indicates his patient brought "creative imagery and expressive capacity" to her analysis. Moreover, "she was an amateur painter and frequently wrote poetry, describing the process as a stream of creative activity without conscious intent" (p. 1002). This case is puzzling, however, for although we are told that the incest depicted was not secret from the mother, all of the memories of the sexual encounters with father *and* of the mother's awareness of them appear to have been recovered from total inaccessibility. The cases of A and Mary are less ambiguous in that absorption in vivid fantasy is specifically noted, without any preexisting memory or external authentication of the recovered trauma. Overall, this evidence seems supportive of fantasy proneness in these patients, but hardly conclusive. There is nothing ambiguous, however, about how these patients experience the therapeutic relationship.

Nearly every published clinical report of recovered memory of trauma comments specifically on one distinctive reaction the patient has to the therapist. Speaking in general of work with recalled or hidden abuse victims, Davies and Frawley (1994) remark upon "the patient's experience of the clinician as a dangerous penetrator of the patient's mind" (p. 91). Williams notes that Mr. B felt that "interpretations were symbolic of 'penetrating' another person" (1987, p. 156), and hence had to be resisted with his analyst. Mary experienced Alpert (1994, p. 231) "as a molester," whose molestation consisted of "verbal intrusions." Alpert writes, "[Mary] did not want interpretations to 'touch' or 'move' her, and she felt compelled to ward off such penetration" (p. 231). In an article on "Seduction Trauma," Gediman observes that for several patients "repeated interpretations [of seduction] tended to be experienced as attempts to crush, to twist words, to recast thoughts in the analyst's terms, to pound into submission, to brainwash, to destroy identity"(1991, p. 396). Such reactions, Gediman writes, identify the "truly traumatized," but she does not indicate the nature of her evidence or the implied counterreferent ("truly traumatized" as opposed to what?).

One might wonder at the openness with which therapists who recover memories of abuse note the patient's experience of them as a dangerous, controlling invader. Any struggle over the meaning of such communications, whatever form they take, is invariably resolved, however, by interpreting them as a replication, in the transference, of the patient's original abuse; thus, transforming a here-and-now experience into a decisive confirmation of then-and-there abuse. As Davies argues, recurrent transference–countertransference "paradigms having to do with mental invasion, penetration, and control . . . among other things should provide the kinds of substantiating evidence the analyst seeks in dealing with her own pervasive doubts" (1996, p. 215). The underlying assumption here is that such therapeutic enactments are not only *re*enactments, but also reenactments of an objective event.

Has this conclusion been carefully extrapolated from existing clinical data on patients who have always known about their abuse? The best one can say is "most likely not." This strong impression is based on several pieces of evidence. As we have seen, analytic clinicians who write about recovering memories of abuse have a definite bias toward that possibility: alternative hypotheses are not seriously entertained; clinical signs which can be misleading are consistently read as indicative; and literature which might call into question these feats of memory is uncited or dismissed. Gediman, for example, cites and endorses a finding from E. Furman (Panel, 1988) that "it is easy . . . to reconstruct, via recapitulation and repetitions in the analysis, what was done to the abused child in the original traumatic situation" (1991, pp. 395–396). Gediman may, however, be imposing her beliefs on Furman. A careful reading of the Panel report reveals no such observation, and as a child analyst, Furman's remarks, if unrecorded, could only be applied to children in treatment. In any event, Gediman's construal or belief could not come from an uncommitted or open mind. In addition, in more general summary writing (Gediman, 1991; Davies and Frawley, 1994; Davies, 1996), no clear distinction can be found in patient vignettes between always remembered and recovered abuse memories. Since this distinction is critical, failure to identify it clearly in print may reflect a failure to identify it clearly in practice. Consequently, memories recovered in therapy, as with Alpert and Williams, may be used to confirm that the patient's intense reaction to feeling invaded and controlled by the therapist represents a reenactment of abuse. The patient's therapeutic experience substantiates the past abuse, while recovered memories substantiate treating the patient's immediate experience as a reenactment. The logic is circular and fails, ultimately, to support the inference of abuse drawn from the clinical data.

AN ALTERNATE HYPOTHESIS: TECHNIQUE AS "ABUSE"

The pieces are now in place to pull together an alternative interpretation of recovered memory of abuse in which the literal is replaced by the figurative, the past by the present, and a distant agent by a proximal one. Psychoanalytic theory has long recognized that particular elements of a patient's experience of the therapeutic relationship may refer to emotionally significant earlier relationships (Freud, 1914, 1915; Greenson, 1967). More recently (Langs, 1981; Gill, 1982), a broader conception of transference communication recognizes that a patient's references to earlier, or extratherapeutic relationships may, in fact, provide an indirect, unconscious commentary on the current therapeutic setting. In other words, specific communications, although manifestly about external, historical relationships and experiences, may be understood as disguised statements about the patient's immediate therapeutic experience. Two circumstances may coalesce to form memories of abuse which mistakenly attribute the patient's present experience to historical events. Let us briefly summarize the preceding discussion.

Strong beliefs about hidden childhood sexual abuse, an absolute link between dissociation and trauma, and a specific "traumatic" memory distinct from ordinary memory impose a kind of rigid zealousness on the therapeutic relationship. Hidden abuse exists, can be reliably detected, and, because of its inherent destructiveness, must be pursued and brought to the light of consciousness. Passively experienced dissociative states provide the key to these encapsulated, guarded chambers and therefore must be encouraged and tracked down. Doubts about the validity of the evidence used to initiate the search for hidden abuse, or the recovered abuse itself, lie too close to denial to be tolerated and are quelled by the therapist's authority and offers of affiliation in exchange for agreement.

Anxious and uncertain enough about themselves to seek therapy, some patients bring complementary sensitivities and cognitive skills into the therapeutic relationship. Oriented toward and taken by fantasy, such patients tend to regard psychic experience as something that happens to them, to which they feel more witness than creator. Reluctance to share this private fantasy life can be seen as having something to hide. Their capacity for divided attention, absorption, and vivid, sensory-rich fantasy mimics clinical dissociation. These patients' subtle attunement to the expectations of significant others makes them fully capable of offering up the kinds of clinical material, in form and content, which the zealous therapist tacitly expects of patients with hidden traumatic experiences.

Within this framework, the recovered literal past abuse is a metaphor, and *only* a metaphor: the patient feels invaded and controlled by a trusted other, the therapist. Things are put into them which do not belong there; a caretaking relationship is violated. The patient feels penetrated by the therapist's rigid, inescapable system of beliefs, and betrayed by invitations to join activities which are misleadingly labeled. Claims lodged against the therapist are acknowledged but reassigned to the past, in effect, silencing the patient's protest. By participating in the temporal relocation and attribution of objective reality to these experiences, the patient may also become a shameful collaborator in his or her own abuse. The violated orifice most often reported is the mouth: Does this mean, more specifically, that patients not only feel unpalatable words have been forced into their mouths, but also that control has been lost over the meaning and intent of their words? This more speculative thought aside, what ultimately results can be thought of as a closed, self-reinforcing circle. Certain firmly held beliefs dictate probing, controlling technical attitudes and procedures; these interventions generate in the patient experiences of being penetrated, trapped, and betrayed, which they resist; and in turn, these resistive responses are interpreted to confirm both the therapist's initial ideas about hidden abuse and the necessity for invasive techniques.

Grace's clinical material now takes on an entirely different cast. Instead of portraying the reenactment of unremembered past traumatic events, Grace's dreams, fantasies, and behaviors can be seen as her desperate efforts to tell me something I could not otherwise hear—that she periodically experienced the therapeutic relationship, and my attendant actions, in themselves, as a terrifying incestuous assault. From her position, intrusive sexual hypotheses were being forced upon her and left her with little alternative but to explode inwardly in rage or go limp and plead for mercy. I was seen as relentlessly "bear"ing down on her and ignoring or discounting my complicity in her wild distress. However benignly I saw my actions and justified them on therapeutic grounds, this was how she felt. The fragmented expression of apparent past incestuous rape was a metaphoric vehicle which required no literal traumatic antecedent.

Furthermore, my perception that I was following the material can now be seen as illusory. Whatever my subjective judgment, I was not following but leading, or more accurately, pushing. My initial impression that the material began to reveal itself more clearly as the apparent truth of sexual trauma was identified turns on its head. From this perspective, the material clarified in tandem with the evolving clarity of my clinical hypothesis. In this Grace unconsciously accommodated to my increasingly articulated explanatory theory and simultaneously conveyed piecemeal her experience of my technical efforts as a sexualized, intrusive betrayal of the therapeutic relationship. Two strands have been joined: Grace absorbed my repeated offerings of the possibility of unremembered sexual trauma while my insistence and pursuit shaped her experience of the process as an abusive one.

This reading inverts the interpretation of certain therapeutic material made by clinicians who recover memory of trauma. The implication of regarding such material as "unsymbolized" (chapter 4) must be that it stands only for itself, with no underlying referent. Sights and sounds refer to nothing else, and in this sense are taken as primary elements of experience. This alternative hypothesis, as it were, reverses figure and ground. What is taken as a literal, concrete self-contained entity, from one perspective, becomes a symbol from the other. Instead of regarding dissociated experiences of literal bodily penetration as an irreducible psychic bedrock, they are taken as metaphoric statements about the patient's therapeutic experience: the "unsymbol" is transformed into the "symbol."

Some of the glue which holds this together is aptly framed by what Spence (1994, p. 107) labels "metalepsis," or the inclination to "look for distant causes of present events." Every therapeutic enactment is taken as a *re*enactment. In fact, if we cannot conceive of being agents of events, in and of ourselves, we have nowhere else to look for causes or explanations than to the past. This is remarkable, however, for we have little difficulty seeing ourselves as agents, in and of ourselves, for the patient's experiences of a positive, growth promoting nature. Logically, we cannot disclaim agency in one circumstance only to claim it in the other.

An interesting historical parallel, familiar to most readers, may be drawn here. Commenting on technique with patients believed to have been victims of childhood sexual seductions, an earlier clinician made use of a penetration metaphor ("if one has not penetrated so far") to describe his therapeutic procedures (Freud, 1896a, p. 153). This view of the process is reinforced in the following clinical observation: "But the fact is that these patients never repeat those stories [of childhood seduction] spontaneously, nor do they ever in the course of a treatment suddenly present the physician with the complete recollection of a scene of this kind. One only succeeds in awakening the psychical trace of a precocious sexual event under the most energetic pressure of the analytic procedure, and against an enormous resistance" (Freud, 1896a, p. 153). The presumption of veiled, guarded experience pulls for energetic efforts to cast the veil aside, while vigorous resistance confirms the presumption.

Freud shortly thereafter reconsidered what has come to be called his "seduction hypothesis." Although recent perspectives (Masson, 1984) have suggested that Freud was right the first time, a careful analysis of Freud's available clinical data indicates (Schimek, 1975b) that "his female patients did not report conscious memories of seduction, but merely memories, thoughts, and symptoms that Freud *interpreted* as the disguised and indirect manifestation of an infantile sexual trauma" (p. 846). The techniques used by Freud included not only hypnosis, but also the firm pressure of his hand on a patient's forehead, accompanied by an authoritative statement about the patient's forthcoming thoughts. In response, Freud's patients "suffer under the most violent sensations, of which they are ashamed" (1896b, p. 204). Schimek (1975b) proposes that they are responding to 'his unrelenting and penetrating pressure to reveal their hidden memories as a seduction," not reliving a past traumatic experience (cf. also Schimek, 1987).

The argument presented here exactly parallels Schimek's contention: the patients' "most violent sensations" may reflect their reaction to the techniques clinicians employ, and feel they must employ, to uncover what they believe to be hidden trauma. A plausible case can be made that what appears clinically as the apparent reliving of a childhood sexual assault has nothing to do with dissociated childhood trauma but rather may be better understood as a vivid commentary on the patient's immediate experience of invasive, controlling technique.

There is, of course, a second alternative to consider. Fragmentary literal depictions of sexual abuse, in dreams, flashbacks, and body enactments, could be taken as depictions of experiences in childhood which did not constitute actual abuse but were felt by the child or youth to be abusive. Portrayals of literal penetrations, then, could be construed as symbolic of psychological penetrations; illustrations of betrayals by caretakers, as symbolic of psychological neglect and malice. This interpretation of the clinical evidence has some appeal (Allen, 1995), in part because it permits a compromise solution between assigning either absolute truth or utter falsehood to recovered memories. In addition and not inconsequentially, it exempts the therapist from any causal role in the production of such memories.

The problem with this solution, however, is that it fails to explain the rather sudden and dramatic clinical appearance of these alleged memory pieces in the past 10 years. As we have seen, references to memories of sexual abuse recovered from purported memory pieces have grown exponentially in recent years. It is not as if clinicians have just come to understand how to interpret these fragments, but rather that the fragments themselves have only recently been evoked or presented in psychotherapy. The explanation that they are to be taken as metaphoric statements about the past does not account for this phenomenon. Something must be happening in the psychotherapy itself, between the patient and the therapist, to explain it.

TRANSFORMING METAPHOR INTO MEMORY

Recent advances in cognitive psychology offer a conceptual basis for the evolution of "honest fabrications" (Belli and Loftus, 1994, p. 429) of traumatic memories. According to the source monitoring framework, "the source of one's memories is not directly specified in the memories themselves, but rather, source information is inferred from various aspects of the content which is contained in the memories" (p. 421). A primary discrimination falls between information generated externally, such as literal perception, and information generated internally, such as fantasy. The source monitoring framework (Johnson, Hashstroudi, and Lindsay, 1993) argues that internally and externally derived information is generally encoded quite differently. Internal information, because it is based in thought, is likely to be coded predominantly with cognitive or reflective properties. By contrast, external information, because it is based on physical stimuli, is likely to be coded with rich perceptual properties.

Such cues allow one to form a judgment about the origin of information (ideas, fantasies, potential memories) which comes to consciousness. Retrieved information packed with sensory qualities is likely to be regarded as originating externally and therefore judged to reflect memory of an actual event. Similarly, retrieved information with primarily cognitive or conceptual qualities is likely to be regarded as internally derived and therefore judged to reflect memory of thought or fantasy. "Source misattributions often occur when the characteristics of the remembered information are not reliable indicants of the source" (Belli and Loftus, 1994, p. 422). Consequently, fantasy which is heavily encoded in perceptual and sensorimotor forms, like that of fantasy prone individuals, runs the risk of having its source, mistakenly, attributed to memory for events which originated externally. Because it is rich in sensory detail, such fantasy also risks being placed erroneously in the category of dissociated memory for trauma. When, in addition, certain technical procedures, like dream analysis or focus on dissociative states, are employed which further enhance the sensory qualities of internally generated experience, the likelihood of source misattribution is compounded. A patient who is capable of deep absorption in vivid fantasy, and a clinician who anticipates hidden trauma and links sensory richness with dissociated memory of trauma, may both misattribute the source of fantasy experience to dissociated memory of trauma.

Both preexisting familiarity with subject matter and conditions which discourage or relax critical judgment further augment source monitoring confusion (Loftus and Pickrell, 1995; Schacter and Curran, 1995). Prior familiarity with certain ideas and circumstances may be taken as false evidence that events have actually occurred. Citing concepts of Conway and Rubin (1993), Schacter and Curran argue that general event knowledge and event specific knowledge are critical in understanding the creation of false memories. General event knowledge functions like the information contained in a file label, giving a broad description of content. Event specific knowledge represents the more detailed, exact contents of the file. For example, remembering going to a ball game would be general event knowledge, while recalling buying a hot dog or seeing a home run would be event specific knowledge. Schacter and Curran propose that "false memories sometimes arise when people mistakenly interpret general event knowledge as evidence of a specific event that did not happen" (p. 729). Similarly, reducing or inhibiting critical awareness also enhances the likelihood of source monitoring confusion (Lindsay and Johnson, 1989; Lynn and Nash, 1994). Urging patients to postpone thinking about whether recovered memories refer to real events, for example, discourages critical reflection. Moreover, the patient's desire to affiliate with the therapist provides a motive to join the therapist in suspending close scrutiny of possible memories.

A facilitating belief system (Ofshe and Watters, 1994) also favors source misattribution. Attributing the source of some clinical material to memory is fostered by a belief, whether tacit or stated, that memory for horrible past events can be lost, embodied in fragments of current experience, and reclaimed by therapeutic exploration. It would not be unfair or inaccurate to say that therapists who recover memories of trauma tacitly endorse a facilitating belief system like van der Kolk's "The body keeps the score" (1994). Nor would it be extravagant to assume (as will be discussed more fully in chapter 8) that patients can identify and absorb these beliefs, even if they are only indirectly revealed.

While these theoretical notions about cognitive operations are plausible, one would not expect the ordinary person under ordinary circumstances to generate false specific memories of abuse simply because of facilitating beliefs, inducements to relax critical judgment, and the background familiarity of ideas about abuse. The dynamics described above, however, reflect extraordinary circumstances—forcefully presented ideas encountering highly suggestible minds. For example, the therapist's belief system, however evidenced, may not just be identified by these patients but rather absorbed wholesale. Furthermore, intensely emotional discussions of abuse, even in the abstract, may well activate general event knowledge about abuse, about mistrust, and about secrecy. This added sense of familiarity may then act as evidence for more specific autobiographical experiences.

The clinical process by which metaphor is transformed into memory would seem to involve interpreting some forms of experience as if they reflected implicit memory for events inaccessible to explicit memory, and gradually constructing explicit memory from these presumed implicit memory fragments. Once this line of reasoning begins, it proceeds insidiously; the initial unfounded presumption (that some experience reflects implicit memory) may be lost to sight, especially when the subsequent mutual process of translating implicit to explicit memory appears to corroborate that initial presumption.

There is no "dangerous Svengali" (Harris, 1996, p. 178) in this view. The hypothesis presented here allocates influence reciprocally and reflexively. Both participants actively influence and are influenced by the other. There need not be a clear-cut suggestor or a clear-cut suggestee. If the patients are reactive and sensitive to the expectations set in motion by the clinicians, the clinicians are equally sensitive to the apparent authenticity of richly elaborated fantasy and segmented consciousness presented by the patients. Such influence, it should be noted, does not require conscious awareness, on either side, of the process or its effects. In fact, it may proceed most effectively when it occurs outside of conscious awareness (Orne, 1962; Bowers, 1984). Both patient and therapist unwittingly contribute to a fabric taken to be objective memory, as unaware of influencing as of being influenced. To imagine otherwise would be to suggest that one or the other is operating in deliberate bad faith. This, frankly, is inconceivable: the woof and warp of this cloth is the stuff of tragedy not evil.

ASSESSING THE EVIDENCE

Two claims can be made on behalf of this hypothesis. First, it accounts for the data in a plausible way. It covers essentially the same observational data as is used to support the recovered memory explanation, without making recourse to a dissociative memory construct extrapolated beyond its established base of evidence. In that regard, the metaphoric reading may be more plausible than the literal one. Second, what is plausible is thereby possible: some therapeutically recovered memories of abuse may be false and arise from the conditions described above. Whether this accounting applies to a few, some, or many instances is impossible to estimate with our present knowledge. The category "none" has been deliberately omitted for reasons that will become apparent in the next chapter. One claim cannot be made. This hypothesis does not demonstrate that wholly inaccessible explicit memory of trauma cannot be recovered from implicit memory with reasonable accuracy. Nevertheless, such a process, as has been shown in chapters 3, 4, and 5, is highly vulnerable to translation error and social influence. Documentary evidence of the accurate recovery of explicit memory is lacking and greatly needed.

The nature of evidence gathered so far to support this hypothesis is by no means conclusive: to say that certain conditions may plausibly cause an event does not mean, in any absolute sense, that they do cause that event. While drawing upon well-established empirical concepts, the evidence is still indirect and the argument speculative. The evidence, however, can be improved upon, and, in the process, the argument strengthened.

As it turns out, this hypothesis can be subjected to a standard type of scientific test. A formulation may be tested by varying what are thought to be its critical elements and seeing if the results accord with what the conjecture predicts. With variables like those at issue here, this type of test is by no means definitive, but nonetheless delivers evidence of a more direct, objective nature.

Present circumstances allow both factors outlined above to be enhanced and the outcome evaluated. Just as patients exist at the extreme upper levels of fantasy proneness or hypnotic susceptibility, there exist therapists whose zealousness and focus on dissociated traumatic memory reaches a comparable extreme. When the two meet, this hypothesis predicts that memories of abuse will be recovered which are heinous to a degree far beyond those considered to this point. With that idea in mind, the phenomenon of multiple personality and its treatment presents itself for examination.

7

MULTIPLE PERSONALITY, INVASIVE THERAPY, AND RECOVERED MEMORY

Controversial issues about early childhood sexual and physical abuse, dissociation, recovered memory, and therapeutic influence distill and concentrate in the diagnostic category of multiple personality disorder (MPD)[1]. No one, it seems, questions the existence of the captivating phenomenology of MPD. The basic question is not whether MPD exists, but rather under what circumstances it exists. Much current research argues for an etiology based on chronic childhood abuse and a powerful dissociative response to this trauma (Braun, 1984; Kluft, 1987, 1991; Putnam, 1989; Ross, 1989). The experience of childhood terror and pain is split off or dissociated from the dominant state of consciousness and, over time, relatively autonomous alter personalities are generated as a memorial and repository for these trauma. These dissociated personalities reemerge under therapeutic conditions to portray the dramatic story of their creation and the burden of their memories. Schwartz (1994, p. 190) reports that this traumatic etiology is a settled issue with "most clinicians."

---

[1]Although redesignated in DSM-IV (APA, 1994) as Dissociative Identity Disorder, the more traditional and well-known nomenclature will be retained here.

CHAPTER SEVEN

There are, however, countervailing views which point to the high degree of hypnotic susceptibility in these patients, give priority to suggestibility and therapeutic influence, and question the role of childhood trauma (Ganaway, 1989, 1994; Mulhern, 1991; Piper, 1995). Taking a wide-angle historical and cross-cultural perspective, Spanos (1994) distinguishes between local and general theories offered to account for multiplicity, or the experience of organized, multiple selves. Local theories provide explanations within a particular culture, such as spirit or demon possession, for manifestations of multiplicity. These local theories, including the current disease model of MPD, fail to account for the variable nature of multiplicity in different cultures. Spanos proposes a general sociocognitive theory which argues that multiplicity in all its variant forms reflects highly ritualized, motivated behavior carefully attuned to and reinforced by the expectations and responses of significant others. Although more philosophical in approach, Hacking's (1995) view of MPD also emphasizes the social, historical, and political contexts in which MPD appears. Sharply divided opinions, like multiple selves, collect around the topic of MPD.

In adding to the debate on MPD, this chapter has a primary and a secondary focus. The primary focus will be to test the alternative hypothesis that therapeutically recovered memories of trauma may be generated by aggressive techniques imposed on malleable patients. This will require demonstrating several things: that MPD patients possess cognitive dexterity and malleability to an extraordinary degree; that therapists who specialize in working with MPD patients represent a correspondingly extreme version of the zealous, controlling therapist; and finally, that, as the model predicts, the recovered memories of non-MPD patients pale in comparison with those recovered, or generated by MPD patients.

Pursuing these tasks essentially outlines a specific alternative etiology for MPD. The contextualist point of view noted above highlights the role of general patterns of social interaction and learning, but leaves undeveloped the individual differences which may enhance the appearance of multiplicity and the specific influences and pathways by which such shaping may occur. The secondary focus of this chapter will be to show that the striking

cognitive capabilities associated with extreme hypnotic susceptibility and fantasy proneness readily interact with particular MPD-
related demand characteristics in the therapeutic situation to promote the appearance of multiplicity.

EXTREME HYPNOTIC SUSCEPTIBILITY AND FANTASY PRONENESS

In the clinical literature, MPD patients are consistently depicted
as highly gifted hypnotic subjects (Bliss, 1980, 1983; Kluft, 1987;
Braun, 1990). The analysis provided by Hacking (1995) places
MPD within the clearly equivalent and more historically
grounded category of susceptibility to trance. This uniformity
raises the possibility that some broader set of cognitive abilities
associated with extreme degrees of hypnotic susceptibility may
play a pivotal role in the emergence of MPD. Taken collectively,
a significant body of clinical (Bliss, 1980, 1983; H. Spiegel, 1974)
and empirical literature (Orne, 1959; Tellegen and Atkinson,
1974; Hilgard, 1977, 1994; Laurence and Perry, 1981; Wilson and
Barber, 1983; Lynn and Rhue, 1988; Lynn, Rhue, and Green,
1988; Rauschenberger and Lynn, 1995) presents a remarkably
rich and consistent picture of the psychological world of people
called variously "hypnotic virtuoso" (Bliss, 1980), "Grade 5 Syndrome" (H. Spiegel, 1974), or "fantasy-prone personality" (Wilson and Barber, 1983).

Identified by exceptionally high scores on a variety of stan-
dardized measures of hypnotic susceptibility, including the appearance of the "hidden observer" phenomenon (Hilgard,
1977), or on tests of fantasy proneness, these subjects are predominantly female and drawn from nonclinical populations. Only
Bliss and Spiegel base their observations on clinical populations.
Such individuals are estimated, roughly, to comprise between 4
percent (Wilson and Barber) and 10 percent (H. Spiegel, 1974)
of the population; more precisely, they comprised 2.6 percent of
Lynn and Rhue's sample of 6000 subjects. Demonstrable psychopathology and self-reports of harsh and abusive childhood treatment are found in a relatively small minority of these individuals

(Lynn and Rhue, 1988). Wilson and Barber characterize their subjects as ranging "in emotional stability or mental health across the entire range of the normal curve" (1983, p. 365). Tellegen and Atkinson (1974) explicitly note that the high degree of hypnotic susceptibility in their subjects is independent of experimental measures of Ego Resiliency and Ego Control.

There appears then to exist a coherent and relatively well-defined set of individuals who are both highly hypnotizable and fantasy prone independent of psychopathology and history of childhood abuse. For the small minority who report difficult or abusive early childhoods, no effort has been made to document these self-reports, and these reports themselves have been questioned (Kihlstrom, Glisky, and Angiulo, 1994; Rauschenberger and Lynn, 1995). These subjects possess powerful, distinctive cognitive abilities which allow for and activate wholesale absorption in vivid fantasy. Two distinctly different capacities are involved (Lynn and Rhue, 1988; Nadon, Hoyt, Register, and Kihlstrom, 1991; Tillman, Nash, and Lerner, 1994). One capacity creates a container or an enclave in consciousness which allows for free rein of thoughts, while the other activates especially gymnastic multisensory, alogical thought patterns. A distinctive interpersonal stance may also accompany these cognitive features.

An enormous ability to focus and encapsulate mental attention supplies the arena for rich fantasy activity. These subjects routinely experience a mental absorption so focused that "the available representational apparatus seems to be entirely dedicated to experiencing and modeling the attentional object" (Tellegen and Atkinson, 1974, p. 273) whether that object is another person or one's own thought. As deeply involved as they may be in immediate internal experience, these people also have an unusual capacity for divided or sequestered attention. They report (Bliss, 1980; Wilson and Barber, 1983) being able to "continue fantasizing without interruption while they are engaged in other activities or interacting with others" (p. 350). These capacities are directly visible in the "hidden observer" phenomenon. A sizable minority of highly responsive hypnotic subjects (Hilgard, 1977, 1994; Laurence and Perry, 1981) report dual or divided awareness: when age-regressed they are aware of being both the regressed age and adult observers; when exposed to experimental pain, both unaware and aware of the sensation of pain. Breuer's highly hypnotizable patient, Anna O, may well provide the earliest depiction of such an individual: she "indulg[ed] in systematic day-dreaming, which she described as her 'private theatre'. While everyone thought she was attending, she was living through fairy tales in her imagination" (Breuer and Freud, 1893–1895, p. 22).

Whether or not this amounts to an ability to induce trance states at will (Bliss, 1980), these people can focus and divide their attention to extraordinary degrees (Bliss, 1983). This process probably is a manifestation of what clinicians regard as dissociation, and may result, as Tellegen and Atkinson state, in "a marked discontinuity between the self and the self during an episode of absorbed concentration on some aspect of the self [so that] we may, indeed, speak of a 'dissociative experience'" (1974, pp. 274–275).

Inside this sequestered, focused cognitive realm, conventional rules of logic abdicate and "trance logic" reigns. Orne (1959) defines "trance logic" as "the ability of the S to mix freely his perceptions derived from reality with those that stem from his imagination. . . . These perceptions are fused in a manner that ignores everyday logic" (p. 295). Like a drama which wins a wholly willing suspension of disbelief, thoughts have free rein and, unchecked by contradiction or critical reflection, are given a degree of credibility not unlike that granted to dreams during sleep (H. Spiegel, 1974; Bliss, 1980). The door opens for extraordinary ideas: without skepticism, reports are offered of the unbelievable (astral travel, past-life identities, intrauterine and birth experiences), the highly dubious (detailed accounts of first birthdays), and the incredible (out-of-body experiences, psychic relocation, and reconstitution as another person) (Bliss, 1980; Wilson and Barber, 1983; Spanos, Burgess, and Burgess, 1994). These ideas so credulously accepted are not to be regarded as psychotic productions nor as reflections of serious mental illness. Rather they reflect a habitual, even creative mode of thought which occurs parallel to the more conventional thinking which allows these people to function in the ordinary world. Some authors (Spanos et al. 1994; Sheehan et al., 1991) posit that such uncritical thinking is induced as much by facilitating instructions (such as to relax and let ones thoughts flow) as by inherent cognitive propensities. Still, a parallel between these facilitating conditions and certain treatment techniques (such as free association or hypnosis) cannot be ignored.

A prodigious gift for detail, immediacy, and what is described as an "excellent memory" (H. Spiegel, 1974, p. 306) also characterizes their cognition (Wilson and Barber, 1983). These people claim to be able to replay memory, in vivid detail, as if it were in present time and space (H. Spiegel, 1974; Wilson and Barber, 1983). One subject (Wilson and Barber, 1983) describes her "echo box" which allows her to replay "entire conversations and lectures in her mind and [she] hears both what she heard originally and also the words and sentences to which she did not originally attend" (p. 357). Such apparent feats of memory extend far back into childhood, as nearly a third of Wilson and Barber's fantasy prone personalities report clear memories for events on or before their first birthday. Very early life is recalled with the same thoughts, feelings, and bodily sensations as were allegedly experienced in the first place.

Are these feats of memory or of invention? The highly plastic, interactive nature of autobiographical memory has been consistently demonstrated, with little evidence of validated memory prior to age 3 (Nelson, 1993; Loftus, 1993c; Kihlstrom, 1994b). Consequently, these subjects' apparent capacity for total, veridical recall may be closer to confabulation in which some elements of reality act as seed crystals to powerful imaginative abilities. Although Wilson and Barber (1983, p. 381) only raise this possibility in a very brief footnote, it is extremely likely that much of what may be presented as memory is fully and indecipherably confounded by fantasy. No corroborations are offered to validate the "excellent memory" of these subjects, and the nature of their fantasy experience argues that what appears as memory may be suffused with invention (Lynn and Rhue, 1988; Orne and Bauer-Manley, 1991; Lindsay and Read, 1994; Spanos, 1994).

Vivid, immediate, detailed, and multisensory fantasy dominates their mental life (Tellegen and Atkinson, 1974; H. Spiegel, 1974; Bliss, 1980; Wilson and Barber, 1983). Almost all of Wilson and Barber's subjects state they spend 50 percent of their waking life absorbed in fantasies which have an "involuntary, automatic, or self-propelling quality" (p. 353). The fantasies are "as real as real"(p. 352), in large part because they are experienced vividly along many sensory channels: not only are their fantasies seen and heard, felt and smelled; these sensations are indistinguishable from those produced by actual, in-the-world, stimuli. Tellegen and Atkinson (1974) label this capacity "syngnosia," an integration of all cognitive and perceptual experience. Their subjects endorse an item (p. 270) which confirms their ability to embellish an incident with elaborations so convincing that the elaborations seem as real, or nearly so, as the actual incident. Wilson and Barber summarize: "their fantasies are typically so realistic that 85% . . . stated that they tend to confuse their *memories* of their fantasies with their *memories* of actual events" (1983, p. 353). Described as "a dreamy and visionary child" (1920, p. 105), Prince's original MPD subject Miss Beauchamp, "so mixed up her daydreams, and imaginings with reality that she did not have a true conception of her environment" (p. 106). Autobiographical memory for these people may consist of an inseparable blend of memory of events and of thought.

This confabulatory style has the greatest impact and sway in the realm of personal, subjective experience. Psychic transformations of or relocations away from the bodily self appear to be routine events. Subjects from Tellegen and Atkinson's study agree with an item which endorses a capacity to alter the sensation of body weight so that it feels immoveable. The vast majority of Wilson and Barber's fantasy prone personalities report having illnesses and physical symptoms which they regard as deriving directly from thoughts and fantasies. Perhaps the most impressive demonstration of the influence of mind over body comes from (false) beliefs of pregnancy reported by 60 percent of these subjects. Typically these women, thinking they were pregnant, developed amenorrhea, breast changes, abdominal enlargement, morning sickness, and "fetal" movement.

One's own body may also be subjectively relocated away from the self. "Realistic out-of-the-body experiences" (Wilson and Barber, 1983, p. 360) are reported by nearly all of the fantasy prone subjects. In addition, some of the out-of-body experiences include transporting the self to other times and places (also Bliss, 1980).

The self may even be relocated in or reconstituted as another person. Tellegen and Atkinson (1974) ground this process in the idea that "objects of absorbed attention acquire an importance and intimacy that are normally reserved for the self and may, therefore, acquire a temporary self-like quality" (p. 275). Weitzenhoffer and Hilgard (1967, p. 57) include precisely such an item ("[Y]ou will no longer be the person you are now. You will have an entirely different name and background") in their Stanford Profile of Hypnotic Susceptibility. Although this item, of all items profiled, is the least likely to receive a maximum score (indicating extreme susceptibility), approximately 10 percent of the subjects used to establish norms received this score. Similarly, Tellegen and Atkinson's subjects endorse a statement that they are "able to forget about my present self and get absorbed in a fantasy that I am someone else" (p. 270).

These rather artificial illustrations of a capacity to reconstitute one's self psychically as another person pale in comparison to those given by Wilson and Barber's subjects. Nearly uniformly, these people report not only pretending during childhood to be someone else, but feeling that they actually became the person or character they pretended to be. One subject felt "not that she was pretending to be a bird, but that she was a bird pretending to be a girl" (p. 347). Two-thirds of these subjects indicated that, as adults, they still pretend to be someone other than themselves, and many describe pretending to be someone else with strangers.

These mental dexterities can be thought of as a confabulatory cognitive style, animated by vivid, multisenory fantasy, governed by "trance logic," and sequestered by enormous powers for focus and absorption. What is imagined is as immediate and real as any current experience. And what is real may be as difficult to discern from the outside (by another) as it is from the inside (by the self). A careful distinction between reality and invention seems irrelevant. These subjects should not be regarded as dishonest or as deliberate liars. Dishonesty and deliberate lying are predicated on a clear awareness of invention. These subjects' notion of truth would appear to resemble genuineness, and as such be more a function of immediate experience. Genuineness is vested primarily in the moment and may flex pliantly in response to changes in context. As moment and context shift, so can what seems most genuine. At times the context to which they seem most attuned is an interpersonal one.

A striking mixture of guardedness and naive trust may characterize the interpersonal posture of these people. Firm resistance coexists with complete openness. Although all were natural hypnotic subjects, some of Wilson and Barber's fantasy prone personalities in fact vigorously resisted hypnotic induction in circumstances which they felt warranted mistrust. Similarly H. Spiegel (1974, p. 308) says of the Grade 5 subjects that they possess "a narrow, hard *fixed core*: a dynamism so fixed that it is subject to neither negotiation nor change." In addition, Wilson and Barber (1983) describe the routine guardedness of their subjects. Sensitive to social norms, all learned early on to "be very secretive about their pretending and their fantasies," and "told virtually no one about the extent or depth of their fantasy life . . . "(p. 348).

This often closed-door attitude toward others who may not understand or appreciate their imaginative gifts opens dramatically under other circumstances. The context in which these subjects "open up" most trustingly appears to be one of active interest and acceptance. Wilson and Barber (1983) recount that, during their interviews, "these women told us secrets they had never told anyone" (p. 366). Several factors are offered by way of explanation for these unprecedented disclosures. First Wilson and Barber asked them questions they had never been asked before and which seemed so perfectly in tune that the subjects felt the researchers were " 'reading' their minds" (p. 366). Second, Wilson and Barber stated that "we were accepting and understanding of everything they told us" (p. 366).

Clearly when such people feel their way of thinking is respected and valued, a "posture of trust" (H. Spiegel, 1974, p. 304) is extended to the other which seems remarkably naive and absolute. Grade 5s, H. Spiegel writes, "exude an intense, beguilingly innocent expectation of support from others" (p. 304). This extension of trust not only provides an open channel through which they share the "secrets" of their fantasy life, but also a channel through which they receive, and expect, direction and support. Thus, "the grade 5s have an incredible ability to *affiliate with new events*—either concrete events or perspectives—an almost magnetic attraction to them" (H. Spiegel, 1974, p. 305).

If these individuals feel a bond of trust with another person, that person may become the "attentional object" (Tellegen and

Atkinson, 1974, p. 274) upon which they are focused and absorbed. This may create, H. Spiegel notes (1974), the opening
for an inventive response: "they tend . . . to look at a simple proposal as a demand, and to concretize a proposal . . . so much so
that they may at times mistakenly use a metaphor as a concrete
command to perform" (p. 312). People with great imaginative
flair, who can "tune in" so totally to the implicit expectations of
trusted others, and who experience metaphors as demands, may
produce exactly what the other is (implicitly) expecting to hear.

DEMAND CHARACTERISTICS AND THERAPEUTIC ATTITUDES

The demand characteristics which fall upon the therapists of
these gifted imaginers are critical. Originally formulated by Orne
(1959, 1962) as an aspect of the hypnotic or psychological experimental situation, the concept of "demand characteristics" has
relevance far beyond these contexts. Demand characteristics—the
unspoken expectations conveyed by one party to another—are to
be found in all social situations and influence all members of
these social arrangements. Formalized relationships between
highly motivated participants such as exist between teacher and
student, experimenter and subject, or patient and therapist bring
forth especially significant demand characteristics which may be
all the more potent because they are not only unspoken but unrecognized by their bearers (Frank, 1973; Bowers, 1984).

The expectations therapists have of MPD patients provides
a measure of the specific demand characteristics borne toward
such patients. These expectations include not only obvious content areas (dissociated early trauma residing in discrete personalities) but also particular dynamics (betrayal of trust) which warrant
specialized therapeutic attitudes (acceptance and belief) and
technical responses (probing and hypnosis). With the exception
of Davies and Frawley, none of the therapists cited here appears
to carry a psychoanalytic orientation as their primary affiliation.
Still, analytic therapists are not immune to finding MPD patients
(Brenner, 1994), nor to taking its purported traumatic etiology
at face value (Davies and Frawley, 1994).

The presumption of many therapists that MPD results from the coalescence of dissociated early trauma into discrete states (Kluft, 1987; Putnam, 1989; Braun, 1990) has several implications. The patient is seen as having suffered the betrayal of early caretakers, as having been left unprotected by others, and as being most likely full of shame. In the therapist's mind, this creates an anticipation of the patient's secrecy entrenched by shame and threat, and of the patient's deep, warranted mistrust in others (Coons and Milstein, 1986; Kluft, 1987; Coons, 1989; Braun, 1990). These people guard against the revelation of terrible experiences, and equally, against the possibility of repeat perfidy.

"Secrecy, suppression, and denial" ought to be expected in the examination and treatment of MPD patients (Kluft, 1987, p. 367). This anticipation of secrecy and deception, wholly understandable in light of presumed history, provides the rationale for a probing, confrontational technique, including the use of hypnosis (Kluft, 1982; Ross, 1984; Braun, 1990). Insistence, interrogation, and cross-examination are acceptable because the patient's full or undivided cooperation cannot be assumed. The therapist, in this situation, "knows" what to expect (resistance in relation to secrets) and therefore can "know" when the patient has failed to cooperate with the treatment.

If the anticipation of secrecy pulls for aggressive and hard-edged technique, the anticipation of mistrust borne of betrayal pulls for a profoundly different attitude. MPD specialists (Summit, 1983; Kluft, 1987; Coons and Milstein, 1986; Braun, 1990) unanimously agree that the prime task of therapy is "trust building" (Coons and Milstein, 1986, p. 109). Since "a multiple was usually abused by a parent or parental figure" (Coons and Milstein, 1986, p. 109), overcoming the mistrust of people in caretaker roles is seen as critical to therapeutic success. They argue that, "Trust is best developed if the therapist uses the following techniques: listening, *believing*, understanding, and empathizing" (p. 109; emphasis added). The therapist's unswerving commitment to these techniques is required, for the possible MPD patient will test that commitment again and again (Summit, 1983).

Belief is an especially important element in trust building. As Davies and Frawley (1991) state, not to believe the "nightmarish memories that begin to flood their waking thoughts (p.

32) . . . represents a secondary betrayal of the child whose original abuse was ignored, denied, and unattended to by the significant adults in his life" (p. 33). The therapist is pulled, and urged (Summit, 1983) toward a position of advocacy and belief because anything less can be seen as a betrayal of trust and therefore as a duplication of the original trauma. Lack of belief, from one vantage point, is seen as tantamount to betrayal; from another, it is seen as a failure of courage. Goodwin (1985) argues that unresolved countertransference anxieties lead clinicians to shy away from believing the terrible tales of childhood abuse. Unable to face the idea of a world in which gruesome actions are perpetrated on children, therapists dismiss the clinical evidence in front of them. As we saw in the last chapter, enormous forces contain the seeds of doubt. Doubt betrays an already mistrustful and frightened patient and also exposes the therapist's lack of moral courage.

The therapist of the potential MPD patient also anticipates "altered states" in which this abuse experience is coded. Further, because the patient might be a "multiple," these altered states, so rich in vivid sensorimotor detail, can be seen as separate from the patient's dominant state of consciousness. For the clinician disposed to MPD, clinical phenomena which might be described as fairly coherent, stable, and episodically experienced "states of mind" (Horowitz, 1988) may become "alters" or separate personality configurations. Regarding such states of mind as "alters" imposes further expectations upon them, such as name, date and circumstances of origin, and function. Thus, the clinician may be inclined to inquire about, expect to hear, and even pull for precisely such details (Bliss, 1986; Putnam, 1989).

The culmination of these demand characteristics upon therapists is that when they do hear, or think they hear material which adds up to discrete personalities and dissociated memories of abuse, they have little choice but to regard both as authentic. It is what they have been expecting to hear, and not to hear it exposes them to accusations of the betrayal of trust. One could argue that the following statement reflects the inevitable position of credulity the therapist must attain: "the more illogical and incredible the initiation scene [of abuse] might seem to adults, the more likely it is that the child's plaintive description is valid"

(Summit, 1983, p. 183). Any measure of skepticism or incredulity is powerfully proscribed, for belief has become the benchmark of acceptable therapeutic attitude.

The patient's ultimate revelation and the therapist's ultimate acceptance of their secrets of abuse and alter personalities become decisive positive reinforcements: the revelation confirms for the therapist that he or she has finally won the trust of this justifiably suspicious patient; the acceptance (belief) of it confirms that the therapist has the moral courage not to flinch from seeing the worst of humanity. Thus Braun (1990) concludes his discussion with this admonition: "The alert therapist focuses [on] . . . the unsettling possibility that the discovery of incest, however reprehensible, may be the clue that still more has occurred, that it may be the 'tip of the iceberg' of the most severe abuse imaginable" (p. 224).

The demand characteristics for the therapist who regards MPD as derived from dissociated early trauma generate a somewhat anomalous mixture of the need for an aggressive, probing technique, an expectation of dissociative experience encoded in "alter" personalities, and the need for absolute belief in the reality of whatever "history" is offered. These are not to be regarded as low voltage demand characteristics, but rather as highly primed expectations. Kluft, for example (1987, p. 367), states: "unless the clinician's index of suspicion for MPD is high, almost inevitably his attention will be held by phenomena that suggest other disorders . . . " (pp. 367–368). In short, the clinician needs to be on full alert for the possibility of MPD. This degree of alertness, however, has the paradoxical effect of opening the therapist to extreme gullibility toward any clinical material which appears to match his or her focused expectations.

THE PRODUCTION OF MPD

A brief digression is warranted. This depiction of the highly imaginative fantasy prone patient and of the therapist committed to the dissociated traumatic origins of MPD, in effect, outlines an etiology for MPD which has nothing to do with early trauma. In the clinical encounter specific cognitive abilities, on the patient's part, dovetail precisely with expectations and demand characteristics on the therapist's part. (1) The capacity of these patients to focus and segment consciousness, often in trancelike states, matches the clinician's anticipation of and template for dissociation which carries the implication of hidden trauma. (2) These patients' "syngnosia" or ability to evoke and meld multisensory experience in "as real as real" fantasy, parallels the clinician's view of dissociated traumatic memory rich in basic sensory properties, only accessible in certain psychological states, and with a likely association with past trauma. Although these "memory" forms may actually have little or nothing to do with memory for actual past traumatic events (Lindsay and Read, 1994), it is clear that many clinicians make exactly that link (Poole, Lindsay, Memon, and Ball, 1995). (3) The guardedness of these patients against revealing the depth and detail of their enormous absorption in fantasy can easily be seen, through the clinician's eye, as mistrust coupled with secrecy about hidden experience. (4) The combination of a practiced talent for highly elaborated and structured fantasy and a well-established ability to "relocate" or "reconstitute" the self in fantasy as another person lines up with the clinician's expectation of discretely organized "alter" personalities which possess specific attributes such as name and personal history. Finally, (5) the exquisite sensitivity of these patients to demand characteristics and their ability to affiliate with new ideas connects quickly with the above, readily definable, and clear-cut demand expectations of clinicians on the alert for MPD. This combination of precisely matched patient and clinician features may result in the clinical phenomena regarded as MPD.

These special patients produce the phenomenology of MPD not because they have "MPD" but because these phenomena are merely an exaggerated reflection of their daily mental experience. Clinicians may confuse the opportunity for expression with the effects of trauma (Wilson and Barber, 1983). Similarly, these patients may also be especially responsive to clinicians interested in MPD because the kinds of things these clinicians are interested in so closely mirror their routine, but shielded fantasy life. In actuality, the mechanisms by which MPD appears may occur outside of awareness so that each participant genuinely feels that it

is a wholly spontaneous unrolling of preexisting structures, processes, and contents.

THERAPEUTIC TECHNIQUES WITH MPD PATIENTS

If the zealous therapist described in the preceding chapter pushes
the limits of standard psychotherapeutic practice, therapists who
treat MPD patients extend those limits to the breaking point.
Technical extensions multiply the might of determined therapeutic attitudes.

Seldom used in conventional psychodynamic therapy, hypnosis is the primary tool employed in the treatment of MPD patients.
Although Braun (1984) points out that some MPD patients have
never been hypnotized, it is nonetheless true that very many have
(Bliss, 1980; Kluft, 1982; C. Ross et al., 1989; Braun, 1990). A
survey of current practice with MPD patients (Putnam and
Loewenstein, 1993) indicates that "all clinician groups ranked
psychotherapy facilitated by hypnosis as the best treatment for
multiple personality disorder" (p. 1051). Hypnosis appeared to
be used by 70 percent of the clinicians. Hypnosis, by its very nature, necessarily involves the resignation of deliberate internal
control and the subjective experience of passive influence.

An experience of submission may not be created by hypnotic
techniques alone. Highly evocative (Lindsay and Read, 1994) and
confrontational (Kluft, 1982) techniques are frequently employed
by a significant minority of therapists (Poole et al., 1995), and
also involve a subjective sense of passive resignation to powers
and forces outside one's immediate deliberate control. Kluft
(1982) notes that his "most common hypnotic instruction is 'ev-
erybody listen' " (p. 236). Ross (1984) describes aspects of his
technique as authoritative and confrontational: "In what I took
to be an appropriately stern interrogator's manner, I cross-exam-
ined Peggy; she soon broke down and admitted she had made it
all up" (p. 227). Kluft makes specific mention of patients' anxiety
as they allow their experience to be shaped passively, and the
clinician's need "to empathize with the terror of passive influence
experience" (1982, p. 235). While Kluft clearly has the force of

alter personalities in mind, it is not unreasonable to turn this view back on itself and replace alter personalities with the confrontational force of regularly employed technical procedures. Bowers (1991) argues that, because of their capacity for dissociated control, highly hypnotizable subjects may be already primed to regard their experience as passively influenced and as having a psychological momentum of its own.

Such techniques may readily induce in the "amenable" patient not only a powerful sense of coercion and "the terror of passive influence," but also a sense of intrusion and invasion. Some evidence for this notion may be found in therapists' accounts of their activity. Describing the treatment course of an MPD patient, Ross (1984) states: "The hypnotherapeutic abreaction acted as an exploratory drill, probing down through previously impenetrable strata of psychic rock, gaining access to the deep source of dissociation" (p. 119). This language can be read as a highly sexualized, phallic-intrusive view of the therapeutic process. Whatever its poetic quality, the language reflects a sexually charged sense of action and reaction: "Probing into Jenny's psyche, always with a therapeutic intention, was a journey into an unexplored region. Behind the wall of her dissociation were memories, feelings, thoughts, and nodes of psychic energy, regions of dense power in the living landscape of her soul" (p. 229). Another, indirect source provides additional support for this contention. Recommendations "to be gentle, patient, and avoid imposing on the patient" (Kluft, 1984, p. 14), and admonitions against "coercion, direction, and control" (Schwartz, 1994, p. 206) both point to the often enacted therapeutic temptation to overpower the potential MPD patient. Generally speaking, warnings are required only where temptations exist.

The details of even more invasive and controlling procedures are seldom revealed in professional journals and books. However, two recent carefully researched publications (Ofshe and Watters, 1994; Pendergrast, 1995) give some inkling of the extreme measures to which MPD patients are subjected. Extended, insistent interviews, sometimes supplemented by hypnosis or sodium amytal, are often required to reveal alter personalities. Putnam, for example, writes that "it may be necessary to spend a large part of the day with some highly secretive MPD patients," during which time the therapist must "continue to probe aggressively" (Putnam [1989], cited in Pendergrast [1995, p. 163]). Six- and eight-hour interviews, sustained without interruption or allowing the patient to avert his or her face, are described by Kluft (Pendergrast, 1995, p. 163). When, in response to such interrogation, a patient reports "feeling smothered, having a sense of terrible internal pressure," Putnam (1989) interprets this as suggestive of dissociative psychopathology (cited in Pendergrast, 1995, p. 163) rather than as the effect of his technique.

Treatment techniques can be even more suggestive and invasive than diagnostic ones. Explicit requests are made for names to be assigned to feeling states, followed by more specific requests to map out and chart personalities (Ofshe and Watters, 1994, pp. 213–214, 218). Once the therapist has decided upon a diagnosis of MPD, insistent discussion may ensue to overcome the patient's reluctance to accept the diagnosis and to convince the patient of its accuracy. Patients may be informed of the virtual certainty that they were abused as children because nearly all multiples are believed to have been abused as children (p. 231).

Efforts to unlock the doors to these memories, which most MPD specialists indicate appear and are credible only after being uncovered in vigorous therapeutic intervention, are both suggestive and relentless. Based on interviews with her and her husband, Ofshe and Watters (1994, pp. 225–251) detail the experience of "Anne Stone" who was treated by two well-known and outspoken MPD therapists. Lengthy and frequent hypnotic trances were commonplace, sometimes lasting up to three hours and occurring as often as several times a day. In addition, Anne reports on more than a few occasions, one or the other of her therapists would "come in after midnight and wake her up before beginning the hypnosis" (p. 235). Once in a hypnotic trance, one therapist would pursue Anne with transparently leading questions: Is your mother around? Are they wearing hoods? Is anyone screaming? Who? Will they be used in the ritual? (p. 234). Having led Anne to the pivotal moment of the ritual, the questions would stop. Nevertheless, it would require little imagination to know what was meant to happen next after Anne "saw herself with a dagger in her hand, standing over a pregnant woman" (p. 234). Ironically, the other therapist at times would be too overcome by Anne's "remembrances" to go on, would hold her hand tenderly, and at the end of a session, kiss her comfortingly on the cheek or forehead. Although such responses might hint at tacit sexual implications, the overwhelming impression left by these actions is of the paramount importance of power and control. Other types of interventions make this clear.

Under the guise of care and protection, treatment techniques may become unmistakably barbaric. One patient, during her hospital stay, was heavily drugged and frequently held in restraints (Pendergrast, 1995, p. 170). According to a nurse on the hospital unit, another patient "was placed in nine-point mechanical restraints for three days . . . not because he was a threat to himself or others . . . but because those three days coincided with some satanic event" (McDonald [1994] cited in Pendergrast, [1995, p. 171]). A young girl is reported to have been confined to one room and denied access to her parents (Pendergrast, 1995, p. 171). Nurses from a dissociative disorders hospital ward indicate that some patients were not allowed to use the phone, to receive mail, to leave the unit, or to see their families (Pendergrast, 1995, p. 177n). Mary S (Pendergrast, 1995, p. 173) states that she was taking "Inderal, Xanax, Prozac, Klonopin, Halcion and several other drugs, all at once." In addition, she reports "when she would not perform properly during an abreactive session, she would be kept in restraints for up to nine hours" (p. 174).

Anne Stone describes similar experiences. Some abreaction sessions took place in a "quiet room" outfitted with a bed with leather restraints for a patient's arms, legs, and torso. Such equipment was thought to be necessary to protect a patient while reliving memories so gruesome that they might injure themselves. A leading therapist (Braun [1992], cited in Ofshe and Watters [1994, p. 246]) announced to a large professional audience that he now limits abreaction sessions to an hour, although in the past they might endure for up to nine hours. Moreover, the same therapist indicates that he "often prescribes his patients a laundry list of drugs" (p. 246), and has on occasion prescribed Inderal at a dosage ten times that of the maximum given to heart patients.

The extreme nature of these allegations requires that one ask how reliable is the information contained in these two publications? With some exceptions (those mentioned by MPD specialists themselves), the allegations are anecdotal, reported second or third hand, and unverified by external corroboration. That some of these practices have been mentioned in public media does not necessarily confirm their occurrence. Standing against these reservations are the reputations of the authors and the quality of their research. Pendergrast, a parent accused of unnamed sexual abuse by one of his adult daughters, is nonetheless an experienced investigative reporter with one critically lauded book already to his credit. Ofshe, a professor of social psychology at the University of California-Berkeley, is well known for his investigations of cults and social manipulation. Ofshe and Watters also indicate that they have checked Anne Stone's story, as much as possible, with her hospital records and the writings of her therapists. Both books are scrupulously documented and referenced. In the end, the reality of these extraordinary procedures will probably be decided in the legal arena where independent evidence such as hospital records can be called upon for substantiation. For the present, the carefulness of the research and the diverse source material upon which it is based argue for the credibility of some of these reports.

At its most extreme, some MPD patients are subjected to a kind of reign of terror, both restrictive and invasive. Physical restraining devices, social isolation, sequestration with other MPD patients, limited access to external information, and multiple drug regimens enforce the therapist's will and point of view. In these respects, the treatment of MPD patients resembles the conditions under which "thought reform" occurs (Singer, 1994). Armed with a powerful array of coercive interventions, the zealous therapist has become an autocrat.

While some of the coercive procedures described above may be in only limited evidence with MPD patients treated on an outpatient basis, even in their mildest forms, the attitudes of MPD specialists remain autocratic. Hypnosis, extended interviews, and confrontational techniques are required because the therapist knows something is hidden and needs to be revealed: secrets emerge and betray their truth only under duress. Ultimately, for some patients, this attitude of conviction alone may be sufficient to produce the phenomenology of MPD and memories of past abuse.

THE RECOVERED MEMORIES

If recovered memories of childhood abuse may be generated by the interaction of aggressive therapeutic attitudes and imaginative, fantasy prone or suggestible patients, the interaction of therapists and patients representing, respectively, extreme zealousness and extreme fantasy proneness should produce memories of unmatched brutality and perversity. As described above, MPD therapists and patients clearly fulfill these conditions. Both general and more specific information is available from a variety of professional and lay sources on the kinds of memories recovered by MPD patients. Although these memories are not always explicitly designated as recovered, nearly all MPD specialists indicate that these patients are unaware of memories of abuse prior to treatment.

Virtually every survey of MPD patients reveals that more than 75 percent eventually recall memories of physical and sexual abuse from childhood (Putnam, Guroff, Silberman, Barban, and Post, 1986; Coons and Milstein, 1986; Ross, Norton et al., 1989; Ross, Miller, Reagor, Bjornson, Fraser, and Anderson, 1990; Boon and Draijer, 1993). When it is possible to determine the percentage who report either physical or sexual abuse, the rate approaches or exceeds 90 percent (Ross, Norton et al., 1989; Ross, Miller et al., 1990; Boon and Draijer, 1993). Many authors (Briere and Conte, 1993; Ross, Miller et al., 1990; Chu and Dill, 1990; Boon and Draijer, 1993) regard even these incidence rates as conservative estimates inasmuch as amnesia is typical for MPD patients and therefore some cases of abuse may remain undisclosed. Remarking on their sample, Boon and Draijer write, "in all cases of sexual abuse [77.5% of the sample], the subjects reported vaginal, anal, or oral penetration before age 5 years" (p. 491).

Although some accounts of individual cases refer to memories in an ambiguous manner, such as "severe preoedipal sexual trauma which continued into late adolescence" (Brenner, 1994, p. 837), others are more specific. Braun (1990) describes several cases. With Miss KM, for example, "mother and grandmother beat the child with sticks, rods, and a doubled electric cord" (p. 234), and at age 4, Miss KM was assaulted by a stranger who forced her to perform fellatio. From the age of 1 to 12, Miss MM was forced to take part in "sadomasochistic child pornography films" (p. 239) in which she was beaten with a whip, forced to perform fellatio and other sex acts with both children and adults, and may have been forced to observe several murders. Miss WM was forced to participate in "satanic cult activities" (p. 241) which included sexual and physical abuse as well as "human sacrifice and cannibalism" (p. 241). Kluft (1987) refers to a woman traumatized by "anal penetration experienced during her exploitation in child pornography" (p. 368).

Claims of satanic ritual abuse like that reported of Miss WM above represent more than isolated instances. Ofshe and Watters ([1994, p. 179], citing Briere [1989, p. 128]) point to a professional text which reports that adult patients "commonly" report childhood activities such as "being forced to publicly masturbate with a crucifix; ceremonial gang rape . . . , sexual contact with or dismemberment of a family pet; demands that the child drink blood or urine . . . ; and ritualistic ceremonies where the child is stripped of clothing, tied to a crucifix or platform, sexually molested, and led to believe that she is about to be sacrificed." Derived from additional sources, similar recovered memories are noted by Pendergast (1995, pp. 176, 188) and Ofshe and Watters (1994, pp. 181–182, 237).

The details of two particular recovered memories are especially revealing. In the "abreaction room" (Ofshe and Watters, 1994, pp. 235–236), Anne Stone recalls being strapped down, her therapist carefully padding her wrists and ankles with towels. While she was restrained and in trance, the therapist would pursue hidden traumatic memory. In one instance, Anne relived "being raped while tied down on an altar." By this account, the exact parallel between recovered memory and therapeutic circumstance was obvious to the patient but not to the therapist.

The second example is, if possible, more chilling and shameful. A therapist who ran a dissociative disorders hospital unit eventually closed down by state health authorities writes (Peterson

[1994] cited in Pendergrast [1995, p. 179]): "I have listened to a mother describe how she tied her small child to the bars of a crib before putting something into every orifice of the body—a rag already in the mouth to prevent screaming." This patient, and her alleged memory can stand for the plight of all patients subjected to virtual torture: in need of care and protection, these patients are mercilessly restrained and invaded by their therapists, while their only means of protest is silenced. Metaphor here approaches reality.

COULD THE MEMORIES BE TRUE?

This line of thought collapses in the face of documentary corroboration that some of the memories recalled by MPD patients are valid and true. In fact, the lack of such evidence is impressive not only by its absence when it is searched for, but also by the pervasive absence of any search. Frankel (1993), in his review of research on MPD patients' recovered memories of abuse, found that efforts to verify their memories were rarely made, and when made, reported in such sparse detail that it was impossible to assess the evidence. The greatest amount of evidence to be found, and the most vigorous pursuit of it occurs in relation to memories of satanic ritual abuse. Lanning (1991), summarizing the FBI investigation which he headed, concludes that after eight years of aggressive search, there was no evidence found to support allegations of ritual abuse. He turns the question back to mental health professionals, to answer why people allege the occurrence of things which have not happened.

Various explanations have been offered for this lack of corroborating support for the memories of MPD patients, including the skillfulness of perpetrators, their understandable reluctance to admit to heinous acts, and the unlikelihood of surviving concrete evidence. Nonetheless, when a clear-cut opportunity to document reports of trauma does occur, it goes unnoticed. Putnam et al. (1986) report that "the witnessing in childhood of a violent death, usually of a parent or a sibling, was reported by 45% of the patients" (p. 290). Not only does it refer to what inevitably must become a public act (violent death), it also cannot be dismissed as the idiosyncratic finding of a single clinician. Putnam et al. collected their data by asking clinicians to fill out a detailed questionnaire using information about a specific patient in their practice. In all, 92 clinicians responded on 100 patients. No mention is made of any effort to document this dramatic finding, although it would seem relatively easy to find explicit documentation (police reports, death notices, newspaper accounts) without causing shame to the patient or intrusion on the family. All the patient would be required to do is give the researcher the name, town, and approximate date of the witnessed death.

In light of these considerations, it does not seem rash to suggest that researchers seem reluctant even to attempt to gather validating external confirmation of trauma. How can this hesitancy be understood? In part, it may reflect a powerful aspect of the demand characteristics attendant to regarding MPD as derived from early abuse. These patients are seen as having been violently exploited and betrayed by caretakers and family. Within this framework, it becomes a further violation of trust to doubt or question the veracity of self-reports of abuse (Coons and Milstein, 1986; Davies and Frawley, 1991). While clinicians may rightly be reluctant to act as detectives, researchers need not share this hesitation. That they do speaks to the powerful demand characteristic created by the perception of the MPD patient as a victim of early betrayal of trust.

CONCLUSION

The alternative hypothesis presented in chapter 6 accurately predicts the more depraved nature of memories recovered by MPD patients, and thus substantiates the contention that recovered memories represent the patient's indirect commentary on his or her immediate therapeutic experience.

It is important to note that just as it is dissociated relationship trauma and experiences which are generally regarded as at the root of MPD, it is relationship dynamics which are seen as at the root of this alternative view. The apparent historical dynamics of coercion, invasion, and betrayal of trust between child and abuser may not be being replicated in the transference dynamics. Rather, they may be being created by the implicit and sometimes explicit relationship of domination and surrender (Schwartz, 1994) established between aggressive, convinced therapists and especially impressionable patients. While there are many differences, the similarities between youthful victims of actual abuse and these adult victims of metaphoric abuse are remarkable.

Sometimes metaphorically, sometimes literally, the contents of recovered memory and the events of treatment bear a striking resemblance. That such powerful ideas, experiences, and imagery can be inculcated without the conscious awareness, in most instances, of either participant, speaks to the extraordinary facility of the mind to influence and be influenced beyond direct perception. This is the topic of the next chapter.

8 SUGGESTION AND INFLUENCE IN THE THERAPEUTIC PROCESS

In the current, highly charged debate about the ultimate validity of therapeutically recovered memories of child sexual abuse, much of the contentiousness has focused on the issue of suggestion (Herman and Harvey, 1993; Loftus, 1993a; Lindsay and Read, 1994; Berliner and Williams, 1994). On one hand, it is argued that the use of a wide variety of technical procedures may have a significant influence in producing material uncritically regarded as recovered autobiographical memory of abuse (Loftus, 1993a,b; Loftus and Ketcham, 1994; Lindsay and Read, 1994). On the other hand, it is argued that few therapists are so biased, and few patients so gullible that something as painful as a recovered memory of abuse could be wholly fabricated (Herman and Harvey, 1993; Berliner and Williams, 1994). The position that such memories fit into an overall clinical picture in a way that makes "intuitive sense" (Briere, 1990) is countered by the position that there is no consistent overall clinical picture which describes victims of consciously inaccessible abuse (Lindsay and Read, 1994).

Both sides share an interest in clarifying and reducing the role of suggestion in therapeutic work with patients who may have been sexually traumatized as children but without direct access

149

to those experiences. To this end, there appears to be a growing consensus that certain technical procedures (such as hypnosis or guided imagery) may be especially likely to have suggestive effects and should be used cautiously if at all (Lindsay and Read, 1994; Berliner and Williams, 1994). Similarly there appears to be a growing appreciation that some people are more vulnerable or responsive to suggestive techniques and that it may be of clinical value to identify these individuals.

Hope that these measures will markedly reduce or eliminate the problem, however, seems premature. Observations that some suggestive factors (Lindsay and Read, 1994), like the authoritative status of the therapist, are inherent in the therapeutic situation, raise the possibility that the problem of suggestion in therapy cannot be easily contained or delimited. Several facets of the therapeutic relationship, and of the process of influence, support the notion that the problem may be deeper, wider, and more subtle than is generally appreciated (Herman and Harvey, 1993). Specifically, it will be argued that a considerable measure of suggestion plays an irreducible role in psychotherapy, that "good" therapy may, in its own way, be just as suggestive as blatantly biased therapy, and that suggestion operates most powerfully as an unconscious reciprocal process.

At the outset, it will be useful to alter the terms of this discussion from the more loaded, and deceptive term *suggestion* to the less pejorative term *influence.* Both concepts convey essentially the same idea, that one makes use of the therapeutic relationship to promote ideas, perceptions, affects, perspectives, or beliefs different from those initially presented by the patient. Suggestion, however, carries with it the connotation of a subject led to believe, often through hypnosis or a comparably heavy-handed medium, something which they did not believe before and should not believe after. It is too easy to think suggestion refers to an active, purposeful therapist who inculcates an idea in the mind of a passive, receptive patient. Much of the debate about recovered memory seems directed toward this domain, which can be labeled as suggestion in a narrow sense, when in fact such suggestion occupies an extreme position on a continuum of interpersonal influence. Interpersonal influence ranges from processes which may be deliberate and undirectional to those which may be wholly unconscious and bidirectional. A good case may be made that powerful interpersonal influence, or suggestion in a broad sense, is distributed unevenly and unpredictably across this continuum. If this idea is valid, even eliminating blatantly suggestive techniques and identifying the most suggestible people, will reduce only a limited amount of influence in therapy. Therapeutic influence does not end with narrowly construed "suggestion"; and suggestion more broadly construed is inseparable from and perhaps identical to therapeutic influence.

INFLUENCE IS UNAVOIDABLE

Framed this way, it seems clear that the heart of any therapeutic encounter is to make benevolent use of one's interpersonal influence. The argument can be made that therapeutic success occurs only with some measure of influence and persuasion. Whether the content of this influence is thought of as a particular theory of technique, of change, of motivation, or of causation matters less than the process by which these ideas affect the patient. It is not a body of abstract ideas or principles which influences a patient, but rather the personal way those ideas are embodied in the therapist's thought, speech, and action. The interpersonal channel between the therapist and the patient provides the pathway for therapeutic action (Loewald, 1960). Influence is a force that clinicians attempt to enhance rather than restrict. The basic premise that change is possible consequent to participating in a therapeutic exchange amounts to an implicit personal statement that alternate, more constructive ways of viewing personal experience are attainable. Hope is offered personally, and if it were not, people would have no reason to participate in psychotherapy. It is a basic misconception of the therapeutic process to think that it can occur in the absence of interpersonal influence (Frank, 1973).

In short, personal influence in the therapeutic relationship cannot be eliminated without eviscerating the process. While such potentially suggestive practices as guided imagery, dream work, and hypnosis (Lindsay and Read, 1994) may be placed out of bounds, the avoidance of these techniques in no way eliminates or even markedly reduces the persuasive dimension of the therapeutic relationship. Simply put, no subset of agreed upon, influence-free therapeutic behaviors can be demarcated, because the defining characteristic of the therapeutic encounter is its absolute reliance upon interpersonal influence. A corollary to this observation is that any factor which augments interpersonal regard also enhances the potential for influence. Thus, typical contextual factors such as patients' perception of the therapist as an authority, their desire for emotional and cognitive affiliation, and their distress and wish for relief cannot help but add to the potential for influence.

INFLUENCE MAY BE POTENTIATED BOTH BY "BAD" AND "GOOD" THERAPY

It has been argued (Herman and Harvey, 1993; Briere, 1994) that suggestion is produced by "bad" therapy and avoided by "good" therapy. "Bad" therapy is to be recognized by its visible bias and preconceived notions urged upon patients, such as a therapist who tells a patient in their first meeting that "people with concerns like yours have often been victims of sexual abuse as children, but have repressed those memories" (Loftus, 1993b). The heavy-handed bluntness of this approach defines "bad" therapy: leading questions pursued relentlessly until the therapist "persuades" a gullible, uncertain patient to produce material which confirms the "truth" of the therapist's preconceptions. Empathy is lost to inculcation.

Few would question that this is "bad" therapy, nor that it is, in fact, suggestive in the narrow sense. Some (Herman and Harvey, 1993; Briere, 1994; Olio, 1994) argue, however, that this observation is basically irrelevant to the current dispute about recovered memory because it is a straw man: few therapists actually behave in this fashion. Some current data challenge this assertion. Books in the popular press (Bass and Davis, 1988; Courtois, 1988; Fredrickson, 1992) promote not only memory recovery techniques known to be highly suggestive (Lindsay and Read,

1994) but also an explicit belief in "robust" repression and the nearly absolute validity of recovered memory. Quite aside from the methods offered by a few extremely visible therapists, an extensive survey of highly qualified American and British practitioners (Poole et al., 1995) counters the straw man claim. A sizable minority of these clinicians believe they can identify patients who deny abuse histories but who were actually sexually abused as children, and often successfully employ a variety of suggestive techniques to recover memory. While this minority acknowledges the possibility of illusory memories, there is widespread belief that those memories recovered by one's own methods and patients are valid.

The problem of untoward influence is not confined within "bad" therapy, however many therapists practice within those borders. Consider the question: What makes "good" therapy? There is probably general agreement that "good" therapy may be characterized as empathic, reflective, and inquiring: the patient leads and the therapist, for the most part, follows. The therapist offers "tell me more" or "how do you feel?" rather than "now we know" or "you feel this." To the extent that conclusions are drawn, whether about the implications of a dream, or a piece of current or past experience, they are arrived at cautiously and collaboratively. This kind of "good" therapy, it might be said, does not reflect narrowly considered suggestive techniques and thereby minimizes suggestive possibilities.

The exact opposite may also be argued. "Good" therapy forges a strong emotional link between a patient and a therapist, precisely because it is "good" therapy; that is, empathic and responsive. This emotional link is the pathway for interpersonal influence, and the stronger the bond, the greater the possibility for interpersonal influence. The corollary from above applies; anything which enhances the conditions for interpersonal regard enhances the potential for influence: "good" therapy creates an empathic bond, enhances interpersonal regard, and therefore augments the potential for influence of whatever sort.

If this influence is thought of as providing opportunities for change and growth, it represents the gain of therapy. If, however, this influence is thought of as providing a pathway for untoward persuasion, it represents the risk of therapy. The risk and the gain are inseparable. Therapy, because it is a process propelled by interpersonal regard, cannot eliminate influence; "good" therapy, precisely because it is good, generates an empathic bond and thereby enhances the possibility of influence.

INFLUENCE IS NOT A CONSCIOUS, ONE-WAY PROCESS

These relatively self-evident arguments present general propositions about the therapeutic relationship and process which enhance the potential for influence. The following discussion presents a broader aspect of human communication which may be greatly magnified in the therapeutic relationship: unconscious communication and perception. Bowers (1984) provides a useful distinction between perceived and noticed information: "perceived" information is registered and influential, while that subset of perceived information which is consciously processed is "noticed." The present discussion focuses on perceived but not noticed information.

In actuality one does not decide consciously nor can one predict exactly what influence will be perceived by the patient. The therapist's unspoken, and perhaps even consciously inaccessible theories about, for example, the roots and cause of psychological distress, will be voiced one way or another. Because of the open channel created by good therapy, these unspoken ideas will not only be perceived but actively listened for and retained. Because the act of sending and receiving an idea may well be invisible to both sender and receiver, ideas which appear to have been generated by clinical data may in fact have invisibly seeded the clinical data.

At the heart of the matter lies the notion that neither suggestion in the narrow sense nor in the broad sense (influence) necessarily involves a visible, deliberate one-way process between a "suggestor" and a "suggestee." In the current debate, obviously, the therapist is thought to fill the former role, while the patient the latter role. Herman's and Harvey's comments (1993) seem to incorporate this view. While it is possible that some suggestive influence fits this model, a great deal of effective therapeutic influence conforms to an antithetical model; that is, it follows a two-way process of perceived but not noticed (consciously) communication (Orne, 1962; Bowers, 1984; Ofshe, 1992). In other words, influence, that is, suggestion in both a narrow and a broad sense, operates most powerfully as a mutually unconscious back and forth process in which both therapist and patient seamlessly lead and follow.

The operative force behind such influence appears to be one of tacit expectations, both sent and received. The potency of tacit expectations was vividly demonstrated in an experiment described by Orne (1962). Subjects were asked to perform routine additions, about two hundred to a page, with a stack of two thousand pages presented to each subject. After five hours, the experimenter gave up before the subjects did and interrupted the process. In a second version, subjects were asked to perform the same task, but to tear up each page as they completed it. Even under these conditions, subjects worked steadily for several hours. What is remarkable is that Orne was trying to find "psychologically noxious, meaningless, or boring" (p. 777) tasks subjects would refuse to do or do only briefly. It became apparent to Orne that a complex and powerful set of "demand characteristics" linked the subject and the experimenter, in this instance forged in part by expectations associated with participating in a scientific study. These expectations completely overrode the subjects' fatigue and tedium.

Demand characteristics refer to the unspoken expectations conveyed to subjects by experimenters. Orne notes that "the demand characteristics most potent in determining subjects' behavior are those which convey the purpose of the experiment *effectively but not obviously*" (p. 780; emphasis added). For this reason, scientific experiments which involve human subjects and researchers in testing treatments or procedures carry the universal expectation that whenever possible the design be "double-blind." Inasmuch as both parties bring explicit and implicit motivations to a research activity, demand characteristics must travel along a two-way street, with experimenters influenced by subjects' complexly motivated responses just as subjects are influenced by experimenters' complexly motivated instructions. Science has long recognized that experimental outcomes can be easily influenced by subtle shades of behavior from researchers in whom various beliefs have been planted (Frank, 1973). Consequently, the strongest test of a hypothesis demands that people on both sides of the experiment be kept unaware of who is receiving which treatment.

Just how subtle these influences can be are illustrated in two studies by Rosenthal (1969, cited by Frank, 1973, pp. 118–120). In the first study, experimenters asked subjects to rate the degree of success or failure reflected in a series of photographs of people's faces. The experimenters, however, were also subjects in that, unbeknownst to them, the previous findings, which they were told this study was designed to try to replicate, were bogus. Although no such relationship existed, some of the experimenters were told the previous findings indicated photographs of success while the others were told the opposite. Both groups of experimenters were given precisely the same instructions and spoke the same words to their subjects. Impressively, most subjects' judgments about the photographs conformed to the bias planted in the experimenter. Those biased toward success induced more judgments of success from their subjects, while those biased toward failure induced more judgments of failure from their subjects. Careful examination of the audio recordings of the process indicated that "deliberate, slight shadings of emphasis" (Frank, 1973, p. 199) were sufficient to bias subjects in one direction or the other. Bowers' (1984) distinction between perceived and noticed information applies here, for the subjects perceived these shadings, but presumably did not consciously notice them.

The second study draws the process of influence into a reciprocal loop. Once again, the designated experimenter was also a subject. The experimenter administered test trials to a sequence of subjects. Unbeknownst to him or her, the initial subjects were programmed to respond in such a way either to support or disconfirm the experiment's hypothesis. Later in the series, naive subjects replaced the programmed subjects. The experimenter's results with these subjects followed the direction of the initial subjects. In other words, the initial subjects influenced the experimenter's manner in such a fashion that the experimenter subsequently led later subjects to perform in a way consistent with those initial subjects. When naive subjects were used throughout, similar trends were visible and later subjects were influenced more than earlier ones. Frank (1973) concludes that "the subjects progressively shaped the experimenter's behavior, leading him to emit increasingly effective cues" (p. 120).

These "interpersonal expectancy effects" (Rosenthal, 1994, p. 177) are subtle, powerful, and widespread. Instigated "by means of unintended nonverbal behavior" (p. 179), expectancy effects are potentiated by several interlocking factors, the primary one being the perceived authority or prestige of the source of the influence. Whether stemming from a need for approval or from high levels of anxiety, "evaluation apprehension" (Frank, 1973, p. 121) also strengthens the receipt of tacit influence. It should not automatically be assumed, however, that prestige is only assigned by the subject to the experimenter, or that "evaluation apprehension" applies only to the subject and not the experimenter. Experimenters, in their own fashion, may prize subjects and, similarly, be anxious about the outcome of personally invested research hypotheses.

Far from being confined to the research laboratory, Rosenthal has identified similar processes in management situations, courtrooms, nursing homes, and in a variety of classroom settings. Real life historical and contemporary examples illustrating these dynamics are not difficult to locate. Precisely such effects were demonstrated by Charcot's hysterical patients (noted in chapter 2). Charcot, his resident doctors, the audiences, and the patients all participated in shaping not only the patients' overt posturing, but also in shaping Charcot and his doctors' behaviors, leading them to "emit increasingly effective cues" about the nature of the behavior the patients were expected to portray. Produced under police interrogation, Paul Ingram's fantastic revelations of satanic ritual abuse (chapter 2) provide a present-day analogue. In both instances, a belief or expectancy emerged in words or deeds through the reciprocal action of mutually unconscious influence.

These enacted beliefs and expectancies may or may not be conscious. If brought to focused awareness by an observer, they may be abhorrent to conscious attitudes and values or even actively disavowed. The current phenomenon of facilitated communication is relevant here. First described in the United States by

Biklen (1990), autistic persons are helped to type messages on a keyboard by the physical support and guidance of a facilitator. Some of the facilitated communications were astounding revelations of sexual abuse, now represented in over one hundred cases in the United States although extremely rare elsewhere (Rimland, Autism Research Institute, personal communication, 1994). The process has been wholly discredited by every scientific research test of its validity (Eberlin, McConnachie, Ibel, and Volpe, 1993; Bligh and Kupperman, 1993; Klewe, 1993; Moore, Donovan, Hudson, Dykstra, and Lawrence, 1993; Shane, 1993). This research conclusively demonstrates that the facilitator alone is responsible for the content of the typed messages.

The few facilitators who have responded to these findings are aghast at being responsible for producing ideas which are entirely unconscious and repugnant to them. Notably, none of the facilitators has alleged that they had been sexually abused as children and were, in fact, recovering previously inaccessible memories of their own (Rimland, personal communication, 1994). Clearly expectancy effects operate unconsciously and may autonomously generate false ideas which are alien to the person's conscious sensibilities. Even in the face of the massive scientific evidence to the contrary, some clinicians hold on to their belief in the potential validity of facilitated communication and dispute the necessary and total influence of the facilitator (Jones, 1994).

INFLUENCE IN THE CLINICAL REALM

The relationship between patient and therapist does not stand apart from these research and real life settings for unconscious influence. The parallel between experimenters and subjects, and therapists and patients seems transparent, and in fact may be extended. Clinicians and patients do not enjoy the "luxury" of working together under even moderately purified or structured conditions. Motivated subjectivity cannot be avoided (Goldberg, 1994). In addition, by virtue of the immediate, personal nature of the therapeutic process it seems highly likely that therapists and patients routinely match or exceed the level of personal involvement and motivation shared by scientists and their subjects. To help and to understand, and to be perceived as helpful and as understanding, may be as compelling a motive for clinicians as being helped and feeling understood is for patients (Mason, 1994). Each may come to regard the other, in some respects, as an authoritative commentator, and desire from the other the affirmation of shared beliefs and reciprocal expectations. If it is true, as Orne argues, that "demand characteristics cannot be eliminated from experiments" (1962, p. 779), they must be an even more potent force and even harder to chart in the much more open and emotionally charged field of the therapeutic dyad. Clinicians and patients simply cannot restrict the densely formed motives and corresponding behaviors by which they consciously and unconsciously influence one another.

Nor do therapists know clearly when and in what way they are subtly influencing or being influenced, as the following clinical examples indicate. Williams (1987) reports on the therapy with a man in which repetitive dreams of dirty buildings and bathrooms, and of a man lying against the patient's back and doing something to his anus, were understood to reflect repressed experience of a childhood seduction. Williams is explicit in her direction to the patient that these dreams had preserved memories of his anal seduction at age 2 by an older male servant. Eventually the patient dreams: "a man who is lying down on a bed is lifting up a little boy whom he suspends horizontally above himself. As the boy looks down, he sees a large erect penis" (p. 154). Williams regards this as a "partial lifting of repression" (p. 154), and as the direct reproduction in the dream of an earlier traumatic experience. By conveying previously inaccessible memory directly in dream content, this dream appears to provide explicit validation of Williams' molestation hypothesis.

Where is the influence in this? Although Williams is quite deliberate in stating her hypothesis, the confirmatory datum—the dream—does not seem forced, nor does it seem likely that something as remote from waking consciousness as a dream could be influenced. Nonetheless, that alternative can be persuasively argued. Although a number of clinical reports reflect the presumption that early memories of trauma may appear directly in dream reports (see also Stewart [1969]; Alpert [1994]), as seen in chapter 2, no independently verified instances of such allegedly veridical dreams can be found in the literature. It is possible that this patient has been sexually traumatized as a 2-year-old child, but it is not possible that these early experiences can be reproduced literally in later dream content. Consequently one salient source for Williams' patient's literal dream is his unconscious collaboration with her hypothesis regarding seduction. It would be unfair not to note that Grace's dreams of explicit sexual exploitation would seem to have followed a similar pattern of derivation. One can only marvel at the facility of Grace's mind to produce dreams so closely in line with my not entirely expressed or consciously formulated thoughts. Clinicians, the author included, may not consider that the dream they hear is not only the one they have been looking for, but the one they have influenced as well. That being the case their thinking, and subsequent therapeutic actions are likely to be heavily influenced in return.

The line of influence invisibly bends and closes on itself: the unwitting "suggestor" becomes the unsuspecting "suggestee." Few therapeutic events are more likely to effect this transformation than the sudden recovery of an apparent memory of early abuse. Often what preceded this revelation of a previously lost memory was a decisive intervention by the therapist—a conjecture ("I stated that I believed it was indeed possible that she had been sexually assaulted . . . " Schuker [1979, p. 569]); a question ("Is that all he taught you to do with your hands?" Bernstein [1990, p. 82]); or a reconstruction ("I reconstructed that she was telling me of being touched, being carried against her will, and being made to touch [or to rub] something [a penis]" [Kramer, 1990, p. 161]) which carried the explicit or implicit expectation that such a buried memory existed. When reported (Sachs, 1967; Schuker, 1979; Bernstein, 1990; Kramer, 1990; Briere, 1994; Brenner, 1994), clinicians describe responding to the ensuing material as if it represented an indisputable piece of validating evidence which substantiated, and therefore reinforced, their immediately preceding comment and its underlying inferential process. In none of these instances did the therapist report turning a skeptical eye on this interactive sequence. If the suggestor here became the suggestee, they were truly unsuspecting.

These clinical examples may lead one to think that unconscious influence is confined to the reconstruction of early experience. This would be erroneous, for the kinds of subtle, mutual influences being considered here are the everyday stuff of clinical exchange. Two ordinary examples demonstrate this.

Over a period of time, a therapist attempted to identify and point out transference links in a patient's current sexual experience. Although the clinical material seemed rather clear and to require little inference, the patient protested that she felt no such link and, rather than being listened to, was being prodded to endorse the therapist's theory. In each such encounter, the therapist reviewed to himself the material which prompted his inference of a transference link and was reassured that the evidence was in the material and not just in his mind. At one point, however, the patient provided indisputable evidence to reveal the therapist's unconscious bias: while many sexual transference links were proposed, few aggressive links were ever proposed. The therapist was wholly unaware of the theory he was behaviorally promoting; namely, that extratherapeutic sexual feelings belonged to the transference while extratherapeutic aggressive feelings did not.

In supervision, another therapist was encouraged to ask a patient to be more specific, since the reported dialogue was filled with rather empty generalities. The therapist attempted to do this, and the patient responded with irritation. The therapist then became aware that this irritation had been manifested all along whenever the therapist was too interested in details. The therapist had unconsciously accommodated to this pattern by restricting his focal interest.

One might discount these clinical examples because they reflect poor technique or inadequate self-scrutiny. Earlier examples might be discounted because they reflect dramatic circumstances. This would miss the larger point, however, that comparable unconscious communications, sometimes subtle, sometimes not, are commonplace in all psychotherapy. Much of the influence in psychotherapy occurs in the realm of perceived but not noticed information. Inadvertent expectancy effects have relatively free play between patient and therapist: therapist and patient routinely shape and influence each other's behavior and ideas in ways neither of them notice.

DISCUSSION

Paraphrasing Orne (1962, p. 780), influence may be most effective when it is clear but not obvious. In the clinical situation the performance of one partner simultaneously shapes and is shaped by the other to become a synchronized pas de deux. Ultimately, neither partner occupies a superordinately objective position from which to view their interaction; neither occupies a position beyond the influence of the other; and neither need be conscious of the most potent forms of influencing or being influenced. Beyond conscious notice, a word or nod from one becomes an idea or an association in the other. A therapist's ideas can be shaped as much by a patient's response as the reverse.

No clinician can realistically declare, as Freud did so authoritatively:

> The danger of our leading a patient astray by suggestion, by persuading him to accept things which we ourselves believe but which he ought not to, has certainly been enormously exaggerated. An analyst would have had to behave very incorrectly before such a misfortune could overtake him. . . . I can assert without boasting that such an abuse of "suggestion" has never occurred in my practice [1937, p. 262].

Even if one eliminates what are recognized as highly suggestive techniques, there can be no assurances against influence because, by its very nature, the therapeutic process is one of personal influence. Even if one practices the best empathic and reflective technique, there are no assurances, because "good" therapy, by its very nature, enhances the potential for influence and suggestion. Even more confoundingly, by their very nature, those influences which are most "effective [are] not obvious."

As has been demonstrated, unconscious communication is capable of conveying, and unconscious perception is capable of perceiving (without noticing), complex, implicit, and even disowned beliefs, feelings, and ideas. The therapeutic process cannot be inoculated against such influence, or suggestion in a broad sense, nor should it be. The deliberate articulation of the patient's implicit ideas and feelings gives psychotherapy some of its restorative power, and this articulation cannot occur in the absence of an openness to precisely the kinds of unconscious communication which are most influential.

When all is said and done, it may be a very difficult task to separate out the beneficial influences from those which are not because the clinical process in both instances may look very much alike. But to avoid throwing the baby out with the bathwater, one needs to be able to distinguish between them. Is there any differentiation to be made, then, between the influence which ultimately benefits the patient from that which operates to his or her detriment?

In all of the material reviewed to this point, one factor stands out as vulnerable to misuse. Although many different systems of meaning are used by clinicians, trouble threatens when clinicians make an implicit or explicit presumption about the root of psychological difficulties, and this cause is taken to be a decisive, objective early event. When, in the absence of explicit memory, this decisive event is presumed to have been an actual betrayal of trust and body by caretakers, such a presumption becomes a quest, and the inherent influence in the therapeutic relationship becomes a direct danger to the patient: Freud's seduction hypothesis error repeated and multiplied a century later. Whether or not the clinician is consciously aware of this decisive internal map, in the end, it is dangerous to follow a quest for "the source of the Nile," having already decided that the source lies in unremembered childhood sexual seduction or physical abuse. When the patient possesses the kinds of intuitive sensitivities characteristic of the fantasy prone patient, the potential arises for the patient to respond accordingly and for belief, to the patient's detriment, to take on the appearance of reality.

9 CONCLUSIONS: REWEIGHING THE EVIDENCE

The preceding chapters have examined the phenomena of therapeutically recovered memories of early trauma. Because the final perspective falls so far, in many ways, from the initial one, the domain for which these concluding remarks apply bears repeating. The memories discussed here have been only those totally inaccessible to explicit memory prior to therapy. Preexisting explicit memory for trauma, whether partial or complete, whether always remembered or only sometimes, is not in question. No clinician and no empirical scientist challenges the validity of these memories.

What initially appeared to be authentic memory derived from empathic and supportive reading of clinical material came to be viewed as the imaginative cross-product of a zealously committed therapist and an anxious, cognitively malleable patient. This complex product entwines, at once, an identification with the therapist's preference for sexual abuse as a causal explanation *and* an enacted response to the technical procedures generated by that causal investment. Suggestion provides the outline while technical pursuit engenders the quality of the patient's experience. What could not be spoken directly about the present was enacted piecemeal and removed to the past. Ultimately, the de-coded message is that the therapeutic relationship has become an invasive, controlling betrayal of therapeutic trust. Having tra-versed this distance along a path of identification, unconscious transformation, and influence, and along a path of different and special memory systems, let us reassess the evidence.

The authenticity of therapeutically recovered memory rests on three propositions. First, experiences of traumatic intensity can fail to register in explicit, autobiographical memory and therefore be inaccessible to consciousness. Second, implicit, as opposed to explicit memory of these experiences is encoded along predictable lines. Finally, these predictable encodings allow the clinician to decipher manifestations of implicit memory and recover explicit memory with a reasonable degree of accuracy.

Support for these propositions is uneven and thin. Aside from trauma which occurs prior to the offset of infantile amnesia, most people retain explicit memory of traumatic experiences with significant accuracy. Nonetheless, one study demonstrates rather convincingly that a minority of childhood trauma survivors fails to recount those events; consequently failure to hold trauma in explicit memory cannot be summarily ruled out. No documented evidence, however, has been found to substantiate the proposi-tion that, in the absence of explicit memory, implicit memory for trauma is literally, accurately, and predictably encoded. Quite the contrary, in dreams, flashbacks, and action sequences, the mind readily transforms these experiences in idiosyncratic, metaphoric terms. These transformed renditions are a kaleidoscopic patch-work in which the literal cannot be separated from the figurative, and the existence of trauma itself cannot be presumed with any certainty from their occurrence.

Ultimately, the presentation of an instance of accurately re-covered, independently verified, and previously inaccessible ex-plicit memory of trauma would challenge these reservations and limitations. Clinical interpretation, after all, can be a finely wrought skill and the tracks left by unremembered trauma, al-though unpredictable, may not be impossible to retrace. Case reports appearing in professional journals fall short of fulfilling these conditions. Some take recovered memory as corroborating evidence in itself; some take the symptoms and circumstantial evidence from which memory is derived as confirming evidence; and some allude to documentation which is not expressly stated or has not been independently reviewed. A case demonstrating the recovery of traumatic memory with reasonably impartial verification could not be located.

An atmosphere surrounds this literature which seems to obscure basic scientific procedures. This is not a casually made observation. Confirmation bias, vested in belief, appears to drive how evidence is viewed. Admittedly this is a sensitive area in which secrecy may abound, but nonetheless both clinicians and researchers seem to shy away from impartial checks upon the data. Active efforts to seek independent evidence not only fail to occur but may be considered as failures to support the patient. Some clinicians bristle at calls for verifying evidence as if such calls reflected a refusal to believe in sexual abuse rather than an essential scientific safeguard. Researchers too sometimes eschew hard, impartial tests of evidence. Publicly recorded traumas (like violent family deaths) are not checked, and no blind tests are reported of the correspondence believed to exist between implicit memory (like dreams, flashbacks, and action sequences) and historically objective accounts or separately elicited explicit memory.

Generally agreed upon scientific standards, it would seem, have fallen victim to less than optimal skepticism. This should not be construed as suggesting that only scientifically tested evidence counts in clinical matters.The therapeutic process is not dictated by science, and its essence may foil the most determined efforts to measure and test it. Still, this does not exempt the process, especially when it claims to make visible previously invisible unconscionable acts of sexual exploitation, from minimal expectations for independent verification. Some clinicians respond to this by declaiming they are not detectives and should not be asked to behave like detectives. If this posture is used, like a shield, to ward off serious consideration of error, it does no service to the patient, to the process, or to the unresolved question of validity.

Does the evidence in favor of the alternative reading stand on any firmer ground? The "suggestion hypothesis," as this reading might be labeled, rests on four propositions. First, memory is not fixed but plastic and subject to considerable modification. Second, unconscious perception, cognition, and communication make possible influence which is in turn unconscious. Third, pairing a therapist with powerful, perhaps disavowed beliefs and a highly responsive, suggestible patient, potentiates unconscious influence and engenders a sense of control and invasion. Finally, communication manifestly taken to be about the past may actually refer only to the present.

The evidence for the first two of these propositions is broad and tested. Far from being an isolated, veridically transcribing instrument, autobiographical memory is considered to be a reconstructive process which can be shaped by personal motives as well as external factors. While this does not mean that autobiographical memory in particular is infinitely malleable, it does mean that it is always reconstituted in the present and subject to the motives of the moment. The empirically identified limits of influence in shaping and creating autobiographical memory have been dictated by ethical considerations and do not reflect inherent boundaries. All of the above are generally agreed upon characteristics of autobiographical memory.

Unconscious perception, cognition, and communication are likewise carefully researched and validated phenomena. Recently, the concept of the "cognitive unconscious" has helped explain far-reaching capacities of the mind to perceive, abstract, evaluate, remember, and deploy enormous quantities of information without representation in consciousness. Implicit memory, automatized motor skills, language development, and the organization of speech all reflect unconscious cognitive procedures. The mind, it appears, is like the proverbial iceberg, with the vast preponderance of its processes occurring below the surface. Inasmuch as the mind, like memory, is an open system, unconscious communication and influence must be inherent processes.

The evidence in support of the latter two propositions is more inferential. Certainly one can identify, from published sources, therapists with relatively single-minded zeal who are primed to read vivid, sensorimotor experience as trauma-derived implicit memory. Similarly, one can also identify people with special cognitive flexibilities who are already absorbed in lively fantasy and sensitively attuned to others' expectations. Just as a firm hand molds a receptive substance, anticipations of and beliefs about unremembered trauma, along with insistent clinical interventions, shape these patients' responses into conforming patterns of apparent memory. Although offering a plausible and possible mechanism of action, this hypothesis is without direct proof. As a hypothesis, however, it gains substantial weight by accurately predicting the heinous memories recovered in MPD by especially zealous therapists from exceptionally pliant patients.

In a reversal of analytic custom, these recovered memories of past trauma are recast as indirect commentaries on the present. Again, this is a plausible hypothesis without direct proof. Indirect support is garnered from two sources: first, no evidence contradicts this hypothesis; that is, no documented corroboration for recovered memories establishes them as valid. If not valid, what could be their source? The second support is the goodness of fit between the content of the alleged memories (of invasion, control, and betrayal) and the therapeutic procedures used to evoke them (single-minded pursuit). We tend to regard axiomatically all therapeutic enactments as reenactments, but this is an inadequately tested assumption. General concordances between past and present experiences do not warrant assuming specific concordances apply, especially when no independent data regarding the past are available to check the equation. If we can represent ourselves as new objects for change, we cannot rule out being sources of new patterns of response, underived from the past. Ill, as well as good, may spring from this fresh soil.

It is important to add here that even if this hypothesis is more or less correct, it does not exclude the possibility that some recovered memories are valid. As apt as the critique of therapeutic recovery might be, this is not an all or none proposition. We can hope that future evidence will identify reliable pathways of recovery, and ways can be found to substantiate real memories and distinguish them from false memories. As long as a dark shadow of uncertainty covers this issue, the integrity of real victims of sexual and physical abuse may be unfairly impeached, and, one must add, the integrity of falsely accused perpetrators as well.

CAPTIVES TO TACIT BELIEFS

Whether or not this alternate reading stands the test of time and the challenge of new data, it raises powerful questions about the nature of influence in the therapeutic process. An uneven tension between the immediacy of the therapeutic moment, and the skepticism of more distant, abstract questions lies at the heart of most therapeutic endeavors. While skepticism may, at any given time, be only weakly represented, its necessity cannot be denied, and for good reason. Because nothing in human experience is pure and objective, psychotherapeutic work is marked by an unavoidable ambiguity. Everywhere subject to personal interpretation, human experience on both sides of the therapeutic couch may be just what it appears to be, but just as easily not at all what it appears to be.

What determines the investment of credibility in apparent memory? What is credible tends to coincide with implicit beliefs about what motivates people and how the world works. In this light, a patient's description of events does not stand apart from the therapist's beliefs, but rather tends to be heard by the therapist in a fashion which reinforces those beliefs. In its inverted form, the adage "seeing is believing" may carry as much or more truth. Especially in matters subject to interpretation and judgment, "believing is seeing" (Snyder, 1984). The beliefs involved, as we have seen, need not be conscious to be influential, and further may remain influential even if disavowed or abhorrent to consciousness. An active skepticism about cherished beliefs stands against the credulity generated by them. When, however, skepticism itself is discredited or seen as injurious, we are indeed at risk not only for believing things of dubious validity, but for creating an atmosphere in which belief is the only alternative.

It would be grossly misleading, however, to think that these dynamics apply only to the distant extremes of the especially zealous, credulous therapist and especially malleable patient. If therapists were impervious to emotional influence and unconscious communication, they would not possess the basic tools to perform psychotherapy; if they were not, in fact, adept at sending and receiving emotional and unconscious information, they would hardly be able to exert therapeutic influence. Consequently, in his and her own way, every therapist may incline toward zealousness, and every patient toward malleability. To think otherwise bespeaks arrogance and courts folly. As was all too evident with Grace's therapist, there was no shortage of cherished and unappreciated beliefs on the therapist's side of the analytic couch.

Regarding oneself as well trained, experienced, and well informed, in fact, may predispose rather than protect one from such arrogance.

We may then be held captive by a steadfast reluctance to acknowledge the power of our cherished beliefs. The result is a potent mixture of rigidity and gullibility: we tend to see that which confirms what we implicitly believe, and that we tend to believe uncritically. More worrisome, we may behave in ways which draw forth exactly what we are primed to believe. It is not false humility to accept that we are not fundamentally different from our patients in this regard.

Active skepticism and a willingness to acknowledge that we can never adequately know our own minds offer some potential protection against unrealized influence, but perhaps more significantly represent an honesty about what we can and cannot know. All therapeutic material and every therapeutic exchange exerts unknown influence and is derived from unknown influence. There is nothing inherently pathological or dangerous in this; it is simply the way minds work. But, to assert that patients who may suffer from unremembered trauma are betrayed by even subtly expressed doubt or caution about the reality of such abuse assaults the integrity of the therapeutic process. Uncritical belief no more warrants and invites the patient's trust than honest doubt warrants and invites the patient's mistrust. To view matters in these polarized terms discourages therapeutic skepticism by unfairly shaming the motives behind caution. Abandoning intellectual integrity may do more disservice to the patient than any amount of caution about what, in the case of recovered memory of trauma, may well be a destructive fiction.

In this regard, clinicians hobble their own skeptical intelligence. The ideas described here about memory, suggestibility, and influence follow pathways well known to empirical scientists, but surprisingly unfamiliar to clinicians. Perhaps it is more accurate to say *dismissed by* than *unfamiliar*, for we hamper ourselves by succumbing to an appealing prejudice that psychotherapy occurs in the real world while empirical research resides in an artificially designed, and therefore unreal world. But while trivial empirical research may exist in abundance, exceedingly relevant empirical and theoretical work is not in short supply. Although working with memory, few clinicians finding and writing about recovered memory are acquainted with the established psychological literature on memory; although working with and through influence, few are acquainted with the established literature on covert influence; although dealing with the concept of dissociation which has many cognitive correlates, few are familiar with the literature on hypnotic susceptibility and fantasy proneness.

A hypothesis without an alternative functions like a belief that necessarily finds confirmation. When clinicians who recover memories of abuse are familiar with some of this literature, contradictory ideas and evidence tend to be peremptorily waved off. It is hard to know which prompts greater harm, ignorance or dismissal, but one potential casualty is the privilege of regarding psychotherapy as a scientifically informed discipline.

Unchallenged belief in one's evidence, the arrogance of presuming to know one's range of influence, and a degree of ignorance born of dismissing scientific literature all contribute, along with broader social factors, to the swelling number of recovered memory cases. No small amount of chagrin attaches to the obvious fact that the writer, as Grace's therapist, embodied all of these factors. No small amount of consternation attaches to the fact that the writer, now, although more informed and actively skeptical, will never know his own mind sufficiently to eliminate the possibility of undue influence.

A SAVING GRACE

While one cannot rule out the possibility that some recovered memories are valid, as yet, the impartial evidence to support this validity, and the process of recovery is virtually nonexistent. Harsh critics have used this to cast much of therapy as, at best, a flimsy house of cards (Dawes, 1994) and, at worst, a pernicious, knowing fraud (Crews, 1995). This is far from the conclusion drawn here. A cry about the absence of scientific support for clinical judgment, and a strident voice raised against blatant suggestion in psychotherapy do bear a resemblance to the criticisms raised here. This resemblance, however, is only skin deep, for these critics fail to appreciate, and some clinicians fail to recognize, the existence of safeguards against sloppy science and rampant suggestion. After all, most clinicians regard the "truth" derived from analytic therapy as a narrative, as opposed to a historical "truth" (Spence, 1982). After all, most analytic therapists do not recover memories of dubious authenticity.

The mantel of scientific inquiry fails to cover much of the body of psychotherapy. Looked at one way, we can deplore the reluctance of clinicians to stretch it as far as it will go. Looked at another way, we must grant that science cannot yet adequately measure explicitly what the mind absorbs and broadcasts implicitly. The heart of what is beneficial in psychotherapy may lie in this uncovered area. The implication of this, though, is not, as some critics would have it, that psychotherapy is necessarily a process run amuck.

Therapy rests upon a foundation of influence from which is built its benefits as well as its liabilities. The expressive intimacy of the psychotherapeutic relationship forms an ideal medium for the development of invisible, mutual influence. We regard identifying aspects of influence as a generally ameliorative feature of analytic therapy. Tracing influence, however, is difficult not only because it is subtle, but also because it has potent emotional consequences for both patient and therapist. As observers we are only somewhat and sometimes more impartial than our patients. In fact, there are occasions when our patients provide us with a more impartial view of our behavior and influence than we are capable of recognizing for ourselves. Such may be the case with recovered memory or sexual trauma: we hear one thing while the patient is trying to tell us another; we hear another time, another place, and another person while the patient is telling us this time, this place, this person.

To benefit from this information, we must shed some of the comfort drawn from seeing the inevitable stamp of past events on the therapeutic present. While there is considerable wisdom in this equation, as unquestioned truth it conceals from us the degree to which we shape and author the process which appears to be unfolding before us. If we but listen, we would learn that patients can be our most informative supervisors. In a reflexive turnabout, their material can reveal to us beliefs and manners we are ignorant of or conceal from ourselves. It takes courage to believe abusive things can happen to people, and to hear the abject stories which accompany these terrible events. It takes as much courage to believe that we can be wholly wrong in our inferences and to hear the desperate stories which reveal our complicity in this terrible truth. As difficult as it may be, our best safeguard against the tide of our own unconscious influence is the uneasy certainty that we may never conclusively know where it lies. The patient can tell us, however, but *only* if we are willing to listen for it.

FINAL WORDS

This book, as much as anything, is an argument in support of informed skepticism. Skepticism, even in so emotionally laden an issue as the recovery of memories of sexual abuse, is not to be confused with disbelief. We perceive our behaviors, beliefs, and effects on others with inevitable bias. The nature of that partiality can be glimpsed only by a skeptical mind turned toward even its most cherished ideas. And only then may we begin to see ourselves as clearly as we hope to view our patients. In the end, our patients may value us more for this skepticism than for any explanatory ideas we have offered.

REFERENCES

Allen, J. (1995), The spectrum of accuracy in memories of childhood trauma. *Harvard Rev. Psychiatry*, 3:84–95.

Alpert, J. (1994), Analytic reconstruction in the treatment of an incest survivor. *Psychoanal. Rev.*, 81:217–235.

——— (1995), Dreams, trauma, and clinical observation: Comments on C. Brooks Brenneis's article. *Psychoanal. Psychol.*, 12:325–328.

American Psychiatric Association (1987), *Diagnostic and Statistical Manual of Mental Disorders*, 3rd ed. rev. (DSM-III-R). Washington, DC: American Psychiatric Press.

——— (1994), *Diagnostic and Statistical Manual of Mental Disorders*, 4th ed. Washington, DC: American Psychiatric Press.

Bass, E., & Davis, L. (1988), *The Courage to Heal: A Guide for Women Survivors of Child Sexual Abuse*. New York: Harper & Row.

Belli, R., & Loftus, E. (1994), Recovered memories of childhood abuse: A source monitoring perspective. In: *Dissociation: Clinical, Theoretical, and Research Perspectives*, ed. S. Lynn & J. Rhue. New York: Guilford Press, pp. 415–433.

Berliner, L., & Williams, L. (1994), Memories of child sexual abuse: A response to Lindsay and Read. *Appl. Cog. Psychol.*, 8:379–388.

Bernstein, A. (1989), Analysis of two adult female patients who had been victims of incest in childhood. *J. Amer. Acad. Psychoanal.*, 17:207–221.

——— (1990), The impact of incest trauma on ego development. In: *Adult Analysis and Childhood Sexual Abuse*, ed. H. Levine. Hillsdale, NJ: Analytic Press, pp. 65–91.

175

176   REFERENCES

Biklen, D. (1990), Communication unbound: Autism and praxis. *Harvard Ed. Rev.*, 60:291–314.

Blank, A. (1985), The unconscious flashback to the war in Viet Nam veterans: Clinical mystery, legal defense, and community problem. In: *The Trauma of War: Stress and Recovery in Viet Nam Veterans*, ed. S. Sonnenberg, A. Blank, & J. Talbott. Washington, DC: American Psychiatric Press, pp. 293–308.

Bligh, S., & Kupperman, P. (1993), Brief report: Facilitated communication evaluation procedure accepted in a court case. *J. Autism & Develop. Disorders*, 23:553–557.

Bliss, E. (1980), Multiple personality: A report of 14 cases with implications for schizophrenia and hysteria. *Arch. Gen. Psychiatry*, 37:1388–1397.

——— (1983), Multiple personalities, related disorders, and hypnosis. *Internat. J. Clin. Exp. Hypnosis*, 25:125–146.

——— (1986), *Multiple Personality, Allied Disorders, and Hypnosis*. New York: Oxford University Press.

Blum, H. (1983), The psychoanalytic process and analytic inference. *Internat. J. Psycho-Anal.*, 64:17–33.

Bonaparte, M. (1947), A lion hunter's dreams. *Psychoanal. Quart.*, 16:1–10.

Boon, S., & Draijer, N. (1993), Multiple personality disorder in the Netherlands: A clinical investigation of 71 patients. *Amer. J. Psychiatry*, 150:489–494.

Boulanger, G. (1985), Post-traumatic stress disorder: An old problem with a new name. In: *The Trauma of War: Stress and Recovery in Viet Nam Veterans*, ed. S. Sonnenberg, A. Blank, & J. Talbott. Washington, DC: American Psychiatric Press, pp. 13–29.

Bower, G. (1987), Invited essay: Commentary on mood and memory. *Behav. Res. & Therapy*, 25:443–455.

——— Mayer, J. (1989), In search of mood dependent retrieval. *J. Soc. Behav. & Personal.*, 4:121–156.

Bowers, K. (1984), On being unconsciously influenced and informed. In: *The Unconscious Reconsidered*, ed. K. Bowers & D. Meichenbaum. New York: Wiley, pp. 227–272.

——— (1991), Dissociation in hypnosis and multiple personality disorder. *Internat. J. Clin. Exper. Hypnosis*, 39:155–176.

Braun, B. (1984), Hypnosis creates multiple personality: Myth or reality? *Internat. J. Clin. Exper. Hypnosis*, 32:191–197.

——— (1990), Dissociative disorders as sequelae to incest. In: *Incest Related Syndromes of Adult Psychopathology*, ed. R. Kluft. Washington, DC: American Psychiatric Press, pp. 227–245.

——— (1992), Taped presentation, Midwest Conference on Child Sexual Abuse. Madison, WI, October 12.

Bremner, J., Southwick, S., Brett, E., Fontana, A., Rosenheck, R., & Charney, D. (1992), Dissociation and posttraumatic stress disorder in Vietnam combat veterans. *Amer. J. Psychiatry*, 149:328–332.

Brenneis, B. (1994a), Can early trauma be reconstructed from dreams?: On the relationship of dreams to trauma. *Psychoanal. Psychol.*, 11:429–447.

——— (1994b), Belief and suggestion in the recovery of memories of childhood sexual abuse. *J. Amer. Psychoanal. Assn.*, 42:1027–1053.

——— (1995), Reply to Alpert. *Psychoanal. Psychol.*, 12:561–563.

Brenner, I. (1994), The dissociative character, *J. Amer. Psychoanal. Assn.*, 42:819–846.

Breuer, J., & Freud, S. (1893–1895), Studies on Hysteria. *Standard Edition*, 2. London: Hogarth Press, 1955.

Briere, J. (1989), *Therapy for Adults Molested as Children*. New York: Springer.

——— (1990), Letter to editor. *Amer. J. Psychiatry*, 147:1389–1390.

——— (1994), Dissociation, "repressed memories," and "false memory syndrone": Working with abuse survivors in the age of denial. Wisconsin Psychological Association, April 16, Milwaukee, WI.

——— Conte, J. (1993), Self-reported amnesia for abuse in adults molested as children. *J. Traum. Stress*, 6:21–31.

Brown, R., & Kulik, J. (1977), Flashbulb memories. *Cognition*, 5:73–99.

Calogeras, R. (1982), Sleepwalking and the traumatic experience. *Internat. J. Psycho-Anal.*, 63:483–489.

Carlson, E., & Rosser-Hogan, R. (1991), Trauma experiences, posttraumatic stress, dissociation, and depression in Cambodian refugees. *Amer. J. Psychiatry*, 148:1548–1551.

Ceci, S., & Bruck, M., (1993), Suggestibility of the child witness: A historical review and synthesis. *Psycholog. Bull.*, 113:403–439.

——— Huffman, M., & Smith, E. (1994), Repeatedly thinking about a non-event: Source misattribution among pre-schoolers. *Consciousness and Cognition*, 3:388–407.

Charney, D., Heninger, G., & Breier, A. (1984), Noradrenergic function in panic anxiety: Effects of yohimbine in healthy subjects and patients with agoraphobia and panic disorder. *Arch. Gen. Psychiatry*, 41:751–763.

——— Woods, S., Goodman, W., & Heninger, G. (1987), Neurobiological mechanisms of panic anxiety: Biochemical and behavioral correlates of yohimbine-induced panic attacks. *Amer. J. Psychiatry*, 144:1030–1036.

Chasseguet-Smirgel, J. (1992), Some thoughts on the psychoanalytic situation. *J. Amer. Psychoanal. Assn.*, 40:3–25.

Christiansen, S-A., (1992), Emotional stress and eye-witness memory: A critical review. *Psycholog. Bull.*, 112:284–309.

Chu, J. (1991), The repetition compulsion revisited: Reliving dissociated trauma. *Psychotherapy*, 28:327–332.

———— Dill, D. (1990), Dissociative symptoms in relation to childhood physical and sexual abuse. *Amer. J. Psychiatry*, 147:887–892.

Cohen, N., & Squire, L. (1980), Preserved learning and retention of pattern-analyzing skill in amnesia: Dissociation of knowing how and knowing that. *Science*, 210:207–210.

Conway, M., & Rubin, D. (1993), The structure of autobiographical memory. In: *Theories of Memory*, ed. A. Collins, S. Gathercole, M. Conway, & P. Morris. Hove, U.K.: Lawrence Erlbaum Associates.

Coons, P. (1989), Iatrogenic factors in the misdiagnosis of MPD. *Dissociation*, 2:70–76.

———— Milstein, V. (1986), Psychosexual disturbances in multiple personality: Characteristics, etiology, and treatment. *J. Clin. Psychiatry*, 47:106–110.

Courtois, C. (1988), *Healing the Incest Wound: Adult Survivors in Therapy.* New York: W. W. Norton.

Crews, F. (1995), The memory wars: Freud's legacy in dispute. *NY Rev. Books.*

Davies, J. (1996), Dissociation, repression and reality testing in the countertransference: The controversy over memory and false memory in the psychoanalytic treatment of adult survivors of childhood sexual abuse. *Psychoanal. Dial.*, 6(2):189–218.

———— Frawley, M. (1991a), Dissociative processes and transference–countertransference paradigms in the psychoanalytically oriented treatment of adult survivors of childhood sexual abuse. *Psychoanal. Dial.*, 2:5–36.

———— ———— (1991b) Reply to Gabbard, Shengold, and Grotstein. *Psychoanal. Dial.*, 2:77–96.

———— ———— (1994), *Treating the Adult Survivor of Childhood Sexual Abuse: A Psychoanalytic Perspective.* New York: Basic Books.

Dawes, R. (1994), *House of Cards: Psychology and Psychotherapy Built on Myth.* New York: Free Press.

DeKoninck, J., & Koulack, D. (1975), Dream content and adaptation to a stressful situation. *J. Abnorm. Psychol.*, 84:250–260.

Dewald, P. (1989), Effects on an adult of incest in childhood: A case report. *J. Amer. Psychoanal. Assn.*, 37:997–1114.

Dowling, S. (1987), The interpretation of dreams in the reconstruction of trauma. In: *The Interpretation of Dreams in Clinical Work*, ed. A.

Rothstein. Madison, CT: International Universities Press, pp. 47–56.

Drinka, G. (1984), *The Birth of Neurosis*. New York: Simon & Schuster.

Eberlin, M., McConnachie, G., Ibel, S., & Volpe, L. (1993), Facilitated communication: A failure to replicate the phenomenon. *J. Autism & Develop. Disorders*, 23:507–530.

Eich, E. (1980), The cue dependent nature of state-dependent retrieval. *Memory & Cog.*, 8:157–173.

——— (1995), Searching for mood dependent memory. *Psycholog. Sci.*, 6:67–75.

——— Metcalfe, J. (1989), Mood dependent memories for internal versus external events. *J. Exper. Psychol.: Learn. Mem. & Cog.*, 15:443–455.

Engel, G., & Reichsman, F. (1956), Spontaneous and experimentally induced depression in an infant with a gastric fistula. *J. Amer. Psychoanal. Assn.*, 4:428–452.

Eyre, D. (1991), Therapy with a sexually abused woman. *Internat. J. Psycho-Anal.*, 72:402–415.

Fahy, T. (1988), The diagnosis of multiple personality disorder: A critical review. *Brit. J. Psychiatry*, 153:597–606.

Felman, S., & Laub, D. (1992), *Testimony*. New York: Routledge.

Fisher, C., & Paul, I. (1959), The effect of subliminal visual stimulation on images and dreams. *J. Amer. Psychoanal. Assn.*, 7:35–83.

Frank, J. (1973), *Persuasion and Healing: A Comparative Study of Psychotherapy*, rev. ed. Baltimore: Johns Hopkins University Press.

Frankel, F. (1993), Adult reconstruction of childhood events in the multiple personality literature. *Amer. J. Psychiatry*, 150:954–958.

——— (1994), The concept of flashbacks in historical perspective. *Internat. J. Clin. Exper. Hypnosis*, 42:321–336.

Fredrickson, R. (1992), *Repressed Memories: A Journey to Recovery from Sexual Abuse*. New York: Simon & Schuster.

Freud, S. (1896a), Heredity and the aetiology of the neuroses. *Standard Edition*, 3:141–156. London: Hogarth Press, 1962.

——— (1896b), The aetiology of hysteria. *Standard Edition*, 3:187–221. London: Hogarth Press, 1962.

——— (1900), The Interpretation of Dreams. *Standard Edition*, 4 & 5. London: Hogarth Press, 1953.

——— (1914), Remembering, repeating and working-through (further recommendations on the technique of psycho-analysis, II). *Standard Edition*, 12:147–156. London: Hogarth Press, 1958.

——— (1915), Observations on transference love (further recommendations on the technique of psycho-analysis, III). *Standard Edition*, 12:159–171. London: Hogarth Press, 1958.

———— (1918), From the history of an infantile neurosis. *Standard Edition*, 17:1–122. London: Hogarth Press, 1955.

———— (1937), Constructions in analysis. *Standard Edition*, 23:255–269. London: Hogarth Press, 1964.

Gabbard, G. (1991), Commentary on "Dissociative processes and transference–countertransference paradigms . . . " by J. M. Davies and M. G. Frawley. *Psychoanal. Dial.*, 2:37–47.

Gaensbauer, T. (1995), Trauma in the preverbal period: Symptoms, memories, and developmental impact. *The Psychoanalytic Study of the Child*, 50:122–149. New Haven, CT: Yale University Press.

———— Chatoor, I., Drell, M., Siegel, D., & Zeanah, C. (1995), Traumatic loss in a one-year-old girl. *J. Amer. Acad. Child Adol. Psychiatry*, 34:520–528.

Ganaway, G. (1989), Historical truth versus narrative truth: Clarifying the role of exogenous trauma in the etiology of multiple personality disorder and its variants. *Dissociation*, 2:205–221.

———— (1994), Transference and countertransference shaping influences on dissociative disorders. In: *Dissociation: Clinical and Theoretical Perspectives*, ed. S. Lynn & J. Rhue. New York: Guilford Press, pp. 395–414.

Gediman, H. (1991), Seduction trauma: Complemental intrapsychic and interpersonal perspectives on fantasy and reality. *Psychoanal. Psychology*, 8:381–401.

Gelinas, D. (1983), The persisting negative effects of incest. *Psychiatry*, 46:312–332.

Gill, M. (1982), *Analysis of Transference: Theory and Technique*, Vol. I. New York: International Universities Press.

Goldberg, A. (1994), Farewell to the objective analyst. *Internat. J. Psycho-Anal.*, 75:21–30.

Goodwin, J. (1985), Credibility problems in multiple personality disorder patients and abused children. In: *Childhood Antecedents of Multiple Personality Disorder*, ed. R. Kluft. Washington, DC: American Psychiatric Press, pp. 1–19.

Greenacre, P. (1953a), A contribution to the study of screen memories. In: *Trauma, Growth, and Personality*. London: Hogarth Press, pp. 174–188.

———— (1953b), The prepuberty trauma in girls. In: *Trauma, Growth, and Personality*. London: Hogarth Press, pp. 189–207.

———— (1956), Re-evaluation of the process of working through. In: *Emotional Growth*. New York: International Universities Press, 1971, pp. 641–650.

Greenberg, M., & van der Kolk, B. (1987), Retrieval and interpretation of traumatic memories with the "painting cure." In: *Psychological*

Trauma, ed. B. van der Kolk. Washington, DC: American Psychiatric Press, pp. 191–215.

Greenson, R. (1967), *The Technique and Practice of Psychoanalysis*. New York: International Universities Press.

Grinker, R., & Spiegel, J. (1945), *Men Under Stress*. Philadelphia: Blakiston.

Hacking, I. (1995), *Rewriting the Soul: Multiple Personality and the Sciences of Memory*. Princeton, NJ: Princeton University Press.

Harris, A. (1996), False memory? false memory syndrome? the so-called false memory syndrome? *Psychoanal. Dial.*, 6(2):155–187.

Hartmann, E. (1984), *The Nightmare: The Psychology and Biology of Terrifying Dreams*. New York: Basic Books.

Herman, J. (1981), *Father-Daughter Incest*. Cambridge, MA: Harvard University Press.

——— Harvey, M. (1993), The false memory debate: Social science or social backlash? *Harvard Ment. Health Letter*, 9(10):4–6.

——— Schatzow, E. (1987), Recovery and verification of memories of childhood sexual trauma. *Psychoanal. Psychol.*, 4:1–14.

Hilgard, E. (1977), *Divided Consciousness: Multiple Controls in Human Thought and Action*. New York: John Wiley.

——— (1994), Neodissociation theory. In: *Dissociation: Clinical and Theoretical Perspectives*, ed. S. Lynn & J. Rhue. New York: Guilford Press, pp. 32–51.

Horowitz, M. (1986), *Stress Response Syndromes*, 2nd ed. New York: Jason Aronson.

——— (1988), *Introduction to Psychodynamics: A New Synthesis*. New York: Basic Books.

Huizenga, J. (1990), Incest as trauma: A psychoanalytic case. In: *Adult Analysis and Childhood Sexual Abuse*, ed. H. Levine. Hillsdale, NJ: Analytic Press, pp. 117–135.

Hyman, I., Husband, T., & Billings, F. (1995), False memories of childhood experiences. *Appl. Cog. Psychol.*, 9:181–195.

Johnson, M., Hashstroudi, S., & Lindsay, S. (1993), Source monitoring. *Psycholog. Bull.*, 114:3–28.

Jones, D. (1994), Editorial: Autism, facilitated communication and allegations of child sexual abuse and neglect. *Child Abuse & Neglect*, 18:491–493.

Jucovy, M. (1986), The holocaust. In: *The Reconstruction of Trauma*, ed. A. Rothstein. New York: International Universities Press, pp. 153–169.

Kanzer, M. (1949), Repetitive nightmares after a battlefield killing. *Psychiatric Quart.* (Suppl.), 23:120–126.

Kihlstrom, J. (1987), The cognitive unconscious. *Science*, 237:1445–1452.
——— (1994a), Hypnosis, delayed recall, and the principles of memory. *Internat. J. Clin. Exp. Hyp.*, 42:337–345.
——— (1994b), The social construction of memory. Presented at American Psychological Society, Washington, DC, July 1.
——— Glisky, M., & Angiulo, M. (1994), Dissociative tendencies and dissociative disorders. *J. Abnorm. Psychol.*, 103:117–124.
Klewe, L. (1993), Brief report: An empiricial evaluation of spelling boards as a means of communication for the multihandicapped. *J. Autism & Develop. Disorders*, 23:559–566.
Kluft, R. (1982), Varieties of hypnotic intervention in the treatment of multiple personality. *Amer. J. Clin. Hypnosis*, 24:230–240.
——— (1984), Treatment of multiple personality disorder: A study of 33 cases. *Psychiatric Clin. N. Amer.*, 7:9–29.
——— (1987), An update on multiple personality disorder. *Hosp. & Commun. Psychiatry*, 38:363–373.
——— (1990), Incest and subsequent revictimization: The case of therapist–patient sexual exploitation, with a description of the sitting duck syndrome. In: *Incest Related Syndromes of Adult Psychopathology*, ed. R. Kluft. Washington, DC: American Psychiatric Press, pp. 263–287.
——— (1991), Clinical presentations of multiple personality disorder. *Psychiatric Clin. N. Amer.*, 14:605–629.
Kramer, S. (1990), Residues of incest. In: *Adult Analysis and Childhood Sexual Abuse*, ed. H. Levine. Hillsdale, NJ: Analytic Press, pp. 149–170.
Krystal, H. (1991), Integration and self-healing in post-traumatic states: A ten-year retrospective. *Amer. Imago*, 48:93–118.
Kuppersmith, J. (1992), Discussion: Assessment and treatment of the unconscious sequelae of sexual abuse. *Psychologist–Psychoanalyst*, 12:21.
Langs, R. (1981), Modes of "cure" in psychoanalysis and psychoanalytic psychotherapy. *Internat. J. Psycho-Anal.*, 62:199–214.
Lanning, K. (1991), Commentary: Ritual abuse: A law enforcement view or perspective. *Child Abuse & Neglect*, 15:171–173.
Lansky, M. (1992), The screening function of post-traumatic nightmares. In: *Essential Papers on Dreams*, ed. M. Lansky. New York: New York University Press, pp. 401–424.
Laurence, J.-R., & Perry, C. (1981), The "hidden observer" phenomenon in hypnosis: Some additional findings. *J. Abnorm. Psychology*, 90:334–344.

Lee, K., Vaillant, G., Torrey, W., & Elder, G. (1995), A 50-year prospective study of the psychological sequelae of World War II combat. *Amer. J. Psychiatry*, 152:516–522.

Levitan, H. (1965), A traumatic dream. *Psychoanal. Quart.*, 34:265–267.

Lindsay, S., & Johnson, M. (1989), The eyewitness suggestibility effect and memory for source. *Memory & Cog.*, 17:349–358.

——— Read, D. (1994), Psychotherapy and memories of childhood sexual abuse: A cognitive perspective. *Appl. Cog. Psychology*, 8:281–338.

——— ——— (1995), "Memory work" and recovered memories of childhood sexual abuse: Scientific evidence and public, professional, and personal issues. *Psychol. Pub. Policy, & the Law*, 4:846–908.

Lipinski, J., & Pope, H. (1994), Do "flashbacks" represent obsessional imagery? *Comprehen. Psychiatry*, 35:245–247.

Lisman-Pieczanski, N. (1990), Counter-transference in the analysis of an adult who was sexually abused as a child. In: *Adult Analysis and Childhood Sexual Abuse*, ed. H. Levine. Hillsdale, NJ: Analytic Press, pp. 137–147.

Loewald, H. (1960), On the therapeutic action of psychoanalysis. *Internat. J. Psycho-Anal.*, 41:16–33.

Loewenstein, R. (1949), A post-traumatic dream. *Psychoanal. Quart.*, 18:449–454.

Loftus, E. (1979), *Eyewitness Testimony*. Cambridge, MA: Harvard University Press.

——— (1993a), The reality of repressed memory. *Amer. Psychologist*, 48:518–537.

——— (1993b), Repressed memories of childhood trauma: Are they genuine? *Harvard Ment. Health Letter*, 9(9):4–5.

——— (1993c), Desperately seeking memories of the first few years of childhood: The reality of early memories. *J. Exper. Psychol.: Gen.*, 122:274–277.

——— (1993d), Presentation, Midwest Conference on Child Sexual Abuse. Madison, WI, Oct. 7.

——— Donders, K., & Hoffman, H. (1989), Creating new memories that are quickly accessed and confidently held. *Memory & Cog.*, 17:607–616.

——— Hoffman, H. (1989), Misinformation and memory: The creation of new memories. *J. Exper. Psychol.: Gen.*, 118:100–104.

——— Ketcham, K. (1994), *The Myth of Repressed Memory: False Memories and Allegations of Sexual Abuse*. New York: St. Martin's Press.

——— Loftus, G. (1980), On the permanence of stored information in the human brain. *Amer. Psychologist*, 35:409–420.

———— Pickrell, J. (1995), The formation of false memories. *Psychiatric Annals*, 25:720–725.

Lynn, S., & Nash, M. (1994), Truth in memory: Ramifications for psychotherapy and hypnotherapy. *Amer. J. Clin. Hypnosis*, 36:194–208.

———— Rhue, J. (1988), Fantasy proneness: Hypnosis, developmental antecedents, and psychopathology. *Amer. Psychologist*, 43:35–44.

———— ———— Green, J. (1988), Multiple personality and fantasy proneness: Is there an association or dissociation? *Brit. J. Exper. Clin. Hypnosis*, 5:138–142.

Maloney, L. (1988), Posttraumatic stresses on women partners of Vietnam veterans. *Smith Coll. Studies in Soc. Work*, 58:122–143.

Marcus, B. (1989), Incest and the borderline syndrome: The mediating role of identity. *Psychoanal. Psychol.*, 6:199–215.

Mason, A. (1994), A psychoanalyst looks at a hypnotist: A study of *folie à deux*. *Psychoanal. Quart.*, 63:641–679.

Masson, J. (1984), *The Assault on the Truth.* New York: Farrar, Straus, Giroux.

McCloskey, M. (1992), Special versus ordinary memory mechanisms in the genesis of flashbulb memories. In: *Affect and Accuracy in Recall,* ed. E. Winograd & U. Neisser. Cambridge, U.K.: Cambridge University Press, pp. 227–235.

McDonald, S. (1994), An ethical dilemma: Risk versus responsibility. *J. Psychosoc. Nursing*, 32:19–25.

Moore, S., Donovan, B., Hudson, A., Dykstra, J., & Lawrence, J. (1993), Brief report: Evaluation of eight case studies of facilitated communication. *J. Autism & Develop. Disorders*, 23:531–552.

Mulhern, S. (1991), Satanism and psychotherapy: A rumor in search of an inquisition. In: *The Satanism Scare*, ed. J. T. Richardson, J. Best, & D. G. Bromley. Chicago: Aldine, pp. 145–172.

Myers, W. (1989), The traumatic element in the typical dream of feeling embarrassed at being naked. *J. Amer. Psychoanal. Assn.*, 37:117–130.

Nadon, R., Hoyt, I., Register, P., & Kihlstrom, J. (1991), Absorption and hypnotizability: Context effects reexamined. *J. Personal. Soc. Psychology*, 60:144–153.

Nash, M., Hulsey, T., Sexton, M., Harralson, T., & Lambert, W. (1993), Long-term sequelae of childhood sexual abuse: Perceived family environment, psychopathology, and dissociation. *J. Consult. Clin. Psychol.*, 61:276–283.

Neisser, U. (1991), A case of misplaced nostalgia. *Amer. Psychologist*, 46:34–36.

———— Harsch, N. (1992), Phantom flashbulbs: False recollections of hearing the news about *Challenger*. In: *Flashbulb Memories: Recalling* the *"Challenger" Explosion and Other Disasters*, ed. E. Winograd & U. Neisser. New York: Cambridge University Press.

Nelson, K. (1993), The psychological and social origins of autobiographical memory. *Psycholog. Sci.*, 4:7–14.

Niederland, W. (1965), The role of the ego in the recovery of early memories. *Psychoanal. Quart.*, 34:564–571.

Nunberg, H. (1932), *Principles of Psychoanalysis*. New York: International Universities Press, 1955.

Ofshe, R. (1992), Inadvertent hypnosis during interrogation: False confession due to dissociative state; mis-identified multiple personality and the satanic cult hypothesis. *Internat. J. Clin. Exper. Hypnosis*, 40:125–156.

——— Watters, E. (1994), *Making Monsters: False Memories, Psychotherapy, and Sexual Hysteria*. New York: Scribner's.

Olio, K. (1989), Memory retrieval in the treatment of adult survivors of sexual abuse. *Trans. Anal. J.*, 19:93–100.

——— (1994), Truth in memory: Comments on Loftus' "Reality of repressed memories." *Amer. Psychologist*, 49:442.

Orne, M. (1959), The nature of hypnosis: Artifact or essence. *J. Abnorm. Soc. Psychology*, 58:277–299.

——— (1962), On the social psychology of the psychological experiment: With particular reference to demand characteristics and their implications. *Amer. Psychologist*, 17:776–783.

——— Bauer-Manley, K. (1991), Disorders of the self: Myths, metaphors, and the demand characteristics of treatment. In: *The Self: Interdisciplinary Approaches*, ed. J. Strauss & G. Goethals. New York: Springer, pp. 93–106.

——— Whitehouse, W., Dinges, S., & Orne, E. (1988), Reconstructing memory through hypnosis: Forensic and clinical implications. In: *Hypnosis and Memory*, ed. H. Pettinati. New York: Guilford Press, pp. 21–63.

Panel (1979), Monica: A 25 year longitudinal study of the consequences of trauma in infancy. *J. Amer. Psychoanal. Assn.*, 27:107–126.

——— (1988), The seduction hypothesis. *J. Amer. Psychoanal. Assn.*, 36:759–771.

Pendergrast, M. (1995), *Victims of Memory: Incest, Accusations, and Shattered Lives*. Hinesburg, VT: Upper Access.

Penfield, W. (1969), Consciousness, memory, and man's conditioned reflexes. In: *On the Biology of Learning*, ed. K. Pribram. New York: Harcourt, Brace, & World.

Person, E., & Klar, H. (1994), Establishing trauma: The difficulty distinguishing between memories and fantasies. *J. Amer. Psychoanal. Assn.*, 42:1055–1081.

Peterson, J. (1994), When the therapists who have sat with shattered souls are themselves shattered. *Treating Abuse Today*, 4(2):26–27.

Piper, A. (1995), A skeptical look at multiple personality disorder. In: *Dissociative Identity Disorder: Theoretical and Treatment Controversies*, ed. L. Cohen, J. Berzoff, & M. Elin. Northvale, NJ: Jason Aronson, pp. 135–173.

Poole, D., Lindsay, S., Memon, A., & Ball, R. (1995), Psychotherapy and the recovery of memories of childhood sexual abuse: U.S. and British practitioners' opinions, practice, and experiences. *J. Consult. Clin. Psychol.*, 63:426–437.

Prince, M. (1920), Miss Beauchamp: The theory of the psychogenesis of multiple personality. *J. Abnorm. Psychol.*, 15:67–135.

Pulver, S. (1987), The manifest dream in psychoanalysis: A clarification. *J. Amer. Psychoanal. Assn.*, 35:99–118.

Putnam, F. (1989), *Diagnosis and Treatment of Multiple Personality Disorder.* New York: Guilford Press.

—— Guroff, J., Silberman, E., Barban, L., & Post, R. (1986), The clinical phenomenology of multiple personality disorder: Review of 100 cases. *J. Clin. Psychiatry*, 47:285–293.

—— Loewenstein, R. (1993), Treatment of multiple personality disorder: A survey of current practices. *Amer. J. Psychiatry*, 150:1048–1052.

Pynoos, R., & Nader, K. (1989), Children's memory and proximity to violence. *J. Amer. Acad. Child Adol. Psychiatry*, 28:236–241.

Rainey, J., Aleem, A., Ortiz, A., Yeragani, V., Pohl, R., & Berchou, R. (1987), A laboratory procedure for the induction of flashbacks. *Amer. J. Psychiatry*, 144:1317–1319.

Raphling, D. (1990), Technical issues of the opening phase. In: *Adult Analysis and Childhood Sexual Abuse*, ed. H. Levine. Hillside, NJ: Analytic Press, pp. 45–64.

Rappaport, E. (1968), Beyond traumatic neurosis. *Internat. J. Psycho-Anal.*, 49:719–731.

Rauschenberger, S., & Lynn, S. (1995), Fantasy proneness, DSM-III-R Axis I psychopathology, and dissociation. *J. Abnorm. Psychology*, 104:373–380.

Renik, O. (1981), Typical dreams, "super-ego dreams," and traumatic dreams. *Psychoanal. Quart.*, 50:159–189.

Revelle, W., & Loftus, D. (1990), Individual differences and arousal: Implications for the study of mood and memory. *Cog. & Emotion*, 4:209–237.

Rhue, J., & Lynn, S. (1988), Fantasy-proneness: The ability to hallucinate "as real as real." *Brit. J. Exper. & Clin. Hypnosis*, 6:173–180.

Rich, C. (1990), Accuracy of adults' reports of abuse in childhood (ltr). *Amer. J. Psychiatry*, 147:1389.

Roediger, H. (1990), Implicit memory: Retention without remembering. *Amer. Psychologist*, 45:1043–1056.

Rosen, V. (1955), The reconstruction of a traumatic childhood event in a case of derealization. *J. Amer. Psychoanal. Assn.*, 3:211–221.

Rosenthal, R. (1969), Interpersonal expectations: Effects of the experimenter's hypothesis. In: *Artifact in Behavioral Research*, ed. R. Rosenthal & R. L. Rosnow. New York: Academic Press, pp. 181–277.

———— (1994), Interpersonal expectancy effects: A 30-year perspective. *Curr. Direct. Psycholog. Sci.*, 3:176–179.

Ross, C. (1984), Diagnosis of mulitple personality during hypnosis: A case report. *Internat. J. Clin. Exper. Hypnosis*, 32:222–234.

———— (1989), *Multiple Personality Disorder: Diagnosis, Clinical Features, and Treatment.* New York: John Wiley.

———— Miller, S., Reagor, P., Bjornson, L., Fraser, G., & Anderson, G. (1990), Structural interview data on 102 cases of multiple personality disorder from four centers. *Amer. J. Psychiatry*, 147:596–601.

———— Norton G., & Wozney, K. (1989), Multiple personality disorder: An analysis of 236 cases. *Can. J. Psychiatry*, 34:413–418.

Ross, R., Ball, W., Sullivan, K., & Caroff, S. (1989), Sleep distance as the hallmark of posttraumatic stress disorder. *Amer. J. Psychiatry*, 146:697–707.

Rynearson, E., & McCreery, J. (1993), Bereavement after homicide: A synergism of trauma and loss. *Amer. J. Psychiatry*, 150:258–261.

Sachs, O. (1967), Distinctions between fantasy and reality elements in memory and reconstructions. *Internat. J. Psycho-Anal.*, 48:416–423.

Schacter, D. (1992), Understanding implicit memory: A cognitive neuroscience approach. *Amer. Psychologist*, 47:559–569.

———— Curran, T. (1995), The cognitive neuroscience of false memories. *Psychiat. Ann.*, 25:726–730.

Schimek, J. (1975a), A critical re-examination of Freud's concept of unconscious mental representation. *Internat. Rev. Psychoanal.*, 2:171–187.

———— (1975b), The interpretation of the past: Childhood trauma, psychical reality, and historical truth. *J. Amer. Psychoanal. Assn.*, 23:845–865.

———— (1987), Fact and fantasy in the seduction theory: A historical review. *J. Amer. Psychoanal. Assn.*, 35:937–965.

Schuker, E. (1979), Psychodynamics and treatment of sexual assault victims. *J. Amer. Acad. Psychoanal.*, 7:553–573.

Schwartz, H. (1994), From dissociation to negotiation: A relational psychoanalytic perspective on multiple personality disorder. *Psychoanal. Psychol.*, 11:189–231.

Shane, H. (1993), Letters to the editor: The dark side of facilitated communication. *Topics in Lang. Disorders*, 13:ix–xv.

Sheehan, P., Statham, D., & Jamieson, G. (1991), Pseudomemory effects and their relationship to level of susceptibility to hypnosis and state instruction. *J. Personal. Soc. Psychol.*, 60:130–137.

Sherkow, S. (1990a), Consequences of childhood sexual abuse on the development of ego structure: A comparison of adult cases. In: *Adult Analysis and Childhood Sexual Abuse*, ed. H. Levine. Hillsdale, NJ: Analytic Press, pp. 93–115.

——— (1990b), Evaluation and diagnosis of the sexual abuse of little girls. *J. Amer. Psychoanal. Assn.*, 38:347–369.

Siegel, A. (1992), Dreaming patterns of firestorm victims. Paper presented at Association for the Study of Dreams, Santa Cruz, CA.

Siegel, D. (1995), Memory, trauma, and psychotherapy. *J. Psychother. Pract. Res.*, 4:93–122.

Simon, B. (1992), "Incest—see under Oedipus complex": The history of an error in psychoanalysis. *J. Amer. Psychoanal. Assn.*, 40:955–988.

Singer, M. (1994), Thought reform exists: Organized, programmatic influence. *The Cult Observer*, 11:3–4.

Snyder, M. (1984), When belief creates reality. *Advances in Exper. Soc. Psychology*, 18:247–305.

Sonnenberg, S., Blank, A., & Talbott, J., Eds. (1985), *The Trauma of War: Stress and Recovery in Viet Nam Veterans*. Washington, DC: American Psychiatric Press.

Southwick, S., Krystal, J., Morgan, M., Johnson, D., Nagy, L., Nicolaou, A., Heninger, G., & Charney, D. (1993), Abnormal noradrenergic function in posttraumatic stress disorder. *Arch. Gen. Psychiatry*, 50:266–274.

Spanos, N. (1994), Multiple identity enactments and multiple personality disorder: A sociocognitive perspective. *Psycholog. Bull.*, 116:143–165.

——— Burgess, C., & Burgess, M. (1994), Past-life identities, UFO abductions, and satanic ritual abuse: The social construction of memories. *Internat. J. Clin. Exper. Hypnosis*, 42:433–446.

Spence, D. (1982), *Narrative Truth and Historical Truth*. New York: W. W. Norton.

——— (1994), *The Rhetorical Voice of Psychoanalysis: Displacement of Evidence by Theory*. Cambridge, MA: Harvard University Press.

Spiegel, D., & Cardena, E. (1991), Disintegrated experience: The dissociative disorders revisited. *J. Abnorm. Psychology*, 100:366–378.

—— Hunt, T., & Dondershine, H. (1988), Dissociation and hypnotizibility in posttraumatic stress disorder. *Amer. J. Psychiatry*, 145:301–305.

Spiegel, H. (1974), The grade 5 syndrome: The highly hypnotizable person. *Internat. J. Clin. & Exper. Hypnosis*, 22:303–319.

Squire, L. (1986), Mechanisms of memory. *Science*, 232:1612–1619.

—— (1994), Memory systems of the brain. Paper presented at Memory and Reality: Reconciliation. Baltimore, MD, November.

Stewart, W. (1969), Comments on the manifest content of certain types of unusual dreams. In: *Monograph Kris Study Group. NY Psychoanal. Inst.*, 3:81–113. New York: International Universities Press.

Summit, R. (1983), The child abuse accommodation syndrome. *Child Abuse & Neglect*, 7:177–193.

Tellegen, A., & Atkinson, G. (1974), Openness to absorbing and self-altering experiences ("absorption"), a trait related to hypnotic susceptibility. *J. Abnorm. Psychology*, 83:268–277.

Terr, L. (1979), Children of Chowchilla: A study of psychic trauma. *The Psychoanalytic Study of the Child*, 34:547–623. New Haven, CT: Yale University Press.

—— (1985), Remembered images and trauma. *The Psychoanalytic Study of the Child*, 40:493–533. New Haven, CT: Yale University Press.

—— (1988), What happens to early memories of trauma? A study of twenty children under age five at the time of documented traumatic events. *J. Amer. Acad. Child Adol. Psychiatry*, 27:96–104.

—— (1990), *Too Scared to Cry*. New York: Harper & Row.

—— (1991), Childhood traumas: An outline and overview. *Amer. J. Psychiatry*, 148:10–20.

Tillman, J., Nash, M., & Lerner, P. (1994), Does trauma cause dissociative pathology? In: *Dissociation: Clinical and Theoretical Perspectives*, ed. S. Lynn & J. Rhue. New York: Guilford Press, pp. 395–414.

Trewartha, M. (1990), On post-analytic amnesia. *The Annual of Psychoanalysis*, 18:153–174. Hillsdale, NJ: Analytic Press.

Tulving, E. (1972), Episodic and semantic memory. In: *Organization of Memory*, ed. E. Tulving, & W. Donaldson. New York: Academic Press, pp. 381–403.

—— Schacter, D. (1990), Priming and human memory systems. *Science*, 247:301–306.

—— Thomson, D. (1973), Encoding specificity and retrieval processes in episodic memory. *Psycholog. Rev.*, 80:353–373.

van der Kolk, B. (1987), *Psychological Trauma*. Washington, DC: American Psychiatric Press.

——— (1994), The body keeps the score: Memory and the evolving psychobiology of posttraumatic stress. *Harvard Rev. Psychiatry*, 1:253–265.

——— Britz, R., Burr, W., Sherry, S. & Hartmann, E. (1984), Nightmares and trauma: A comparison of nightmares after combat with lifelong nightmares in veterans. *Amer. J. Psychiatry*, 141:187–190.

——— Kadish, W. (1987), Amnesia, dissociation, and the return of the repressed. In: *Psychological Trauma*, ed. B.van der Kolk. Washington, DC: American Psychiatric Press, pp. 173–190.

——— van der Hart, O. (1989), Pierre Janet and the breakdown of adaptation in psychological trauma. *Amer. J. Psychiatry*, 146:1530–1540.

——— ——— (1991), The intrusive past: The flexibility of memory and the engraving of trauma. *Amer. Imago*, 48:425–454.

Wakefield, H., & Underwager, R. (1992), Recovered memories of alleged sexual abuse: Lawsuits against parents. *Behav. Sci. & Law*, 10:483–507.

Weitzenhoffer, A., & Hilgard, E. (1967), *Revised Stanford Profile Scales of Hypnotic Susceptibility Forms I & II*. Palo Alto, CA: Consulting Psychologist's Press.

Wetzler, S. (1985), The historical truth of psychoanalytic reconstructions. *Internat. Rev. Psychoanal*, 12:187–197.

——— Sweeney, J. (1986), Childhood amnesia: A conceptualization in cognitive-psychological terms. *J. Amer. Psychoanal. Assn.*, 34:663–685.

Williams, L. (1994), Recall of childhood trauma: A prospective study of women's memories of child sexual abuse. *J. Consult. Clin. Psychol.*, 62:1167–1176.

Williams, M. (1987), Reconstruction of early seduction and its aftereffects. *J. Amer. Psychoanal. Assn.*, 35:145–163.

Wilmer, H. (1982), Vietnam and madness: Dreams of schizophrenic veterans. *J. Amer. Acad. Psychoanal.*, 10:47–65.

——— (1986), Combat nightmares: Toward a therapy of violence. *Spring*, 46:120–139.

Wilson, S., & Barber, T. (1983), The fantasy-prone personality: Implications for understanding imagery, hypnosis, and parapsychological phenomena. In: *Imagery: Current Theory, Research, and Applications*, ed. A. Sheikh. New York: John Wiley, pp. 340–387.

Winograd, E., & Neisser, U., Eds. (1992), *Flashbulb Memories: Recalling the "Challenger" Explosion and Other Disasters*. New York: Cambridge University Press.

Witkin, H., & Lewis, H. (1965), The relation of experimentally induced presleep experiences to dreams. *J. Amer. Psychoanal. Assn.*, 13:819–849.

Wolf, E., & Alpert, J. (1991), Psychoanalysis and sexual abuse: A review of the post-Freudian literature. *Psychoanal. Psychology*, 8:305–327.

Wright, L. (1993a), Remembering Satan. *The New Yorker*, 64(13): 60–81.

——— (1993b), Remembering Satan. *The New Yorker*, 64(14):54–76.

NAME INDEX

Aleem, A., 32
Allen, J., 118
Alpert, J., xiv, 14, 15, 18, 27, 28, 29, 30,
    43, 45, 46, 55, 56, 57, 62, 66, 76,
    90–92, 102, 104, 106, 111–112,
    114, 159
Anderson, G., 144
Angiulo, M., 128
Atkinson, G., 127, 128, 129, 130, 131–
    132, 133–134

Ball, R., 138, 139, 153
Barban, L., 144, 146–147
Barber, T., xv, 36, 112, 127–128, 129,
    130–131, 132–133, 138
Bass, E., 152
Bauer-Manley, K., 130
Belli, R., xvi, 119
Berchou, R., 32
Berliner, L., 149, 150
Bernstein, A., 18, 27, 29, 42, 43, 54, 56,
    57, 59, 62, 160
Biklen, D., 157–158
Billings, F., 48
Bjornson, L., 144
Blank, A., 29, 33, 70, 71, 89
Bligh, S., 158

Bliss, E., 127, 128, 129, 130, 131, 136,
    139
Blum, H., 43, 48
Bonaparte, M., 20, 21–22
Boon, S., 144
Boulanger, G., 37
Bower, G., 67, 68
Bowers, K., 122, 134, 140, 154, 155, 156
Braun, B., 30, 35, 65, 125, 127, 135,
    137, 139, 142, 145
Breier, A., 35
Bremner, J., 35
Brenneis, B., 28, 71, 89, 92
Brenner, I., 29, 30, 62, 66–67, 76, 134,
    145, 160
Brett, E., 35
Breuer, J., 129
Briere, J., 97–98, 102, 104, 144, 145,
    149, 152, 160
Britz, R., xiv, 20, 27, 30, 70–71, 82,
    84, 91
Brown, R., 86
Bruck, M., 75
Burgess, C., 129
Burgess, M., 129
Burr, W., xiv, 20, 27, 30, 70–71, 82,
    84, 91

Calogeras, R., 99
Cardena, E., 35
Carlson, E., 35
Ceci, S., xiv, 74, 75
Charcot, J. M., 33–34, 49, 157
Charney, D., 34–35, 67, 68, 70–71
Chasseguet-Smirgel, J., 21
Chatoor, I., 92, 93
Christiansen, S.-A., 82, 85, 86
Chu, J., 29, 30–31, 35, 36, 144
Cohen, N., 64
Conte, J., 144
Conway, M., 120
Coons, P., 135, 144, 147
Courtois, C., 152
Crews, F., 172
Curran, T., 120

Davies, J., 30, 35–36, 50, 51, 55, 56–57,
    62, 64, 65–66, 81, 82, 99, 102–
    103, 104–105, 106–110, 111,
    112, 113, 134, 135–136, 147
Davis, L., 152
Dawes, R., 172
DeKoninck, J., 21
Dewald, P., 29, 33, 43, 53, 55, 56, 62,
    66, 102, 112
Dill, D., 35, 36, 144
Dinges, S., 71
Donders, K., 45
Dondershine, H., 30, 38
Donovan, B., 158
Dowling, S., 18, 99
Draijer, N., 144
Drell, M., 92, 93
Drinka, G., 33–34, 49–50, 71, 90
Dykstra, J., 158

Eberlin, M., 158
Eich, E., 55, 67, 68
Elder, G., 37
Engel, G., 54
Eyre, D., 18

Fahy, T., xv

Felman, S., 24
Fisher, C., 20
Fontana, A., 35
Fraiberg, S., 51
Frank, J., 75, 134, 151, 156, 157
Frankel, F., 32–33, 37, 39, 58, 71, 146
Fraser, G., 144
Frawley, M., 30, 35–36, 50, 51, 55,
    56–57, 62, 64, 65–66, 81, 82, 99,
    102–103, 104–105, 106–110,
    111, 112, 113, 134, 135–136,
    147
Fredrickson, R., 152
Freud, S., 4, 18, 20, 23, 27, 29, 43, 44,
    61–62, 97–98, 99, 114, 117–118,
    129, 162
Furman, E., 113

Gabbard, G., 57
Gaensbauer, T., 92, 93–96
Ganaway, G., 126
Gediman, H., 81, 112–113
Gelinas, D., 29
Gill, M., 114
Glisky, M., 128
Goldberg, A., 158
Goodman, W., 35
Goodwin, J., 136
Green, J., 127
Greenacre, P., 18, 27, 99
Greenberg, M., 18
Greenson, R., 44, 114
Grinker, R., 23
Guroff, J., 144, 146–147

Hacking, I., 126, 127
Harralson, T., 36
Harris, A., 121
Harsch, N., 86
Hartmann, E., xiv, 20, 27, 30, 34, 37,
    70–71, 82, 84, 91
Harvey, M., 99, 149, 150, 152, 154
Hashstroudi, S., 119
Heninger, G., 34–35, 67, 68, 70–71
Herman, J., 15, 29, 58, 99, 149, 150,
    152, 154

Hilgard, E., 127, 128, 132
Hoffman, H., 45
Horowitz, M., 23, 26, 29, 136
Hoyt, I., 128
Hudson, A., 158
Huffman, M., 74
Huizenga, J., 17, 27
Hulsey, T., 36
Hunt, T., 30, 38
Husband, T., 48
Hyman, I., 48

Ibel, S., 158
Ingram, P., 49, 51, 157

Jamieson, G., 129
Johnson, D., 34, 67, 68, 70–71
Johnson, M., 119, 120
Jones, D., 158
Jucovy, M., 18

Kadish, W., 35
Kanzer, M., 23, 25, 26
Ketcham, K., 149
Kihlstrom, J., xiv, 44, 63, 64, 75, 77, 128, 130
Klar, H., 29, 30, 62, 66–67, 76, 81, 102, 103, 106, 111
Klewe, L., 158
Kluft, R., 6–7, 14, 35, 65, 125, 127, 135, 137, 139–140, 141, 145
Koulack, D., 21
Kramer, S., 18, 29, 30, 33, 43, 46, 53, 55, 56, 62, 66, 160
Krystal, H., 36
Krystal, J., 34, 67, 68, 70–71
Kulik, J., 86
Kupperman, P., 158
Kuppersmith, J., 29, 43

Lambert, W., 36
Langs, R., 114
Lanning, K., 146
Lansky, M., 84
Laub, D., 24
Laurence, J.-R., 127, 128

Lawrence, J., 158
Lee, K., 37
Lerner, P., 36, 128
Levitan, H., 23
Lewis, H., 20–21
Lindsay, S., xiv, 72, 76, 119, 120, 130, 138, 139, 149, 150, 151, 152–153
Lipinski, J., 84
Lisman-Pieczanski, N., 18, 21
Loewald, H., 151
Loewenstein, R., 24, 26, 139
Loftus, D., 68
Loftus, E., xiv, xvi, 41, 44, 45, 48–49, 75, 119, 120, 130, 149, 152
Loftus, G., 44
Lynam, D., xvi
Lynn, S., 36–37, 120, 127–128, 130

Maloney, L., 32
Marcus, B., 18
Masson, J., 29, 117, 159
Mayer, J., 67, 68
McCloskey, M., 86
McConnachie, G., 158
McCreery, J., 30, 32, 71
McDonald, S., 142
Memon, A., 138, 139, 153
Metcalfe, J., 67, 68
Miller, S., 144
Milstein, V., 135, 144, 147
Moore, S., 158
Morgan, M., 34, 67, 68, 70–71
Mulhern, S., 126
Myers, W., 18, 27

Nader, K., 32, 71
Nadon, R., 128
Nagy, L., 34, 67, 68, 70–71
Nash, M., 36, 120, 127, 128
Neisser, U., 86
Nelson, K., 130
Nicholaou, A., 34, 67, 68, 70–71
Niederland, W., 18, 99
Norton, G., 30, 139, 144
Nunberg, H., 18, 99

Ofshe, R., 45, 49, 120, 140, 141–142, 143, 145, 155
Olio, K., 29, 30, 152
Orne, E., 71
Orne, M., xvi, 71, 122, 127, 129, 130, 134, 155, 159, 162
Ornstein, P., xiv
Ortiz, A., 32

Paul, I., 20
Pendergrast, M., 140, 141, 142, 143, 145–146
Penfield, W., 44, 97
Perry, C., 127, 128
Person, E., 29, 30, 62, 66–67, 76, 81, 102, 103, 106, 111
Peterson, J., 145–146
Pickrell, J., 48, 120
Piper, A., 126
Pohl, R., 32
Poole, D., 138, 139, 153
Pope, H., 84
Post, R., 144, 146–147
Pulver, S., 27, 53
Putnam, F., 125, 135, 136, 139, 140–141, 144, 146–147
Pynoos, R., 32, 71

Rainey, J., 32
Raphling, D., 18
Rappaport, E., 21, 22–24, 84
Rauschenberger, S., 127, 128
Read, D., 72, 76, 130, 138, 139, 149, 150, 151, 152
Reagor, P., 144
Register, P., 128
Reichsman, F., 54
Renik, O., 19, 20, 27
Revelle, W., 68
Rhue, J., 36–37, 127–128, 130
Rich, C., 97
Rimland, B., 158
Roediger, H., 63, 69, 71
Rosen, V., 18, 54, 99
Rosenheck, R., 35
Rosenthal, R., 156, 157

Ross, C., 30, 125, 135, 139, 140, 144
Rosser-Hogan, R., 35
Rubin, D., 120
Rynearson, E., 30, 32, 71

Sachs, O., 18, 55, 56, 99, 160
Schacter, D., 63, 69, 70, 71, 120
Schatzow, E., 15, 58
Schimek, J., 44, 83, 97, 99, 117–118
Schuker, E., 18, 30, 43, 46, 50, 55, 56, 160
Schwartz, H., 125, 140, 148
Sexton, M., 36
Shane, H., 158
Sheehan, P., 129
Sherkow, S., 18
Sherry, S., xiv, 20, 27, 30, 70–71, 82, 84, 91
Siegel, A., 21, 22, 25, 26
Siegel, D., 65, 81, 92, 93
Silberman, E., 144, 146–147
Simon, B., 14
Singer, M., 143
Smith, E., 74
Snyder, M., 170
Sonnenberg, S., 29
Southwick, S., 34, 35, 67, 68, 70–71
Spanos, N., 126, 129, 130
Spence, D., xv, 117, 173
Spiegel, D., 30, 35, 38
Spiegel, H., 127, 129, 130, 133, 134
Spiegel, J., 23
Squire, L., 52–53, 55, 63, 64, 67, 72
Statham, D., 129
Stewart, W., 18, 27, 99, 159
Summit, R., 135, 136, 137
Sweeney, J., 57

Talbott, J., 29
Tellegen, A., 127, 128, 129, 130, 131–132, 133–134
Terr, L., 5, 14, 20, 23, 25, 26, 29, 30, 33, 51, 54, 70, 71, 79, 82, 89, 92–93
Thomson, D., 55, 64

Tillman, J., 36, 128
Torrey, W., 37
Trewartha, M., xiii, 57
Tulving, E., 55, 63, 64, 69, 71

Underwager, R., 41

Vaillant, G., 37
van der Hart, O., 29, 34, 64–65, 71, 79, 80–81, 82, 87–90
van der Kolk, B., xiv, 5, 18, 20, 27, 29, 30, 34, 35, 64–65, 70–71, 79, 80–81, 82, 84, 87–90, 91, 121
Volpe, L., 158

Wakefield, H., 41
Watters, E., 120, 140, 141–142, 143, 145
Weitzenhoffer, A., 132

Wetzler, S., 57, 61
Whitehouse, W., 71
Williams, L., 58, 85, 96, 149, 150
Williams, M., 18, 27, 29, 30, 45, 46–47, 51, 55, 56, 62, 66, 76, 103, 105–106, 112, 114, 159–160
Wilmer, H., 21, 23, 84
Wilson, S., xv, 36, 112, 127–128, 129, 130–131, 132–133, 138
Winograd, E., 86
Witkin, H., 20–21
Wolf, E., 14, 18, 29, 43
Woods, S., 35
Wozney, K., 30, 139, 144
Wright, L., 49

Yeragani, V., 32

Zeanah, C., 92, 93

SUBJECT INDEX

Altered states, 136
Alternative hypotheses, 172
Analytic dyad
    influence in, 158–162
    in recovered memory, 45–48
Anna O case, 129
Anne Stone case, 141–142, 145
Arousal, extreme, 62
    defense against, 64
Association, presented as memory, 46
Autobiographical memory, 63, 65–66
    plasticity of, 130, 168
    retrieving of, 73–74
    social influences on, 75

Behavior, shaped, 49–50
Behavioral reenactments, 14, 31–34, 54
    exact, 70–71
    ritual, 90
    trauma-driven, 93–95
Belief
    enacted, 157–158
    in multiple personality disorder patients, 135–137
    in recovered memories, 52–59, 59–60

therapist's, 169–172
    in trust building, 135–136
Betrayal, by early caretakers, 134–135
Body memory, 76
Brain, permanent, accurate record of experience in, 97–98

Central nervous system, response to trauma, 34–35
Challenger explosion, memories of, 86
Childhood sexual abuse. *See* Sexual abuse
Childhood trauma. *See* Sexual abuse; Trauma
Chowchilla children's dreams, 25
Clarity, 50–51
Clinical literature, xiv–xv
    on multiple personality disorder patients, xv–xvi
Closure, 50–51
Coercive therapy
    with multiple personality disorder patients, 141–144
    recovered memories as metaphor of, 145–146, 147–148
Cognitive unconscious, 168–169
Combat memories, 35

Combat veterans, posttraumatic stress disorder in, 35, 37
Compulsive rituals, 33
Concentration camp experience dream, 22–24
Confabulatory cognitive style, 130–132
Confirmation bias, 167
Confrontational techniques, 140, 143
Countertransference, maladaptive, 51
Covert influence, xvi

Declarative memory, 52
Demand characteristics, xvi, 134–137, 155–156, 159
Denial, 104
Dishonesty, versus multisensory fantasy, 132
Dissociation, 35–37, 56–57
  between implicit and explicit memory, 72
  during sexual abuse, 91
  as sign of traumatic memory, 69–70, 102–103, 105
  trauma and, 65, 114–115
Dissociative state, 5–6
  focus on, 120
  mimicking trauma, 73–74
Doubt
  destructive action of, 105–107
  suggestion and, 58
Dreams. See also Nightmares
  of abducted Chowchilla children, 25
  combat, 22–23
  of concentration camp experience, 22–24
  as exact replica of trauma, 20
  Freudian interpretation of, 18
  homomorphic traumatic, 23–26
  images in, 21
  influence in, 159–160
  interpretation of, 46–47
  isomorphic traumatic, 19–23
  lion hunter's, 21–22
  phases in production of, 19–20
  posttraumatic stress disorder and, 29–31

presleep stimuli and, 20–21
  repetitive, anxiety-provoking, 17, 27, 66–67, 84–85, 101–102
  repetitive playback, 14
  repressed memory in content of, xiv
  sexual, 4, 11–12, 27–28
  of sexual exploitation, 11–12
  sexual exploitation symbols in, 4
  sexually explicit, 27–28
  transformed memories in, 166
  traumatic, 17–19, 20–28, 90–92
  violence in, 6

Evaluation apprehension, 157
Examination dreams, 27
Expectancy effects, 156–158
  in clinical practice, 159–162
Expectations
  attunement to, 111
  enacted, 157–158
  unspoken, 155–156

Fantasy
  multisensory, xv–xvi, 130–131, 132
  as source of information, 119–120
Fantasy proneness, 36–37, 110–111, 123
  facilitating conditions in, 130
  in multiple personality disorder, 127–134
Firestorm evacuee dream, 25
Flashbacks, 31–34, 84, 101
  biochemical pathways in, 35
  exact fit of, 70–71
  personality factors in, 37–38
  transformed memories in, 166
Flashbulb memory, 85–87
Focused mental absorption, 128–129

Guided imagery, 150

Hidden observer phenomenon, 127
Homicide witness, responses of, 32
Homomorphic traumatic dreams, 23–26
  data on, 33

Homomorphism, 18–19
Honest fabrications, 119
Hypnogogic hallucinations, 67
 normalizing of, 109
Hypnosis
 in false recovered memories, 50
 fantasy proneness and, 130
 memory produced under, 71
 with multiple personality disorder
  patients, 139–140, 141–142,
  143
 recovered memories in, 88–89
 suggestion in, 150
Hypnotic susceptibility, 37–38, 123
 in multiple personality disorder,
  126, 127–134
Hysteria
 behaviors of, 33–34
 infantile scenes of, 97
 postural concomitants to, 49–50

Imaginative proficiency, 37–38
Imaginative thought, 111
Incest. See also Sexual abuse
 reconstructed history of, 90–91
 recovery of memories of, 57
 unremembered, xiv
 validation of memories of, 57–58
Influence, 173. See also Suggestion
 in clinical realm, 158–162
 potentiated by bad and good therapy, 152–154
 in therapeutic process, 150–163
 as two-way process, 154–158
 unavoidability of, 151–152
Information
 misattribution of source of, 120–121
 source of, 119–120
Interdisciplinary dialogue, 76
Interpersonal expectancy effects, 156–
  158
 in clinical practice, 159–162
Interpersonal influence, 150–151
 in good and bad therapy, 152–154
 as two-way process, 154–158
 unavoidability of, 151–152

Invasive techniques
 with multiple personality disorder
  patients, 125–148, 140–141
 recovered memories as metaphor
  of, 145–146, 147–148
Irene case, 87–90
Isolation, suggestion and, 58
Isomorphic traumatic dream, 19–23

Learning, state-dependent, 67–69
Lifeguard image, 8–9

Memory, xi–xii
 accurate versus false, 74
 assumptions about nature of, 44
 burned in, 92–93
 complexity of, xi
 declarative versus procedural, 52–53
 dream content and, xiv
 dynamic, plastic, 44–45, 52, 130,
  167–168
 error-proneness of, 52
 experimentally implanted, 48–49
 explicit, 63, 64, 81–84
 explicit versus implicit, 68, 69–74,
  93–96, 101
 false versus genuine, 59–60
 flashbulb, 85–87
 highly detailed, 130
 implicit, 63–64, 81
 inconsistencies of, 104
 indelible, static, 44
 intact implicit and impaired
  explicit, 81–85
 as multisensory, 52–54
 procedural, 55–56
 reconstruction versus retrieval of,
  61–62
 recovered. See Recovered memories
 repressed, 1–15
 sensorimotor, 52–54
 social influence on, 89–90, 101
 state-dependent, 55–56, 67–69
 systems of, 63–67
 transforming metaphor into, 119–
  122

Memory equivalents, 102–103
Metalepsis, 117
Metaphor
versus hidden sexual abuse, 115–116
sexual abuse as, 145–146, 147–148
transforming into memory, 119–122
Motor enactments, 53
Multiple personality disorder (MPD), 169
demand characteristics and therapeutic attitudes in, 134–137
etiology for, 125–127
external validation of, 146–147
hypnotic susceptibility and fantasy proneness in, 127–134
literature on, xv–xvi
production of, 137–139
recovered memories and, 144–148
therapeutic techniques with, 139–144

Narrative memory, 88
Neurological abnormality, 35
Nightmares. See also Dreams
chronic, 84
frequent disruptive, 27

Out-of-the-body experiences, 131

Panic disorder, 35
Passionate attitudes, 33–34
Patient, malleable, 110–114, 150, 165, 170
Patient-therapist relationship, 158–162. See also Analytic dyad; Therapeutic relationship
Pattern recognition, 63–64
Penetration, symbolic, psychological, 118–119
Permeable psychological boundaries, 37–38
Personality variables, 37–38
Posttraumatic reactions, generalized, 93–95
Posttraumatic stress disorder

dreams and symptoms of, 29–31
flashbacks and behavioral reenactments in, 31–34
personality variables in, 37–38
systemic responses of, 34–35
Posttraumatic symptoms, 80
Presleep stimuli, 20–21
Primal scene, 61
Procedural knowledge, 52–53, 55–56
Psychoanalysis, in reconstructing trauma memories, 61–77

Reconstruction, 61–62
Recovered memories
alternative explanations for, 108–109
analytic dyad in, 45–48
authenticity of, 165–174
belief in, 41–43, 52–59, 59–60
dream interpretation in, 46–47
evolving thinking about, xii–xiii
expectation of, 160–161
extracting from dreams, 28
false, 49–51
false versus genuine, 59–60
malleable patient in, 110–114
mechanism of, xv–xvi
as metaphor for therapeutic techniques, 169
multiple personality and, 125, 144–148
versus reaction to technique, 101–123
suggestion in, 41–51
transforming metaphor into, 119–122
validity of, xii, xvii, 14–15, 97–99
zealous therapist in, 102–110
Repetitive behavior, 33–34
Repressed memories, partial, 41–42
Restraints, with multiple personality disorder patients, 142, 143
Retrieved memory
versus reconstruction, 61–62
validity of, 76
Ritual satanic abuse, 145, 146

Rupture, images of, 6

Satanic cults, 141–142, 145
Scientific standards, 167, 171–173
Secrecy, 104–105
Seduction hypothesis, 117–118
Selection, 89
Self, relocation of, 131–132
Sensorimotor memory, 52–54, 81–82
  traumatic, 82–83
Sexual abuse. *See also* Incest
  accuracy of reports of, 97–98
  belief and suggestion in recovered
    memories of, 41–60
  dissociation and, 35–36
  evidence of, 8–13
  failure to recall, 85
  false memory of, 49
  in multiple personality disorder
    patients, 144–148
  nature of, 61
  prevalence of, xiii, 76
  reconstructed history of, 90–91
  recovered memories of, xi–xii
  recovered memories of, versus re-
    action to technique, 101–
    123
  repressed memory of, xiii–xiv
  sensitivity of, xi
  validity of evidence of, 14–15
Sexual exploitation dreams, 4, 11–12,
    27–28
Sexually suggestive techniques, 153
Shame, 104–105
Sitting duck syndrome, 6–8, 14
Skepticism, 171–172
Sleep, disrupted, 30
Social influences, 89–90
  covert, 75
Somatic memories, 53, 66
  normalizing of, 109
Source monitoring theory, xvi
Stereotyped actions, 33
Stimulus
  overwhelming, 79–81
  state and sensory, 64–65

unsymbolized, 64
Subject-experimenter influence, xvi,
    155–158
Suggestibility, 37–38, 121, 150
Suggestion, 165–166. *See also* Influence
  analytic dyad in, 45–48
  continuum of, 43–44
  dilemma of, 59
  doubt and uncertainty in, 47
  hypothesis of, 167–168
  isolation and doubt in, 58
  in recovered memories of child-
    hood sexual abuse, 43–51
  in therapeutic process, 149–163
  as unconscious process, 154–155
Suicide, thoughts about, 3–4
Syngnosia, 131

Therapeutic enactment, 115, 117
Therapeutic relationship. *See also* Ana-
    lytic dyad
  influence in, 173
  suggestion and influence in, 149–
    163
Therapeutic techniques
  as abuse, 114–119
  influence in, 152–154
Therapist
  attitudes toward multiple personal-
    ity disorder patients, 134–
    137
  beliefs of, 102–103, 169–172
  biased, 152
  with multiple personality disorder
    patients, 139–144
  as penetrating invader, 112–113,
    115–116
  zealous, 102–110, 123, 169, 170–171
Therapy
  foundation of, xvi–xvii, 173–174
  influence in, 173
Trance logic, 129–130
Transference, images in, 8–10
Transformation, 89, 166
  bypassing, 19–20
  between trauma and dreams, 24–26

Trauma. *See also* Posttraumatic stress disorder; Sexual abuse; Traumatic dream; Traumatic memory
absence of explicit memory in, 81–82, 84
behavioral reenactments of, 31–34
dissociation and, 35–37, 65, 114–115
dreams and, 17–19
evidence of, 5–13
explicit memory of, 82–84
falsely implanted memory of, 48–49
flashbacks and, 31–33
impact of, 62
massive, repeated, 14–15, 24
memory markers of, 81–82
in multiple personality disorder, 137–139
psychoanalytic retrieval of memories of, 61–77
recovered memories of, xi–xii
recovered memories of, versus reaction to technique, 101–123
somatic memory of, 53
symptoms of, 29–39
systemic responses to, 34–35
unremembered, 1–15
validity of recovered memories of, xvii
Traumatic dream
concept of, 18–19
homomorphic, 23–26
identifying, 26–28
isomorphic, 19–23
Traumatic memory
always remembered versus recovered, 113–114

clinical implications of, 74–77
cue-triggered, 79–80
demonstration of, 92–96
dreams and, 90–92
explicit, 93–96
implicit versus explicit memory in, 68, 69–74
indirect, 79–80
memory systems and, 63–67
paradigm for, 87–90
sensorimotor encoding of, 82–83
special form of, 80–100
state-dependent learning and, 67–69
transforming metaphor into, 119–122
Trust, 133–134
with multiple personality disorder patients, 135–136

Unsymbolized material, 116–117

Validation
versus belief, 54–55
of clinical evidence of abuse, 107–108
of reconstructed memory, 57–58
of recovered memories, 76, 97–99, 172–174
of trauma in multiple personality, 146–147
Victimization, 6–7
Vietnam veterans, 37–38
Violence, dream, 6

Wolf man, dreams of, 97

Yohimbine, 35